Y0-AAT-742

LANGUAGE ▲ LITERATURE ▲ MEDIA

PRENTICE-HALL CANADA INC.

Canadian Cataloguing in Publication Data

Main entry under title:

In flight
(Destinations)
ISBN 0-13-456153-8

1. English language. 2. English language – Composition and exercises. 3. Communication – Problems, exercises, etc. I. Robinson, Sam, date. II. Series: Destinations (Scarborough, Ont.).

PE1408.I5 1991 808'.042 C90-094312-2

Prentice-Hall, Inc., Englewood Cliffs, New Jersey
Prentice-Hall International, Inc., London
Prentice-Hall of Australia, Pty., Ltd., Sydney
Prentice-Hall of India Pvt., Ltd., New Delhi
Prentice-Hall of Japan, Inc., Tokyo
Prentice-Hall of Southeast Asia (PTE) Ltd., Singapore
Editora Prentice-Hall do Brasil Ltda., Rio de Janeiro
Prentice-Hall Hispanoamericana, S.A., Mexico

ISBN 0-13-456153-8

Research & Marketing Manager: David Steele
Managing Editor: Alan Simpson
Editors: Lavinia Inbar and Susan Sopcek
Contributing Writers: Mary Beth Leatherdale and Elise Levine
Permissions: Sharon Houston and Dorothy Melly
Manufacturing: Crystale Chalmers
Design & Composition: Derek Chung Tiam Fook
Picture Research: Francine Geraci
Cover Photo: The Image Bank/Hans Wendler
Printed and bound in Canada by D.W. Friesen & Sons Ltd.

1 2 3 4 5 6 D.W.F. 96 95 94 93 92 91

DESTINATIONS

Destinations is an English/Language Arts program developed for use in senior high-school English courses. Each level consists of a student text, accompanying anthology, and a teacher resource book.

LANGUAGE LITERATURE ▲ MEDIA	▲	STORIES ▲ ARTICLES POEMS ▲ PLAYS
FAST FORWARD STUDENT TEXT TEACHER RESOURCE BOOK		**ACCELERATE** ANTHOLOGY
STRAIGHT AHEAD STUDENT TEXT TEACHER RESOURCE BOOK		**OVERDRIVE** ANTHOLOGY
IN FLIGHT STUDENT TEXT TEACHER RESOURCE BOOK		**GLIDE PATH** ANTHOLOGY

ANNOTATED TABLE OF CONTENTS

TABLE OF CONTENTS

RESOURCE UNITS

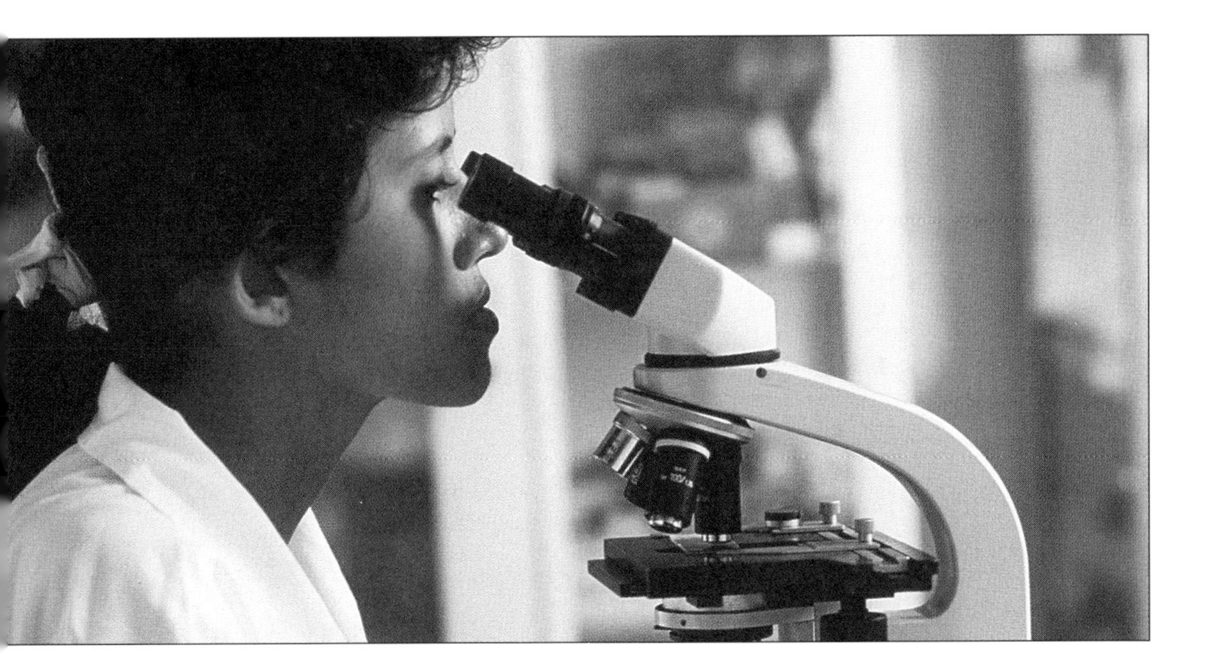

LITERATURE CONTENTS

HOW TO USE THIS BOOK

As you experience the content and activities of *In Flight,* you will grow in your ability to exercise your English-language skills. You will also have the opportunity to examine your attitudes and ideas about Canadian and world issues. You may also discover something about who you are and where you are going.

ORGANIZATION

- This book is comprised of Core units and Resource units. Each Core unit focusses on an interesting topic or issue. Resource units focus on a particular process such as writing, reading, listening, speaking, viewing, working in groups, and studying.

- This book is flexible and has been designed to be used in any order or sequence depending upon your own interests and needs.

- Each unit is divided into sections containing reading selections, visuals, and activities. The section titles appear in purple ink. Sections within units are linked together by topic and theme, but they also stand alone and can be used independently, if you desire. The names of all the units and sections are listed in the Table of Contents.

LITERATURE

- All reading selections in this book are highlighted with a yellow screen. These selections offer a variety of short stories, poems, essays, articles, plays, and autobiographies that explore a particular theme.

- All the reading selections are listed in the Literature Contents at the beginning of the book.

VISUALS

- This book also includes a wide variety of photographs, paintings, illustrations, advertisements, and cartoons.

- Each visual has a caption that asks you to think about the image and its relationship to the unit.

ACTIVITIES

- This book contains a variety of activities. These activities are highlighted with a turquoise-coloured activity number in the margin and are designed to allow you to explore a theme through reading, writing, listening, speaking, and viewing. Sometimes you may be asked to complete the activities independently. In other cases you will work with a partner, a small group, or the whole class.

- The last activity in each Core unit includes a list of possible Extension Ideas for the unit. These activities suggest larger projects that will help you continue your exploration of the theme through independent study or group work.

INFOBOXES

- Throughout the book you will notice infoboxes highlighted with a blue border. These boxes offer information about literature, language, and media that relate to the topic of the unit and help you complete the activities in the unit. A list of these boxes is provided in an Index at the back of the book.

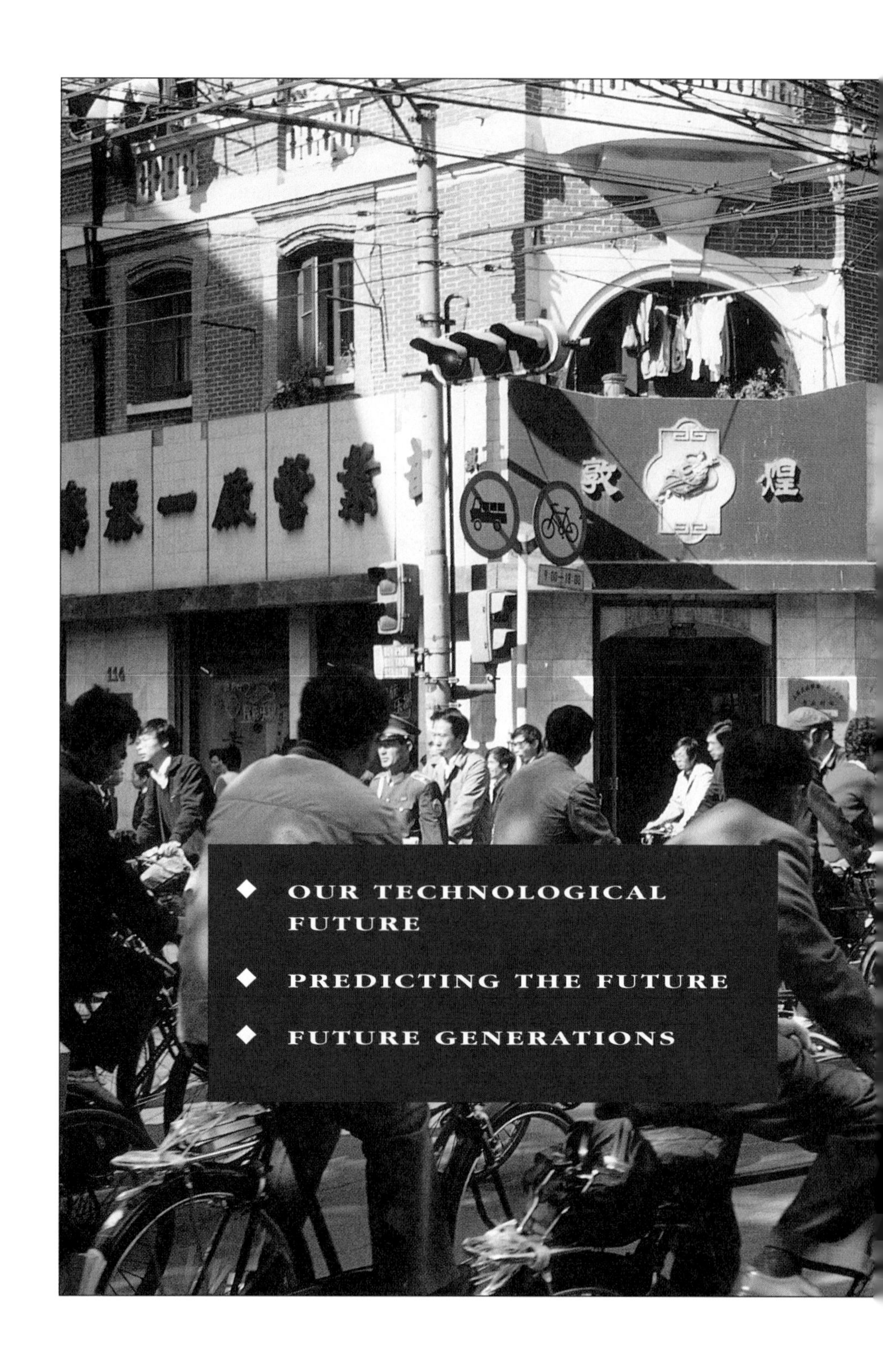
◆ OUR TECHNOLOGICAL FUTURE
◆ PREDICTING THE FUTURE
◆ FUTURE GENERATIONS
敦 煌

UNIT 1

WHAT'S AHEAD

As you head towards a new stage in your life, it is natural to wonder about what lies ahead. You may have begun to set goals and to establish your priorities for the future. But the future holds many changes that will have a great impact on how you live your life.

In this unit, you will think, talk, read, and write about the future. By reflecting on your personal goals and the changes you may have to adapt to, you will be better able to face the challenges ahead.

OUR TECHNOLOGICAL FUTURE

Many short stories, movies, and songs explore the idea of life in the future. In *Star Wars*, the wisdom of the past is used to deal with situations in the future.

Planning for your future can be a rather daunting task. You can't begin to imagine all the changes that are in store for you in your lifetime. Technological and social changes are occurring at a rapid rate. Old familiar routines are disappearing and changing. In this section, you'll have an opportunity to think about your future as well as reflect on some of the technological developments of the twentieth century.

ACTIVITY 1
CHANGES

1. What does the future hold in store? Explore your thoughts on this subject in a journal entry. What personal goals do you have? What changes do you foresee in your daily routines and your career choices as a result of technological developments and changing social structures? How will your life differ from that of your parents or grandparents?

2. If possible, interview an older relative or friend about the changes that have occurred in his or her lifetime. Consider going to a senior citizens' home and asking if any of the people there would like to share their stories with you. Prepare your questions ahead of time. Ask open-ended questions such as:
   - What changes have occurred in modes of transportation in your lifetime? How do you feel about these changes?
   - What was your daily routine like when you were my age?
   - What has remained consistent throughout your life?
   - Do you have any advice to give about adapting to a changing world?

3. Discuss the interviews with your classmates. Which responses did you find most interesting? Were you surprised by any of the changes described? Why or why not?

4. a) Did the subject's attitude towards the changes he or she has faced affect your feelings about your future?
   b) Refer to the journal entry you wrote for question 1. Have your feelings changed at all? Why or why not?

The following personal essay describes one individual's response to technological innovation. It explores the impact of technology on society by asking a fundamental question: Is technological advance necessarily good? This essay may challenge some ideas that you take for granted.

WENDELL BERRY EXPLAINS WHY HE IS NOT GOING TO BUY A COMPUTER

Wendell Berry

Like almost everybody else, I am hooked to the energy corporations, which I do not admire. I hope to become less hooked to them. In my work, I try to be as little hooked to them as possible. As a farmer, I do almost all of my work with horses. As a writer, I work with a pencil or a pen and a piece of paper.

How could I write conscientiously against the rape of nature if I were, in the act of writing, implicated in the rape?

My wife types my work on a Royal standard typewriter bought new in 1956 and as good now as it was then. As she types, she sees things that are wrong and marks them with small checks in the margins. She is my best critic because she is the one most familiar with my habitual errors and weaknesses. She also understands, sometimes better than I do, what *ought* to be said. We have, I think, a literary cottage industry that works well and pleasantly. I do not see anything wrong with it.

A number of people, by now, have told me that I could greatly improve things by buying a computer. My answer is that I am not going to do it. I have several reasons, and they are good ones.

The first is the one I mentioned at the beginning. I would hate to think that my work as a writer could not be done without a direct dependence on strip-mined coal. How could I write conscientiously against the rape of nature if I were, in the act of writing, implicated in the rape? For the same reason, it matters to me that my writing is done in the daytime, without electric light.

I do not admire the computer manufacturers a great deal more than I admire the energy industries. I have seen their advertisements, attempting to seduce struggling or failing farmers into the belief that they can solve their problems by buying yet another piece of expensive equipment. I do not see that computers are bringing us one step nearer to anything that does matter to me: peace, economic justice, ecological health, political honesty, family and community stability, good work.

What would a computer cost me? More money, for one thing,

than I can afford, and more than I wish to pay to people whom I do not admire. But the cost would not be just monetary. It is well understood that technological innovation always requires the discarding of the "old model" – the "old model" in this case being not just our old Royal standard, but my wife, my critic, my closest reader, my fellow worker. Thus (and I think this is typical of present-day technological innovation), what would be superseded would be not only something, but somebody. In order to be technologically up-to-date as a writer, I would have to sacrifice an association that I am dependent upon and that I treasure.

What would a computer cost me? More money, for one thing, than I can afford, and more than I wish to pay to people whom I do not admire.

My final and perhaps my best reason for not owning a computer is that I do not wish to fool myself. I disbelieve, and therefore strongly resent, the assertion that I or anybody else could write better or more easily with a computer than with a pencil.

To make myself as plain as I can, I should give my standards for technological innovation in my own work. They are as follows:

1. The new tool should be cheaper than the one it replaces.
2. It should be at least as small in scale as the one it replaces.
3. It should do work that is clearly and demonstrably better than the one it replaces.
4. It should use less energy than the one it replaces.
5. If possible, it should use some form of solar energy, such as that of the body.
6. It should be repairable by a person of ordinary intelligence, provided that he or she has the necessary tools.
7. It should be purchasable and repairable as near to home as possible.
8. It should come from a small, privately owned shop or store that will take it back for maintenance and repair.
9. It should not replace or disrupt anything good that already exists, and this includes family and community relationships. ▼

Everyone faces the challenge of deciding how to adjust to technological changes.

ACTIVITY 2
RESPONDING TO A PERSONAL ESSAY

1. Summarize Berry's thoughts on technological innovation. Do you agree with him? Why or why not? What would you do if you were in his situation?
2. With a partner, discuss your reactions to the essay by Wendell Berry. Are your reactions similar? Are they different? How do you account for the similarities and the differences?
3. Look at the cartoon on this page. What does the cartoon say about technological innovation? Compare and contrast the ideas presented in the essay and in the cartoon. Which one makes its point more effectively? Explain.
4. Form a group of four to discuss your ideas about technology further. Choose a perspective to argue, such as, to promote technological innovation at any cost or to resist technological innovation. Debate the issue. Try to support your opinions.

PREDICTING THE FUTURE

The future has become the subject of highly specialized study in universities and private industry around the world. In the twenty-first century, the futurists expect technology to develop even more rapidly than it has during the past 100 years. In this section, you will make your own predictions about life in the twenty-first century and compare your ideas to what the experts are saying.

With pollution and traffic congestion threatening the industrial world, the bicycle may become the vehicle of tomorrow.

This solar and electric car was built at the University of Waterloo.

Turkey may be the fast-food star of the future. It is moist, nutritious, and low in cholesterol and calories.

Of 80 000 species of edible plants in the world, about twenty to twenty-two feed the world. Rice, wheat, and corn alone account for the bulk of our food supply.

ACTIVITY 3
PREDICTING

1. What changes do you think you will see in your lifetime? Consider the areas of communication, transportation, food, climate, and family life. Refer to the photographs on page 25 for ideas. Brainstorm a list of the possible changes.
2. Share your thoughts with a partner. Together, choose one of your ideas about the future to develop further. How will this change affect your life? Will you benefit from it, or not?
3. Prepare an oral presentation for the class, describing your prediction and its impact on life in the future. You may want to create illustrations to use in your presentation.

The following imaginary account about life in Vancouver in 2060 is based on interviews with several experts including Frank Ogden of Vancouver, co-founder of the Canadian chapter of the World Future Society. The World Future Society provides services for professional forecasters and planners. Also interviewed was Christian de Laet, a consultant at Montreal's Gamma Institute which carries out future-oriented studies for government and industry.

Each person's vision of the future lies in his or her imagination.

A DAY IN THE YEAR 2060

Rae Corelli

> ...No one could have foreseen recorded history's worst earthquake, which killed more than thirteen million Japanese...

Linda Harrison had been wrestling with the problem for a week. Now, as she placed raw vegetables on a plate, she found herself more and more attracted to the idea of applying to the North Vancouver Genesis Centre for permission to have a third child. She put the plate under the 30.5 cm-diameter sonic dome and brushed the sensor with her hand, activating the low-pitched melodious tone that would heat her lunch. Harrison left the kitchen and stood in the transparent ceramic sphere of her living room, absently watching the rain and the swirling mists that obscured the upper flanks of Grouse Mountain. As the sky darkened, detectors automatically turned up the light levels in the apartment. Perhaps, Harrison reflected, the federal law empowering the provinces to limit the size of families was justified. After all, the North American economy was only now beginning to revive following its total collapse in 2047. There had been no economic safeguards that could have protected the West against Japan's overnight withdrawal of almost $995 billion in foreign investment. But then, no one could have foreseen recorded history's worst earthquake, which killed more than thirteen million Japanese and led Tokyo to repatriate its assets to rebuild the shattered nation.

Still, Harrison felt that it would be unfair if the centre ruled that Rolfe, nine, and Peter, four, were enough children – especially for a woman only forty-six and still in her prime with a life expectancy of at least 125 years – forty-five years longer than the Canadian female average in 1990. Perhaps, Harrison thought, she could argue that she wanted a daughter to give the family better balance.

Harrison realized that, for some time now, the tone from the sonic dome had been telling her that her vegetables were ready. While she ate and watched the rain, her preoccupation with having a daughter led her to think of her own childhood in the second decade of the twenty-first century when she could vaguely remember her mother actually boiling *water* to cook vegetables. She guessed that genetic engineering – which had led to the development of new strains of green beans and mushrooms and dozens of other things that heated themselves in response to sound – was truly one of the marvels of the mid-twenty-first century.

She punched the head-office co-ordinates into the control panel of her electric car and pressed the activator.

But her children were marvels on a far more impressive scale. Rolfe had been conceived in the old-fashioned natural way in 2051 – during a relationship now long gone in a society where marriage was a rarity – but Peter had been nurtured in an artificial womb at the Genesis Centre, which had fertilized her egg with an anonymous donor's sperm cell that had been genetically altered to correct minor abnormalities. So having a daughter would be a simple process – if her application were approved. An obstacle might be her capacity to support a larger family. Still, while her $250 000-a-year salary was modest enough, it provided a good life in the five-room apartment in the seven-storey apartment cluster in the Upper Lonsdale district. Which was just as well: she would never be able to afford the $7 million for an average three-bedroom house in neighboring West Vancouver.

Her reverie was interrupted by the musical murmuring of the phone. She put her plate aside and pressed the receive button on the console beside her chair, hoping it was Kurt calling from the lunar engineering laboratory. But the holographic projector in a panel above her head flashed a full-size three-dimensional image of Nancy Wong into the middle of the living room. Her boss smiled tentatively; people always did while waiting for someone to answer. Harrison pressed a second button, and the transmitter across the room glowed pale amber.

Wong told Harrison that three senior officials of the firm they worked for had just flown in from Hong Kong, Frankfurt and Singapore. Now, Wong wanted Harrison to bring her team to company headquarters for a conference on developments in consumer robotics. They disconnected. Harrison called the three members of her group, shut down the video communications system in the room that had been her office for three years and rode the building's centre-core elevator on a cushion of compressed air to the basement garage. She punched the head-office co-ordinates into the control panel of her electric car and pressed the activator. The five-centimetre screen began flashing STANDBY, and for nearly a minute the car did not move. Then the display changed to ACTIVATING, the garage door slid noiselessly sideways, and the little car – its occupant sitting with her hands folded – sped to the nearby Lonsdale Avenue intersection where it paused briefly until the Greater Vancouver segment of TrafCon, the nationwide traffic-control computer, located an opening and fed it into the traffic.

...The latest fashion fad among Caucasian women was to have their eyes surgically altered to give them an Eastern cast.

Speeding down Lonsdale fifteen centimetres behind the car ahead, Harrison skimmed the news in *The Electronic Sun* on the car's InfoScreen. Another robots-in-sports scandal: this time the New York Yankees had been fined $30 million for using a disguised Generation VII robot at third base. They would not have been caught if the robot had not malfunctioned in his second at-bat and driven a ball through the centre-field scoreboard. She flicked the screen off and played her usual game of trying to guess which of the six acrylic tunnels under Burrard Inlet between North Vancouver and the city TrafCon would slot her into. She whooshed out of the tunnel and spiralled up the ramp to the fourth level of the parking terminal at Howe and West Georgia. The nine kilometres had taken nearly eight minutes. No wonder the metropolitan region's eight million residents were up in arms over traffic delays. She could not imagine what it must have been like decades ago when people had to leave their homes every day and travel long distances just to work.

On West Georgia, in the shadow of the four-block-square indoor ski centre, she was surprised to discover that the Eyes Right chain had opened yet another outlet. With Asians making up seventy per cent of the people who lived in Greater Vancouver, the latest fashion fad among Caucasian women was to have their eyes surgically altered to give them an Eastern cast. She wondered how so many people could afford the procedure: only about forty per cent of the adult population had the skills needed to qualify for a job at a time when total human knowledge was doubling every nine months.

The meeting at FuturEngineering lasted about ninety minutes. Most of it revolved around the success of the Singapore team in extracting a crude but unmistakable emotional response from an FE3000 series domestic robot. The experiment had involved programming the FE3000's artificial intelligence with an index of activities, which had been rated on a scale from "most desirable" to "least desirable." When the robot had been promised and then denied the opportunity to engage in the "most desirable," it had knocked the team leader unconscious. That was interpreted as disappointment. Harrison was asked to explore the market for emotionally reactive robots.

The huge creature had been cloned from a single cell in 30 000-year-old tissue unearthed from the frozen Siberian wasteland.

To Harrison, the project made no sense. She headed for her car, remarking to a friend, "Science spends more than seventy years developing artificially intelligent robots that unquestioningly perform tasks ranging from guarding prisons to housework, and now we want to make them disagreeable." She recalled the Pleistocene-age mastodon she and the children had seen bellowing in its enclosure at the Los Angeles SuperZoo. The huge creature had been cloned from a single cell in 30 000-year-old tissue unearthed from the frozen Siberian wasteland. If the world wanted a new class of serfs, why not clone them from the centuries-old remains of people who actually had been serfs? She concluded that she was likely just jealous of the billionaires whose lives beneath the vast climate-controlling ceramic dome covering West Vancouver were made immeasurably easier by household robots.

After work, when TrafCon brought Harrison's car out of the parking garage, she discovered that the rain had given way to a blizzard. The temperature had dropped sharply. Such drastic weather changes were becoming increasingly common and unpredictable. Year by year, the tree line across the North

American continent was receding and cold polar air was pushing farther and farther south. That cold air eventually encountered warm air generated by the global greenhouse effect, and the result was constant atmospheric turmoil, especially over the northern British Columbia desert. Tomorrow, Harrison mused as the little car sped into the Burrard tunnel leading to North Vancouver, it would probably be hot and sunny. TrafCon shunted her off onto a northbound Lonsdale exit ramp, and she looked up from her car's InfoScreen in time to see the apartment clusters – perched on carbon and concrete stems and resembling gigantic bunches of grapes – come into view. The snow had eased off, but accelerating forty-eight-kilometre-an-hour winds were driving what remained of it.

She heated and ate two of the large mushrooms that tasted like hamburger and climbed into bed.

Harrison's body heat failed to open the apartment entranceway; perhaps the infrared detector was acting up again. Last week, the delicate mechanism had malfunctioned and the panel had opened every time the neighbor's dog walked by. She pressed her palm against the autolock and the panel opened, closing silently behind her. Harrison checked the message centre in the communications room: Rolfe and Peter were spending the night with a friend under the dome in West Vancouver.

Feeling lonely suddenly, Harrison wandered aimlessly around the apartment, missing Kurt and wondering whether she should try to get on a moon shuttle the next day and pay him an unexpected visit. But Harrison decided that was not a good plan; Kurt hated surprises. She toyed with the notion of exploring the 500 worldwide channels of holographic television where the night before she had been both fascinated and appalled by a historical documentary from Madrid describing a bloody twentieth-century ritual called bullfighting. She turned away and decided instead on an early night. She heated and ate two of the large mushrooms that tasted like hamburger and climbed into bed. The snow had turned to rain that coursed down the outer translucent shell of her bedroom sphere, forming patterns on the interior wall opposite the bed. She dimmed the lights, turned on the old-fashioned two-dimensional monitor and called up the classic novel that Nancy

Wong had recommended. It was entitled *Nineteen Eighty-Four* and had been written by somebody called Orwell. Harrison thought the plot was pretty farfetched. ▼

ACTIVITY 4
LIFE IN 2060

1. Jot down a list of the predictions presented in this imaginary account. To organize your thoughts, spend a few minutes thinking about each of the following topics: transportation, food, mass media, communication devices, climate, entertainment, economy, workplace, and family life and daily routines.
2. In a small group, discuss the predictions by topic. Do the predictions seem reasonable to you? Why or why not? How do you feel about this vision of the future? Explain your response.
3. What do you think of the way the character Harrison is depicted? How do her values compare with present-day social values? Do you think Harrison's concerns perpetuate a stereotype? Why or why not? How would the account differ if Harrison were male? Explain.
4. How did the predictions you made in Activity 2 compare with those presented in the fictional account? How do they differ? How do you account for the similarities and the differences?
5. Does this article remind you of any other articles, short stories, or novels you have read, or movies or television programs you have seen? If so, describe one to a partner. How is it similar? How does it differ? Why do you think futuristic settings are so popular in literature and films?

FUTURE GENERATIONS

Writers often use their talent to express their concerns about problems they see around them. In the following poems, two well-known Canadian poets Gwendolyn MacEwen and Miriam Waddington reach out to future generations with their messages.

Future generations may become more concerned with the existence of chemicals in food. The product pictured here is wholly organic.

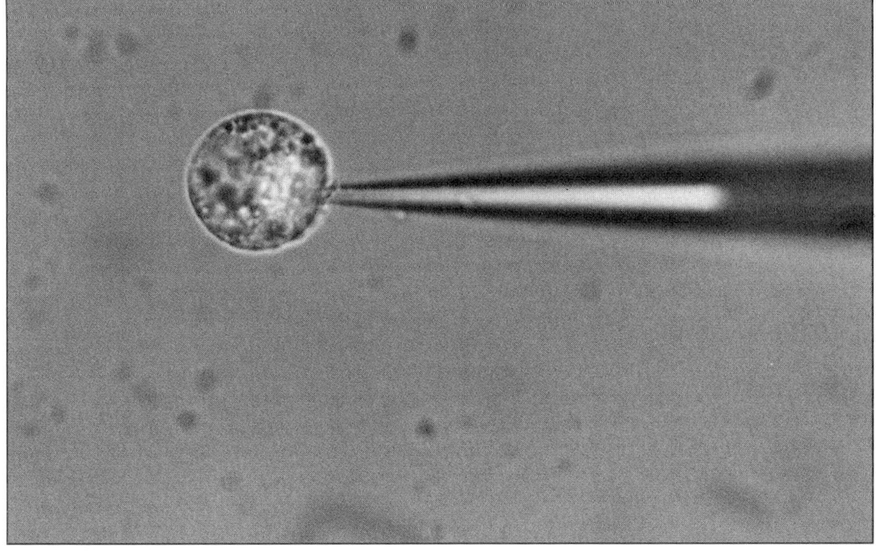

Future generations will have to deal with the moral issue of tampering with nature. Here, a foreign gene is being implanted into a live plant cell.

LETTER TO A FUTURE GENERATION

Gwendolyn MacEwen

we did not anticipate you, you bright ones
though some of us saw you kneeling behind our bombs,
we did not fervently grow towards you
for most of us grew backwards
sowing our seed in the black fields of history

avoid monuments, engrave our names beneath your own
for you have consumed our ashes by now
for you have one quiet mighty language by now

do not excavate our cities
to catalogue the objects of our doom
but burn all you find to make yourselves room,
you have no need of archaeology,
your faces are your total history

for us it was necessary to invent a darkness,
to subtract light in order to see,
for us it was certain death to know our names
as they were written in the black books of history

I stand with an animal at my left hand
and a warm, breathing ghost at my right
saying, Remember that this letter was made
for you to burn, that its meaning lies
only in your burning it,
that its lines await your cleansing fire –
understand it only insofar
as that warm ghost at my right hand breathed
down my blood and for a moment wrote the lines
while guns sounded out from a mythical city
and destroyed the times

ADVICE TO THE YOUNG

Miriam Waddington

1

Keep bees and
grow asparagus,
watch the tides
and listen to the
wind instead of
the politicians
make up your own
stories and believe
them if you want to
live the good life.

2

All rituals
are instincts
never fully
trust them but
study to im-
prove biology
with reason.

3

Digging trenches
for asparagus
is good for the
muscles and
waiting for the
plants to settle
teaches patience
to those who are
usually in too
much of a hurry.

4
There is morality
in bee-keeping
it teaches how
not to be afraid
of the bee swarm
it teaches how
not to be afraid of
finding new places
and building in them
all over again.

ACTIVITY 5
COMPARING POEMS

1. Read "Letter to a Future Generation" and "Advice to the Young." Summarize in your own words each poet's message.
2. In what ways are the two poems similar? In what ways are they different? Which poem do you prefer? Why?
3. When asked about this poem, Waddington said that it "is an ironic and dramatic poem based on the duality of the world as it is and the world as it should be." Summarize in your own words what you think she means. Does reading this quote affect your response to her poem? Explain.
4. What advice would you give to future generations? Your message could be in the form of a letter or a poem.

END THOUGHTS

In this unit, you have had the opportunity to think, talk, read, and write about the future. By exploring how you want to live your life and the changes that may occur, you are better able to meet the challenges of the future.

ACTIVITY 6
EXTENSION IDEAS

1. Create a collage to illustrate what you think will be the important elements of your life in the future.
2. Prepare a scrapbook of articles and photographs about new advances in technology.
3. Write an essay describing an ideal future society.
4. Write an advice column for high-school graduates giving them advice on how they should prepare for life in the future.
5. Invite a panel of students from your school who have graduated and enrolled in a technical or business school to talk with your class about their experiences. Ask them to focus on the skills they needed to learn on the job.
6. If you have a career in mind, see if you can spend a day "job shadowing" a person in that career. Job shadowing means that you spend a day following the person in his or her job, observing all that he or she does. Keep a record of the various things involved in doing the job. Make a list of those abilities that you will need to acquire to be successful in the job.
7. Watch a futuristic video such as *Star Wars*, *Star Trek*, *Blade Runner*, *1984*, *Dune*, *Brazil*, or *Hardware*. Write a report about the vision of the future that is presented in the movie. Do you think the vision is accurate? Why or why not? Would you like to live in such a world? Give your reasons.

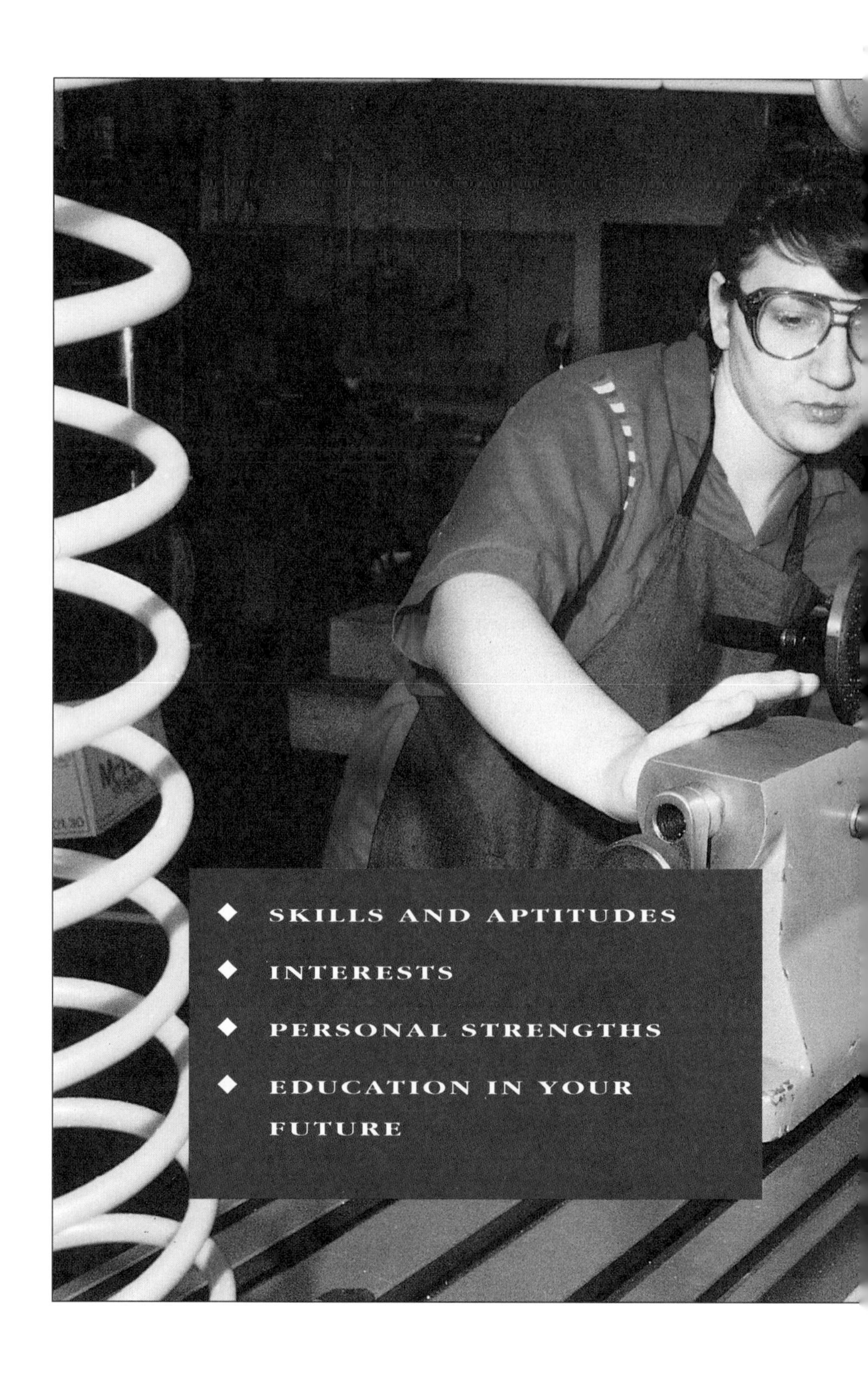
SKILLS AND APTITUDES
INTERESTS
PERSONAL STRENGTHS
EDUCATION IN YOUR FUTURE

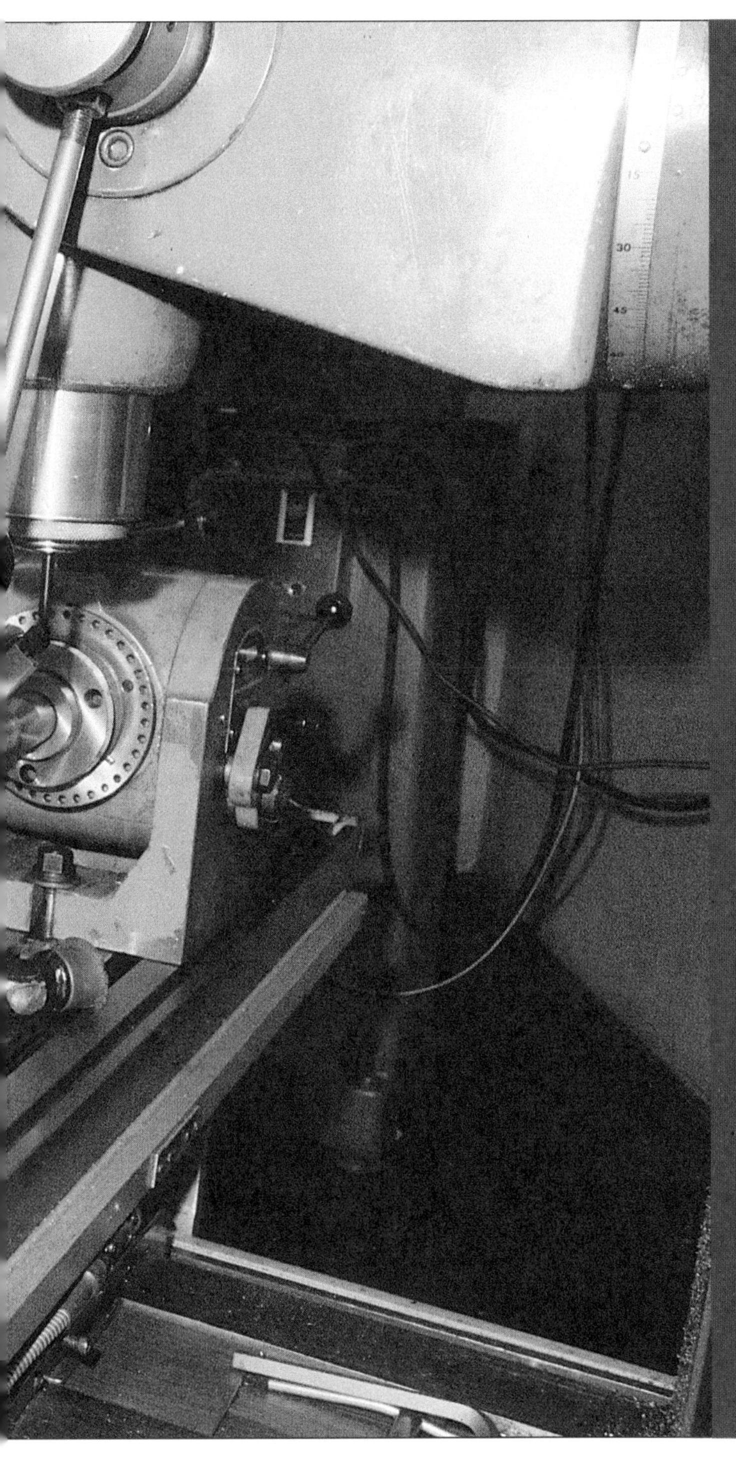

UNIT 2

TAKING STOCK

What does the future hold? It's up to you. You have the power – and the responsibility – to make decisions that will affect your future.

In this unit, you will take stock of your talents, skills, interests, and personal style. The information you gain in your self-inventory will help you to consider career options and determine what immediate actions may be required to achieve your long-term goals.

SKILLS AND APTITUDES

At this point in your life you have already acquired a number of different skills. You have also shown talent in specific areas. You have the aptitude, or the potential, to develop skills in those areas.

The following broad categories provide an inventory of skills and aptitudes. You can use these categories to think about the skills you have and the aptitudes you may develop.

Interpersonal Skills: These are the skills that you use when interacting with people. Helping, serving, motivating, encouraging, leading, selling, persuading, or speaking require interpersonal skills. Do you like to talk with new people? Do you enjoy working in groups? If so, you probably have strong interpersonal skills.

Business Skills: You use business skills for any of the various operations or details of trade or industry. Handling facts, figures, or records requires strong business skills. If you like to manage, record, plan, copy, file, keep records, organize, or budget you may want to consider developing your business skills.

Manual Skills: These are skills that you perform with your hands. Operating, repairing, or building machinery or equipment requires manual skills. When you use your hands to manufacture or produce a product, you are using your manual skills. If you like to sew clothing, repair computers, prepare food, or work on motors then you have an aptitude for manual skills.

Creative Skills: You use creative skills to solve problems and express thoughts or feelings in original ways. If you like to invent, paint, write stories, or make music then you probably have an aptitude for creative skills.

A high-school student developed the following chart to take stock of her skills and aptitudes.

Inventory of Skills and Aptitudes

	Interpersonal	Business	Manual	Creative
At home	babysit my younger sister; keep her happy and occupied		operate lawn mower	
At school	can get people to share ideas when doing group work	accounting is my best subject		enjoy creative writing
Part-time work	serve customers at fast food restaurant	balance till at end of evening	operate cash register, deep fryer	
In the community	volunteer at animal clinic	make out monthly bills	clean animal cages	
Through hobbies			build model cars	write poetry
Through clubs	secretary for church group	record minutes		

This chart provides an inventory of one student's skills and aptitudes.

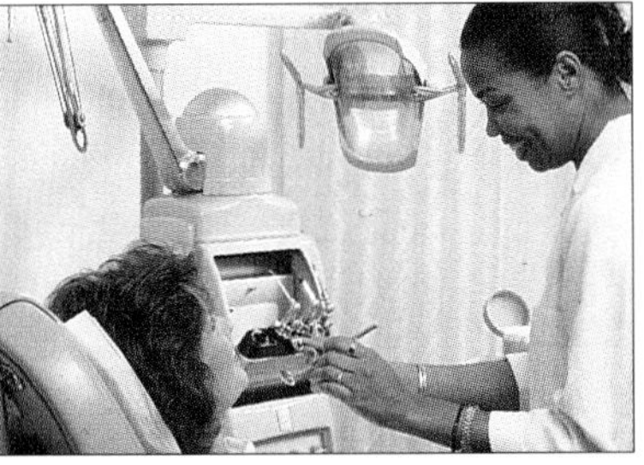

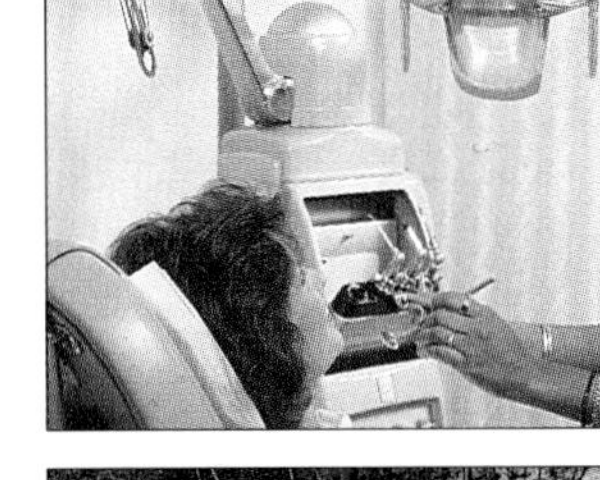

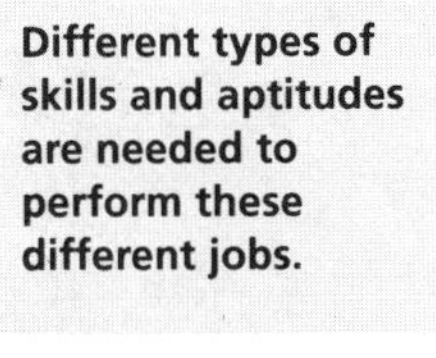

Different types of skills and aptitudes are needed to perform these different jobs.

ACTIVITY 1 INVENTORY OF SKILLS AND APTITUDES

1. Brainstorm a list of your skills and aptitudes. The four categories of skills (Interpersonal, Business, Manual, Creative) may help to organize your thoughts.
2. Using the *Inventory of Skills and Aptitudes* on page 41 as a model, develop your own self-inventory chart. Try to be as specific as possible when you are recording your skills and aptitudes.
3. When you have completed your chart share it with someone who knows you. Ask that person to suggest any skills or aptitudes that you may have left out.
4. Review your chart. Indicate the five items that you feel are your strongest skills and aptitudes or that you enjoy doing most of all. Think about how you would like to develop them further in the future. Record your thoughts in your notebook.

Open the door to your future by recognizing your strong and weak points.

INTERESTS

Your interests will also play an important part in your selection of future goals. The following chart will help you to consider where your interests in a particular subject or area might lead.

Art	photographer, interior designer, lithographer, cartoonist, jeweller, illustrator, art historian...
Business Education	accountant, systems analyst, accounting clerk, cashier, administrative assistant...
Biology	dietitian, game warden, paleontologist, arborist, medical illustrator, dentist, bacteriologist...
Chemistry	textile technician, film developer, diagnostic radiologist, assayer, atomic scientist...
English	performer, travel agent, research director, teacher, speech pathologist, reporter, auctioneer, author...
Family Studies	food services, fashion retailer, nursing attendant, day-care worker, psychologist...
Physical & Health Education	horse industry, coach, lifeguard, athletic therapist, medicine...
Mathematics	teller, statistician, seismologist, pharmacist, pilot, electronic technician, biologist, computer programmer...
Modern Languages	flight attendant, courier, anthropologist, export clerk, singer, salesperson...
Music	recording technician, librarian, choreographer, composer, orchestra conductor, disc jockey...
Physics	ophthalmologist, medical technologist, electroplater, astrophysicist, audio engineer...
Social Studies	lawyer, criminologist, journalist, demographer, social worker, economist, historian...
Technical Education	computer graphics, tool-and-die maker, pilot, engineer, architect, aircraft mechanic...

ACTIVITY 2
PURSUING YOUR INTERESTS

1. Read through the list of careers on page 43. Identify the subject areas in which you have the greatest interest. Are there any careers listed which you would like to learn more about? If so, what are they? Why do they interest you? If not, can you think of another career that you would be interested in learning more about?
2. How would you obtain more information about a particular career? In a group of three or four students, brainstorm some ideas. Consider the resources you have within your school and your community.
3. Choose a career which you would like to learn more about. Research, using the resources available in your school and community, to find out what skills and aptitudes are needed and what formal training is required. Would you like to pursue the career further? What immediate actions would be required to achieve your long-term goal?
4. Review your response to question 3 in Activity 2. Are there any similarities between the skills and aptitudes you considered developing further and the skills and aptitudes needed for the career you researched? If so, describe the similarities. If not, how do they differ? How do you account for the similarities and the differences?
5. Has considering your interests as well as your skills and aptitudes changed your thoughts of what you might like to do in the future? Explain your response to a partner.

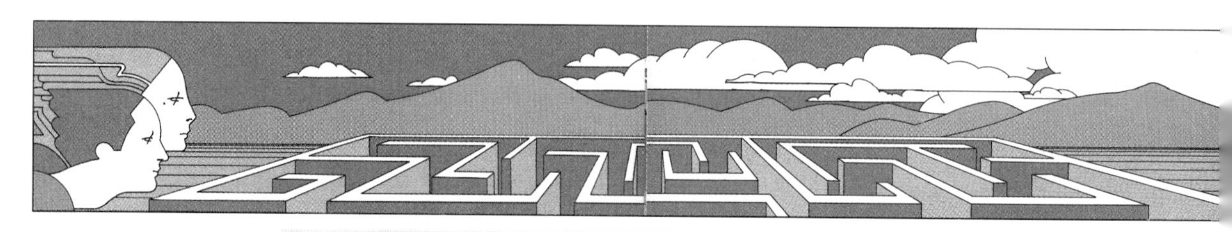

The future may sometimes seem like a maze. Find your way by thinking about what career interests you.

PERSONAL STRENGTHS

When are you at your best? In what kinds of situations are you most comfortable? What kind of behaviour is typical of you? For example, when working in a group are you usually more talkative or less talkative than the other group members? Do you prefer to deal with people or with tasks? It is important to take stock of your personal style as well as your skills, aptitudes, and interests when thinking about your career and educational future. This section will help you to consider your personal strengths and how to use them to your advantage. It will help you, too, to recognize your weaknesses and consider ways of dealing with them.

ACTIVITY 3
PERSONAL STYLE

1. How can your attitude at the beginning of a task affect its outcome? Write about a personal experience where your initial attitude affected the outcome. Your experience might be either positive or negative.
2. List three of your strengths. In a journal entry, describe personal experiences where you have used your strengths to your benefit. Consider how your strengths might be used to your advantage in the future. For example, *I'm very persuasive. I was able to convince our principal to start a recycling program at our school. In the future, I'd like to work on a fund-raising campaign for a cause I believe in.*
3. List three weaknesses that you believe you have. In a journal entry, explore how you could deal with those weaknesses in the future. For example, *Sometimes I fly off the handle. When I am under pressure at the restaurant I often blow up at my co-workers. In the future, I'll try to remain calm, listen to my co-workers, and remember we're all in it together.*
4. Has considering your personal strengths and weaknesses affected your thoughts on what you might like to do in the future? Discuss your response with a partner.

WHEN ARE YOU AT YOUR BEST?

Susan Perry and Jim Dawson

All living organisms, from mollusks to men and women, exhibit biological rhythms. Some are short and can be measured in minutes or hours. Others last days or months. The peaking of body temperature, which occurs in most people every evening, is a daily rhythm. The menstrual cycle is a monthly rhythm. The increase in sex drive in the autumn – not in the spring, as poets tell us – is a yearly rhythm.

...The time of day when a person receives X-ray or drug treatment for cancer can ultimately mean the difference between life and death.

The idea that our bodies are in constant flux is fairly new – and goes against traditional medical training. In the past, many doctors were taught to believe the body has a relatively stable, or homeostatic, internal environment.

As early as the 1940s, however, some scientists questioned this view of the body. Franz Halberg, a young European scientist working in the United States, noticed that the number of white blood cells in laboratory mice was dramatically higher and lower at different times of the day. As this kind of research spread to the study of other rhythms in other life forms, the findings were sometimes startling. For example, the time of day when a person receives X-ray or drug treatment for cancer can ultimately mean the difference between life and death.

The scientific and medical communities are beginning to review their ideas about how the human body works, and what had been considered a minor science just a few years ago is now being studied in major universities and medical centres around the world. This is *chronobiology*, and the evidence supporting it has become more persuasive.

Chronobiologists are teaching us things that can literally change our lives – by helping us organize ourselves so we can work *with* our natural rhythms rather than against them. This can enhance our outlook on life, as well as our performance at work and play. Because they are easy to detect and measure, more is known about daily rhythms than any others. The most obvious daily rhythm is the sleep/wake cycle. But there are other daily cycles as well: temperature, blood pressure, hormone levels. Amid the body's changing rhythms, you are simply a different person at nine in the morning than what you are at three in the afternoon. How you feel, how you work, your level of alertness, your sensitivity to taste and smell, how much you enjoy food or take pleasure in music – all change throughout the day.

Some people feel most alert around noon. Soon after that, alertness declines, and sleepiness may set in by mid-afternoon.

Amid the body's changing rhythms, you are simply a different person at nine in the morning than what you are at three in the afternoon.

Your short-term memory is best during the morning – in fact, about fifteen percent more efficient than at any other time of day. So, students, take heed: It pays to review your notes right before that morning exam.

Long-term memory is different. Afternoon is the best time for learning material that you want to recall days, weeks or months later. Politicians, business executives and others who must learn speeches would be wise to do their memorizing at that time of day. If you are a student, you should try to do more studying in the afternoon. Many students believe they memorize better while burning the midnight oil, their short-term recall being better in the wee hours of the morning than it is in the afternoon. But short-term memory won't help them much if they face an exam several days later.

By contrast, we tend to do best on cognitive tasks – things that require the juggling of words and figures in one's head – during the morning hours. This includes balancing a chequebook and solving logical problems.

Your manual dexterity – the speed and co-ordination with which you perform complicated tasks with your hands – peaks in the afternoon. Such work as carpentry, typing or sewing will be slightly easier at this time of day.

What about sports? During the afternoon and early evening, your co-ordination is at its peak, and you're able to react the quickest to an outside stimulus – like a baseball speeding towards you at home plate. Studies have shown that late in the day you will also *perceive* a physical workout to be easier and less fatiguing. You are more likely to work harder during a late-afternoon or early-evening workout, and therefore benefit more from it.

In fact, all of your senses – taste, sight, hearing, touch and smell – may be at their keenest during late afternoon and early evening. This could be why dinner usually tastes better than breakfast, and why bright lights irritate us at night.

Not only does it seem to fly when you are having fun, but to fly even faster if you are having that fun in the late afternoon or early evening, when your body temperature is also peaking.

Even our perception of time changes from hour to hour. Not only does it seem to fly when you are having fun, but to fly even faster if you are having that fun in the late afternoon or early evening, when your body temperature is also peaking.

While all of us follow the same general pattern of ups and downs, the exact timing varies from person to person. It all depends on how your "biological" day is structured – how much of a morning or night person you are. The earlier your biological day gets going, the earlier you are likely to enter and exit the peak times for performing various tasks. But the difference is relatively slight: An extreme morning person and an extreme night person have daily cycles that are no more than a few hours apart.

Each of us can increase our knowledge about our individual rhythms. Learn how to listen to the inner beats of your body; let them set the pace of your day. You will live a healthier and happier life. ▼

Some people believe that your month of birth determines your bio-rhythmic highs and lows.

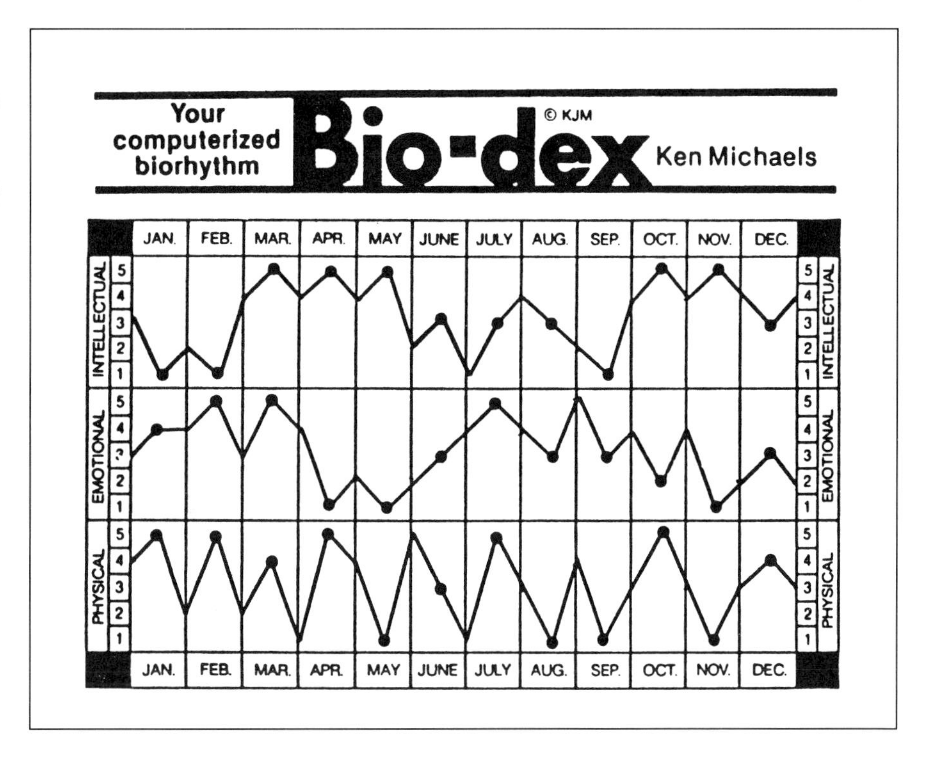

ACTIVITY 4
RESPONDING TO THE ARTICLE

The previous article presents some interesting ideas about when you are at your best.

1. What do the authors mean when they refer to biological rhythms? Give two examples of biological rhythms that are mentioned in the article. What is the study of these rhythms called?

2. According to the article, when is your short-term memory best? What does this tell you about preparing for an exam? Why do the authors suggest that you do more of your studying in the afternoon?

3. Most professional sporting events are played at night or in the afternoon. According to the article, is this a good time for these events? Why?

4. Do you agree with the ideas presented in this article? If so, have you noticed differences in how you feel, how you work, or your level of alertness at different times throughout the day? Will you change your habits based on the article? If you do not agree with the ideas presented, why not? Explain your position to a partner.

EDUCATION IN YOUR FUTURE

How will your training and education affect your future? The following tables provide some facts that you might want to consider as you make your training and education plans.

UNEMPLOYMENT RATES BY AGE, 1989/90
(percentage)

	25 years and over		15-24 years	
	Male	Female	Male	Female
Newfoundland	12.7	14.6	25.7	21.6
P.E.I.	—	—	—	—
Nova Scotia	9.7	10.5	18.1	11.9
New Brunswick	12.5	10.8	24.3	18.1
Quebec	7.9	9.1	14.4	11.8
Ontario	3.9	4.9	8.5	7.4
Manitoba	6.4	4.7	14.4	11.4
Saskatchewan	7.1	6.2	14.1	—
Alberta	5.7	6.1	13.7	11.6
British Columbia	6.8	6.6	16.3	14.3

(Figures not available for some provinces and the territories.)

INCOME BY AGE, 1988

	19 years and under	64 years and under
Canada	$ 4927	$ 20280
Newfoundland	3801	15251
P.E.I.	4100	15008
Nova Scotia	3766	17227
New Brunswick	3860	16143
Quebec	4638	18003
Ontario	5444	22917
Manitoba	4291	19064
Saskatchewan	3913	18249
Alberta	5175	24957
British Columbia	4455	20427

(Figures not available for the territories.)

INCOME BY EDUCATIONAL LEVEL, 1988

Income Groups	0-8 years		Secondary and some post-secondary		University degree	
	Male	Female	Male	Female	Male	Female
Under $2000	3.6%	7.1%	4.9%	8.9%	1.0%	4.7%
$2000 - $2999	1.2	3.1	2.2	4.0	0.4	1.4
3000 - 3999	1.1	3.7	2.1	4.2	0.6	1.8
4000 - 4999	2.3	5.3	2.3	3.6	0.8	2.3
5000 - 7449	8.8	20.3	5.9	10.3	3.6	5.2
7550 - 9999	11.5	22.9	4.9	11.4	3.0	5.4
10000 - 12499	11.6	14.8	5.4	10.4	3.1	5.9
12500 - 14999	8.6	6.3	5.1	7.2	2.9	4.4
15000 - 17499	7.2	5.6	5.8	7.1	3.3	4.7
17500 - 19999	5.5	3.7	5.4	6.6	2.6	5.6
20000 - 22499	5.4	2.4	5.7	6.4	3.8	4.5
22500 - 24999	4.9	1.4	5.2	4.9	3.7	5.9
25000 - 29999	8.3	1.7	9.7	6.3	8.2	9.7
30000 - 39999	12.0	1.1	17.7	6.3	16.9	17.2
40000 - 49999	5.3	0.4	9.6	1.5	15.0	11.9
50000 and over	2.6	0.3	7.9	1.0	31.0	9.4
Average income	$19239	$9970	$25130	$14273	$42035	$26301

ACTIVITY 5 EDUCATION, EMPLOYMENT, AND INCOME

Examine the three tables *Unemployment Rates by Age, Income by Age,* and *Income by Educational Level* on page 50 and this page and answer the following questions.

1. a) What is the unemployment rate in your province for people twenty-five years and over? What is it for the fifteen to twenty-four-year age group? Answer for both male and female.
   b) Which provinces have the highest and the lowest unemployment rate for males and females over twenty-five years? What might be some of the causes of such a difference in unemployment rates?

2. a) What is the average income for all people sixty-four years and under in Canada? What is it for people nineteen years and under? What reasons can you suggest to account for such a difference between the two groups?
   b) What is the average income for people across Canada in the nineteen years and under age group? Now look it up for your province.

3. What is the average income of each of the different educational levels for males and females?

This illustration by Douglas Fraser shows women at work.

4. If you had to quit school at the end of grade eight, what, on the average, would you expect your salary to be?

5. Based on the figures provided in the table *Income by Educational Level*, calculate the difference in average lifetime earnings between males or females at different educational levels.
   Example: Calculate the difference in earnings over thirty years between a female with grade eight schooling and one with a university education.

University degree average income	\$26 301
Grade 8 average income	- \$ 9 970
	\$16 331

   Over thirty years the difference for a female is (30 x \$16 331)= \$489 930.
   a) Calculate the difference in earnings over thirty years between a male with grade eight schooling and a male with a university education.
   b) On average, what will the difference be in earnings over thirty years between a person with some secondary-school education and someone with a university education? Calculate for both males and females.
   c) Calculate on the average how much you will earn in thirty years based on the level of education you hope to attain

6. Form groups of three or four to discuss the following:
   a) Were you surprised by the information in the tables on pages 50 and 51 such as regional differences, differences in the earnings of males and females, differences in earnings by educational level?
   b) Does this information affect your plans for the future in any way? Explain your response.

END THOUGHTS

In this unit, you examined your skills, aptitudes, interests, and personal style. You also explored your career and educational goals. You may have acquired a clearer understanding of your goals and the actions required to achieve those goals. Throughout your working life, you will be constantly reassessing your skills, interests, and goals. The ability to assess your strengths and determine your goals will make you better able to improve your chances for a satisfying lifestyle.

ACTIVITY 6
EXTENSION IDEAS

1. Use the information you have gathered about yourself to prepare for an interview. Role-play an interview situation with a partner. Take turns interviewing each other, asking questions about skills, interests, personality traits, and training. Answer the interviewer's questions in complete sentences. Create a positive picture of yourself for the interviewer.
2. Invite an employer to your class. Ask that person to tell the class what he or she is looking for when hiring an employee.
3. If possible, visit a Canada Employment Centre and have them demonstrate the General Aptitude Test Battery (GATB). Report what you discover about this test to your class.
4. Think about yourself at the age of thirty. Write a résumé for yourself at that age. Include current occupation, previous occupations, marital status, education, community activities, hobbies, and any special accomplishments. Save this résumé and dig it out and look at it when you turn thirty.
5. You will accumulate skills and experiences throughout your life. Select pages at the back of your notebook and label them: (1) skills and aptitudes, (2) interests, (3) educational and future training plans. As you become aware of or develop new attributes, date them and add them to these pages.
6. Talk with your parent(s) or guardian about your future plans. Share with them your self-inventory to see whether they share your description of your skills and aptitudes.
7. Working with a small group, choose a TV character. Complete a self-inventory for this character. Be prepared to share your inventory with your class. Or, complete this inventory on a character in a novel which most members of your class have read.

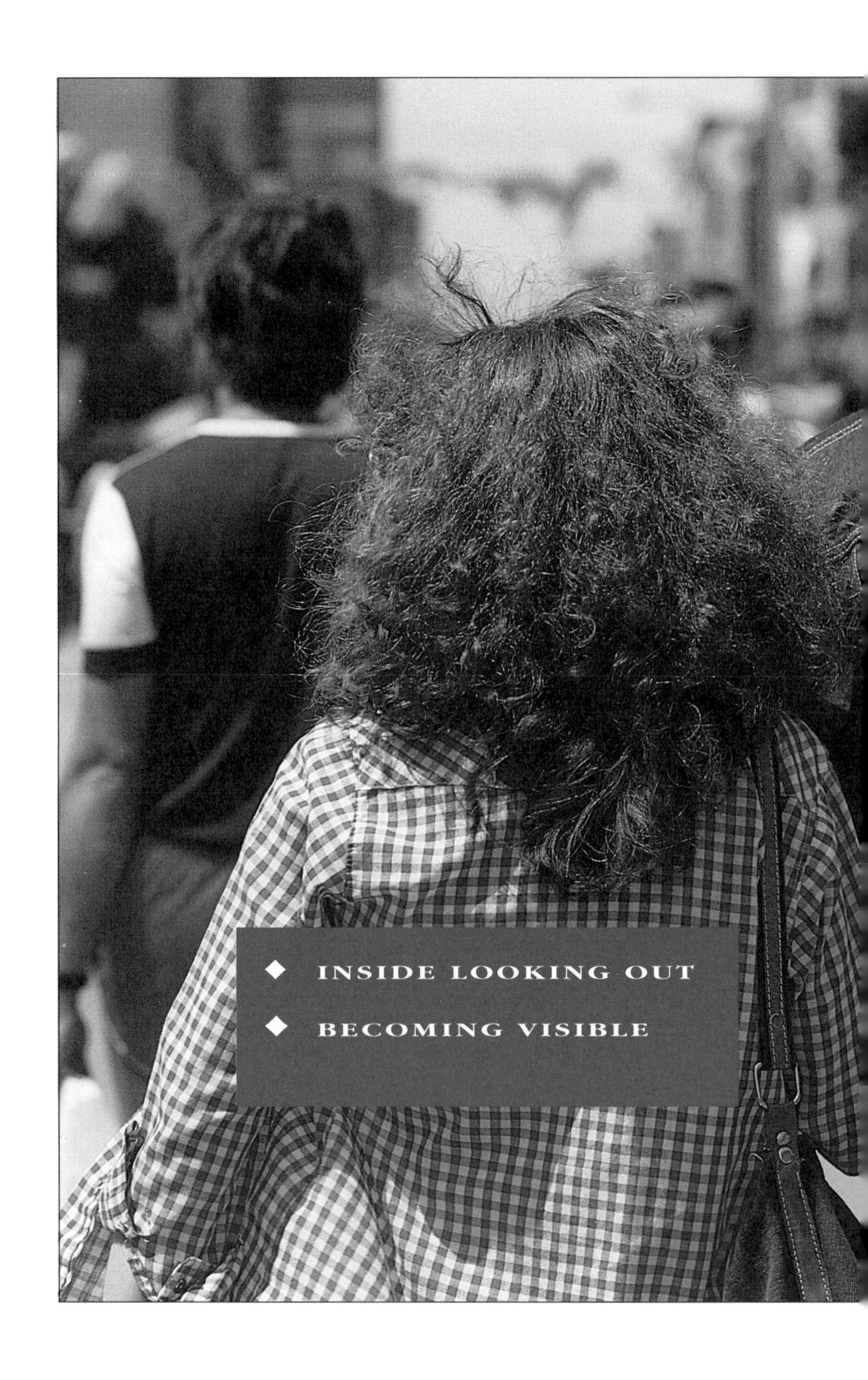
◆ INSIDE LOOKING OUT
◆ BECOMING VISIBLE

UNIT 3

BEING VISIBLE

Looking outward and seeing your surroundings clearly is important. But looking inward and understanding yourself is equally important because it enables you to share your experience and perceptions. Being visible means expressing yourself to others.

In this unit, you will use your reading, writing, group interaction, and viewing skills to consider the ways in which people are visible. You will explore ways in which artists and writers have examined obstacles to becoming visible, and the effects of these obstacles. You will also examine what happens when people choose to become visible through the expression of their own unique experience.

INSIDE LOOKING OUT

Being visible begins with self-examination and leads to self-expression. Consider the self-portraits on this page. How would you describe each of the people? What clues does each self-portrait contain about the artist's personality? Now consider how you present yourself to others. What do you choose to show?

Communicating with someone you trust can help you gain a more accurate picture of how you present yourself to others. Try the following activity to see if the way you perceive yourself matches the way others perceive you. Then read the poem on page 59 by black American writer Audre Lorde. How does she explore the theme of looking inside/looking outside?

***Self-Portrait* by Deborah Samuel.**

***Self-Portrait* by Joyce Wieland, 1978.**

***Self-Portrait* by Norval Morriseau, 1**

ACTIVITY 1
SIGNATURES

1. With a partner check your visibility by filling out a signature chart like the one below. Under each of the headings, note what you believe to be your and your partner's "signature" look, behaviour, and verbal expression. In other words, use the chart to define what makes you, and your partner, look unique.
2. Compare your finished chart with your partner's. How similar were your perceptions of each other? Be sure to explain your opinions. Did any of your perceptions surprise your partner? Did your partner's surprise you?
3. With your partner, brainstorm a list of ways to make yourself more visible.

SIGNATURE CHART

My partner's name:

My partner's signature look	Jean jacket, buttons with environmental slogans.
My partner's signature behaviour	Brushes bangs out of eyes with right hand.
My partner's signature expression	Says "No way!" and "you've got to be kidding!" loudly and quickly.

My name:

My signature look	Black, baggy clothes.
My signature behaviour	Wipe glasses frequently.
My signature expression	"That's neither here nor there" and "Seen any good films lately?"

You can convey your interests and opinions by the clothes you wear. This young man is concerned about nuclear power.

This advertisement shows a young woman conveying an image. How do you express your image?

CONTACT LENSES

Audre Lorde

Lacking what they want to see
makes my eyes hungry
and eyes can feel
only pain.

Once I lived behind thick walls
of glass
and my eyes belonged
to a different ethic
timidly rubbing the edges
of whatever turned them on.
Seeing usually
was a matter of what was
in front of my eyes
matching what was
behind my brain.
Now my eyes have become
a part of me exposed
quick risky and open
to all the same dangers.

I see much
better now
and my eyes hurt.

ACTIVITY 2 RESPONDING TO A POEM

1. Think of a time when your perception of an issue or situation was influenced by your feelings or first-hand experience (for example, the anger you might have felt at the dumping of toxic waste near your home). How was your perception affected? Explain your experience to a partner.
2. With your partner, think about the distinction Lorde makes between "Seeing usually" and seeing now that her "eyes have become/a part of me exposed." What do you think each way of seeing involves? To help you consider this, make a list of words that Lorde uses to describe each way of seeing.
3. Discuss the following questions with your partner, and record your answers.
   a) Why do you think the poet says that "Now my eyes have become/a part of me exposed" that "I see much/better now"?
   b) Why do you think Lorde feels there is risk involved in the second type of seeing? What dangers do you think she is referring to?
4. a) Why do you think Lorde says, "Lacking what they want to see/makes my eyes hungry" and "my eyes hurt"? What might her eyes want to see?
   b) What relationship is Lorde suggesting exists between our personal feelings and experience, and our response to the world around us?
5. Form a small group with another pair and compare answers for numbers 1, 2, and 3.

Mohawk demonstrators.

The 1988 Special Olympics.

Being proud of who you are gives you the confidence to make others understand you better.

Johnny Clegg and Savuka band member.

BECOMING VISIBLE

A number of writers and artists have explored the theme of becoming visible through self-expression. For many, it is a difficult process fraught with barriers. For some, the barriers are personal and for others, the barriers are social. In this section, you will have the opportunity to consider how various artists and writers view the process of becoming visible.

Read the autobiographical account on page 62, "Nei um lung, ma? (Aren't you cold?)," to see how the writer explores her barriers to self-expression. Then read the short story "Golden Girl" on page 67 to consider how this selection deals with the theme of self-expression.

Being able to express yourself to others begins with accepting who you are and where you come from.

NEI UM LUNG, MA? (AREN'T YOU COLD?)

May Yee

I stared at the large black and white photographs of her taken by my big brother. It has been over seven years now. Grandmother. In the photographs she looked so small and fragile, sitting in the kitchen chair in our old apartment, leaning her head on her hand over the kitchen table. Yet her shrunken figure filled my mind with overpowering memories. It was her face – so small and lined, framed by her thin, black hair which I used to trim so carefully. Her eyes – deep with age and things I do not know. And her clothes – embroidered Chinese slippers (from Father's store downstairs), striped flannel pyjamas, covered with a sweater that had only the top two buttons done up.

On our way to school my little brother and I (little then too) would always undo those consipicuous top buttons, like they were strangling us, undo the gesture of love.

Grandmother used to always ask me, and my seven brothers and sisters, if we were cold, telling us to put on a sweater, and when we had one on, she would button only the top two buttons at the neck for us, leaving the unbuttoned part of sweater below to flare to either side, revealing a triangle of the shirt beneath. On our way to school my little brother and I (little then too) would always undo those conspicuous top buttons, like they were strangling us, undo the gesture of love.

And so many years later, and older, don't we still bristle defensively when Mother asks us if we are cold? Are we still waiting for those words we saw blonde mothers telling freckled kids on TV? Still waiting to hear the magic words, "I love you," while reacting in anger to the real thing expressed through such unromantic words of concern – "aren't you cold?" ("Nei um lung, ma?")

Grandmother, if I could answer you now I would say, "Ngen, ngoi lung...." Yes, I feel cold in my denial of your warmth.

"Ngen" – Grandmother. Her name sounds almost the same as the Chinese word for "people." How appropriate, because she embodied for me the people of China, so unknown to me, yet evoking a feeling captured in the word "home," an unknown home. And "home" ("aw kei") was what she used to call China, the land of her birth and life.

Does that make Canada, where my Grandmother spent her last ten years, the land of her dying? Where she died of cancer (such a Western-sounding and modern disease) so far away from "home," in a large Toronto hospital. Her small face, brown and lined with age and pain, like the earth in winter, while all around her was so unlike the earth – the sterile and controlled decay of the white hospital corridors, doors of glass, ways of concrete.

> **...I felt for the first time a real insurmountable distance from him – a gulf where the different colour of our skins was only the surface of depths unplunged.**

Yet this Western city which entombed my Grandmother in her bedroom, then her hospital room, is my "earth," the only earth that my senses know. The corridors of the hospitals she was in were not unlike the corridors of the schools I have daily passed through in my life. The "white ghosts" ("wuq gui") my Grandmother watched from car windows, and even whiter around her hospital bed, I speak to every day in a language that was unknown to her – they are my friends, my teachers, my co-workers.

Yet, sometimes I wonder if I will always feel alien in these white cities, white streets, white corridors, white rooms, amidst unslanted eyes that always first (and always after?) recognize my difference, forever keeping me feeling like an observer on the outside looking in. Eyes that say, "You don't belong here," while mouths ask, "Where do you come from?" – denying me a home here, telling me to return to an unknown home. Do those eyes look at mine and see within them a billion people, see within them my Grandmother, whose only place in this society, outside our family circle, was a hospital bed paid for by Medicare?

Maybe I am exaggerating the restrictions of her life here since, after all, our family circle was quite large, and her feet, which I washed, manicured and massaged for her, had never been bound. Yet the alienation seems total, taken as a measure of her distance from me and my distance from the world without.

When I was with my closest friend, looking at those haunting photos of my Grandmother, I felt for the first time a real insurmountable distance from him a gulf where the different colour of our skins was only the surface of depths unplunged. Gripped by a fear of drowning, I looked at him, the one I always had turned to to save me, and saw a stranger (or am I the stranger?). He sensed my withdrawal. I tried to explain.

But I know that in a way I was grieving also for myself – not for my inevitable physical death, but for the suffocation of some deeply rooted part of my spirit.

I told him about Grandmother, (not about the loneliness in her eyes, but) about how she used to make us put on sweaters, and would not let us go outside with wet hair; how she always complained when the children spoke English to each other in front of her; how she slept on a hard, box-like, black lacquered pillow which she had brought from China; how she kept a small, multicoloured plastic purse filled with little red envelopes for "happy money" ("feng bao"), to be given to all of us on Chinese New Year and birthdays (including her own) – we would thank her, wish her good health, and later, after taking out the money, return the little red envelopes to her to be used again.

Then I told my friend about how Grandmother used to often ask us, her youngest grandchildren, to massage her shoulders and back, to literally, in Chinese, "hammer the body" ("up sien"). It was difficult to describe the punching motion involved, so I went behind my friend and demonstrated on his shoulders. And the strange, but oh-so-familiar motion opened floodgates of so many years another world ago.

And I cried..., wracked by grief I am not even sure I understand – cried in a way I had not been able to seven years ago when Grandmother died, months after we knew she would, from cancer. But I know that in a way I was grieving also for myself – not for my inevitable physical death, but for the suffocation of some deeply rooted part of my spirit. "Ngen," I cried over my denial of you, over the forgetting of memories of you and your world, and of what we share. I cried in recognition of collective memory and shared pain.

And yet I cannot forget that we also denied so much to each

other in turn. As children, we hid the wounds when the outside world hurled names at us like stones. I could never cry in front of any of my family the way I cried in front of my friend. At home, when I used to share a room with my sister and Grandmother, I cried alone, locked inside the bathroom, locked inside my pain, my shame. And I assumed others in my family did the same, or did not cry at all. For the longest time, I wrongly believed the latter.

How many different worlds we find ourselves forced to live or are torn apart in, when we are not allowed to be at "home" in our skins. What different parts of ourselves do we deny to different people, to ourselves, while something deep within us cries out to be whole? What masks do we wear to hide the pain of knowing ourselves to be different, knowing ourselves to be unknowable?

"Ngen," all voyages of self-discovery should be dedicated to you.... And I hope that you are never cold. "Ngoi hei mong nei um lung...." ▼

ACTIVITY 3
BREAKING DOWN THE BARRIERS

1. Who is telling this story? What do you think he or she looks like? What does this person do for a living? for recreation?
2. Do you know anyone like the grandmother? Who is this person? Describe him or her.
3. The narrator says, "...I wonder if I will always feel alien in these white cities...amidst unslanted eyes that always first (and always after?) recognize my difference...." Why do you think the narrator feels this way? What is your reaction to this statement?
4. Explain this line from the story: "...I was grieving...not for my inevitable physical death, but for the suffocation of some deeply rooted part of my spirit." What do you think the narrator means?
5. In a group of three or four, discuss the following questions: Why does Yee say, "'Ngen,' all voyages of self-discovery should be dedicated to you..."? What changes does Yee feel she needs to make in order to "be whole"?

6. Examine the photographs on page 60. In what ways are the people in these photographs concerned with becoming more visible? Why do you think these people feel it is important to become visible? In a small group of three or four people, make a chart in which you list reasons for becoming visible and various methods for doing so. (Have each person in your group make their own copy of the chart.) Your chart might look like the one below. An example of an entry is provided.

REASONS	METHODS
preservation of language, culture	writer's program in schools

GOLDEN GIRL

Janette Turner Hospital

Now I notice colours much more than before. I think I used to let everything rush by my eyes in a heedless swirl, believing there would always be time for the particular. People too – always there, a blizzard of confetti, a festive out-of-focus backdrop to the event of me. It must have been that way.

I note the flash of green and gold in eyes smarting with sudden sun, the blue of winter fingertips, the mottled bloodlessness of a lip bitten with embarrassment.

It's hard to remember.

I look at photographs of myself taken before it happened and I try to enter the picture, to look out at the photographer. I can rarely recall who it was. It does not matter, I suppose. People liked to take my picture. It gave them pleasure and their pleasure pleased me.

Now that I have dwindled to my eyes, I record the world mercilessly and passionately, seeing it for the first time. I mark each wince and the way a face recomposes itself politely. I note the flash of green and gold in eyes smarting with sudden sun, the blue of winter fingertips, the mottled bloodlessness of a lip bitten with embarrassment. I don't recall noticing any of this before.

I do remember that I used to wake greedily each morning, gulping in the day like a glutton. The sun who adores me, who waits upon me hand and foot, what delectations has he prepared for me this day?

There is a heavy penalty for that sort of thing, of course, though I do not believe I was guilty of *hubris*, being only a child, wildly eager. Epiphanies rode on the clock hands; I breathed impatience. I loved the way words and ideas dropped into my mind like rapiers. And I did love being beautiful, I admit it. I exulted in it. Oh I realize it now, I had more than my fair share, I was heavily in arrears. The golden girl herself – a prime case for auditing.

I don't mean I was vain in the ordinary sense, though I was intolerant of slow thinkers. I never looked in mirrors, except surreptitiously. I didn't need to. It was the sighing of eyes, bending my way like grasses before a wind, that sustained me. I could havc livcd on admiration, growing slender and translucent, fragile as a moon flower, my pale hair swaying like corn silk.

She's brilliant too, people whispered.

I would hoard the murmured comments like a lyre-bird lining its nest with forbidden objects.

I always knew my destiny would be extraordinary.

Shortly after it happened I had a curious vision.

There was fire everywhere, the earth crackling and blackening like a turkey forgotten in a hot oven, flames snaking along the ground, wrapping themselves like bracelets around the ankles, licking the walls of buildings, the bottoms of clouds.

There was fire everywhere, the earth crackling and blackening like a turkey forgotten in a hot oven, flames snaking along the ground, wrapping themselves like bracelets around the ankles, licking the walls of buildings, the bottoms of clouds.

The three of us were there – Christina, Wendy, and myself, flailing about and screaming.

And then there were the stairs that went both up and down. We had to choose. Christina ran up, and Wendy and I ran down, all of us mad for the absence of heat. It is hard to say who made the better choice. It is hard to be sure that Wendy and I are lucky to be alive.

They told me I was delirious most of the first few weeks, but I have had the dream again recently. Several times.

It must be Hallowe'en. I look like the bride of Tutankhamen, all wrapped in white and driving dead lovers crazy.

The mask itself is the artwork of a medical school famous for its research. For this I am supposed to consider myself lucky, I am supposed to meditate upon the fact that a mere two years ago a case like mine would have been fatal. I am, in a way, becoming fond of my unquestionably distinctive and traffic-stopping headgear. Resting delicately on a neck brace, it encloses my entire head in a stylish arc of glistening plaster, white as a virgin's underwear. (*She hath no loyal knight and true....* No. That way madness lies.) Round black holes suggest the locations of my eyes, nose, and mouth; and radiating downwards in a dazzling display of pleats and folds and overlaps, the white bandages guard every nook and cranny.

Of course I am as curious as anyone to know what will hatch from this egg.

I have, you see, been rearranged in the most unexpected of ways. I am told that layers of skin like Kleenex tissues have been taken from my thighs and buttocks and stitched to my forehead, cheeks, ears, chin. I cannot imagine how this was done, nor what the end product will be, but I can vouch for the details. This is how I obtained them from the surgeons who reconstructed me like a jigsaw puzzle:

I am told that layers of skin like Kleenex tissues have been taken from my thighs and buttocks and stitched to my forehead, cheeks, ears, chin.

In the beginning there was only pain and nausea and hallucination. On the seventh or perhaps seven hundredth day, faces floated from the void.

"Let there be form," I said to a recurrent pair of eyes. "And conversation."

The eyes seemed startled and excited. "Who are you?" I asked them.

They were crying with that stupid happiness of people who are winning television game shows.

"Young lady, you are remarkable, quite remarkable. It makes one humble...to have saved the brain.... It would have been such a waste, a criminal waste.... Progressing very nicely, very nicely indeed. You will pull through."

"What shall I pull through, doctor?"

"I mean...you will pick up the threads of your life again. And Dr. Norris also has done, I can assure you, an excellent job. The scarring will be minimal – I mean, given the extent of the damage."

"I see. What damage is this?"

"Ah," he said nervously, patting the bed.

"Ah...I think you are ready to talk with Dr. Simon."

"And who is Dr. Simon?"

"He will help you to handle these things. He will answer your questions. But thank God the mind is safe. That is the main thing.

The rest...such a mind will cope with the rest."

I don't let go so easily. I made all of them answer to me. How do you mean, repairing my face? What was it like without skin? How did you know what I looked like? Did you work from a photograph? How do I know if I am still me? What do my thighs look like, so gallantly doffing their cloak of flesh to cover my cheeks?

Did you put my dimples back?

Are my eyebrows there?

I think, when one has been singled out in this extraordinary fashion, one can only be analytical. I should, however, confess that I have irrational moments. The first time I saw myself in a mirror was one of these. It was the disproportion my new headgear gave me that shocked me, the esthetic jarring. I mean, it is a natural law that the head should be only one-seventh of body size, and a human body which violates this principle can only be called treacherous.

...It is a natural law that the head should be only one-seventh of body size, and a human body which violates this principle can only be called treacherous.

I behaved very badly – so I am told – and had to be sedated, a pleasing experience. This is what happened: a warm wave, golden green, wells up like love from the floor and washes me right to the cave of safety. I slid back into my dreams.

Wendy came to visit one day. It is difficult to say when it was, time swimming about me the way it does now. After several weeks? A month? Three months? Longer than that? She was terribly nervous, unwilling to meet my eyes.

"You look good," I said.

It seemed to embarrass her, and she turned away as though insulted or wounded. Apologetically she murmured: "It was mainly my hands and arms."

"When do your bandages come off?"

"I don't know. I don't...I almost don't want them to come off."

"I know what you mean. But we'll manage, Wen. We'll just have to make long sleeves the in thing. Remember when the three of us decided to wear shirts and men's ties and everyone copied us? And Christina wore that gaudy thing of her father's, four inches wide? I don't think you should have cut your hair so short, though."

Her eyes leaped about the way I have seen rabbits buckle upward when boys are out with their pellet guns.

"So many things I never used to notice," I told her. "Like your jack-rabbit eyes, Wen. And your hair. You know we liked it long. Why did you do that?"

"Cilla, my hair...my hair, too, you know. Don't you remember?"

In the large, slow-falling, pear-shaped drops trickling down Wendy's face, I could see myself, the chilling, unseeable seer.

A new thought occurred to me, and I reached upward with surprise, forgetting I would feel only the plaster cage.

"Oh, Wen! Mine, too?"

And yet of course I must have known that. Somehow, seeing only the white egg, I hadn't pictured myself hairless within it. This is too much, too much.

"I wish you hadn't told me," I said angrily, accusingly.

"Please, Cilla!" She waved her mummified arms in distress, turning away, mumbling, crying.

"Stop whining. I can't hear you."

"Christina, Christina! Oh, what will we do?"

Always Christina. And Wendy the marionette, her adoring lap-dog. But I was, and am, and ever will be the leader, amen.

"Christina, Christina," she moaned childishly.

Distress is a phenomenon in which I have become inordinately interested. It is fascinating, the sense of drama possessed by the tear ducts. First a moat rings the eyes, a meniscus forms, quivers, hesitates, spills over. In the large, slow-falling, pear-shaped drops trickling down Wendy's face, I could see myself, the chilling, unseeable seer.

"I had a dream about Christina and us," I told her dispassionately. "The world was burning while we fiddled on a staircase...."

"Oh God, Cilla, please! Oh God, oh God...." It began as a moan, and then I watched her sobs curl upward in a plume of hysteria. A nurse had to come in and take her away.

"Poor girl," the nurse said. "They shouldn't have let you two....

It was too soon. She blames herself, of course."

I do not know what she is talking about. Clearly we were all in some accident, though I cannot recall the details, and blame is, in any case, pointless. If Wendy is living with it, however, it will not go away with her bandages.

This is not entirely honest. How dare she claim Christina as her special private loss. Perhaps I am jealous because I cannot cry, I will not mourn.

Fragments of event float by me in sleep, and waking too, like jetsam on a flooded river. I clutch at them, lifebelts, and swim against chaos.

I was deliberately vicious. After all, Wendy still has the use of her face. I wanted to even the score, to make her lose control. One: one.

I am trying to remember what happened. Fragments of event float by me in sleep, and waking too, like jetsam on a flooded river. I clutch at them, lifebelts, and swim against chaos.

Christina's face, whole for an instant, radiant as gold in a refiner's fire.

And yet, as I try to comprehend, to remember what happened before and after, as I concentrate on her face, seeing her there transfigured, she recedes into the past and I am racing, racing to catch her. We are running along staircases, up and down, feet flying...subway stairs, so many days of our lives.... Here we are on a particular September morning, both of us late...running backwards, years into the past....

One could never keep up with Christina. Everything, the seconds and minutes themselves, lured her off into byways and tangents, waylaid her with pleasures, with concerns, with ministrations. The thing about her to be loved and hated was that, quite simply, she had only good impulses. She never stopped to think, never weighed things, never had to. Her actions came out pell-mell and pure.

On the subway stairs that day, a furtive Italian widow, toothless and dressed in black and smelling of garlic, mumbling her rosary, half squatting against the wall, jabbered something at us. A curse perhaps. Careful, was my instant, wary thought. Not uncharitable exactly. Just unwilling to – ah yes, the sudden ripe smell of urine in a puddle below her. As one might have known.

I ran on to the turnstile.

"Quick!" I called. "There's one coming! If we get it, we can be on time after all."

But there, inevitably, was Christina helping the old hag up to the street, hailing a taxi.

...I hear horns and a shouting taxi driver and a stream of shrill Italian. Christina is off like a wraith of smoke, flames rising from her heels like streamers.

"Christina! Really! We *are* running late, you know!"

Pausing, telling the taxi to wait, here she comes breathless and trailing clouds of gorgeous self-consciousness, as always when caught out doing good.

"Oh, Cilla, can you imagine? The poor thing. The embarrassment! And the discomfort! And she doesn't even speak English. Obviously I'll have to take her home."

"Oh, obviously."

Flushing again. (Was Christina beautiful? Probably not, though one always believed so. A matter of blushes and vivacity, of illusion.)

"But imagine how you'd feel, Cilla!"

"No. Frankly, I can't imagine. It simply isn't a possible situation, peeing in public places."

"Oh, Cilla." Her brows had a way of puckering, not reproachful really, more not quite believing me, not comprehending the less than totally generous.

Now, as I remember this, I hear horns and a shouting taxi driver and a stream of shrill Italian. Christina is off like a wraith of smoke, flames rising from her heels like streamers.

"Christina! Wait! We were at the lake, remember? What happened? I can't remember what happened!"

But she continues running up stairs, ascending in conflagration, transfigured.

Every day, Dr. Simon asks me: "Do you want to talk about your night terror?"

"I don't have any night terrors," I tell him. "Only that dream I've already told you about. The three of us on the stairs. There's a fire, but it's not frightening."

"The fire doesn't frighten you?"

"No."

"*Something* frightens you every night."

"No," I lie.

"Do you remember what happened?"

"Yes." I am lying again.

"You were very harsh with Wendy. She was deeply upset."

"Wendy hasn't changed."

"Ah. What does that mean, exactly?"

(So transparent, so glib, these counsellors. As if I don't know what he is trying to make me admit.)

"She was always like that. It was impossible not to hurt her feelings. Well, impossible for me not to. Christina of course...that's different.... And Wendy is the kind of person who can never get enough friendship. Ruthless in her own way. Insatiable. Always tagging along, the third wheel, and Christina indulging her. Now I'll have her in tow forever."

Every evening I silently implore the night nurse to douse me with sufficient sedative so that sleep will rush me on an express ride right through to morning, no stops.

"I don't think so. Wendy is extremely ill."

"Wendy? She was here. She hasn't changed at all."

"She is extremely ill. She believes it was all her fault. She believes you blame her for what happened, though we both know that would be ridiculous."

Entrapment! (What happened? What happened?)

"Of course," I say lightly, haughtily.

"It is probable that you are the only person who can help her."

"I don't see how."

I am lying about the night terror.

Every evening I silently implore the night nurse to douse me with sufficient sedative so that sleep will rush me on an express ride right through to morning, no stops. Yet I am too proud to ask her, to admit that I am afraid of the dark. And every night there is a derailment somewhere before sunrise.

The ward is black and still as death, and I try desperately not to look out of the window. I push my egg head back against the pillow, forbidding it to turn. But it turns against my will and sees the street where the street lamp burns like a coal against the sky, a devil's eye. My attention is riveted helplessly to it, I cannot turn away. Sheer terror rams through me at high voltage and my body begins to convulse, even the bed goes into spasms. It is impossible to breathe.

The night nurse comes running with medication.

In the morning Dr. Simon begs me once again to confide in him, but the street light is watching. Menacing. Mocking: See my innocuous daytime disguise? Who will believe you?

Sheer terror rams through me at high voltage and my body begins to convulse, even the bed goes into spasms.

I am afraid of being thought crazy.

"I don't have night terrors," I tell Dr. Simon. "Only that dream I already told you about."

The days have grown fins and swim around me in circles. I remember the white dress with blue ribbons that I wore for my eighth birthday party. I remember (is it possible, or do I only remember the retelling?), I remember the day – I was only three years old – when I said yes I would ride in the side-car of my father's old motorcycle, and when he made it roar I was terrified and wouldn't get in. I remember the day my mother grew pale and slumped into tears, wasting away like a snow woman in spring. That was today, I think. And my father blighted with anguish, pretending that all was well. Was that today?

At night the planets collide and give off sparks. Red eyes stare in at windows and bounce off bed covers.

Sometimes the days seem to be braiding themselves over me like smoke plumes, twisting, dizzying.

I have floated willy-nilly on time to this amazing point: I have been discharged. My mother, consumed with tenderness, instead of the night nurse, hovers by me. My father, over breakfast, sighs for what cannot be believed. It is a good thing that I have this heavy responsibility of my parents. Behind the mask, I program myself for action.

I have to see Dr. Simon, whom I tell nothing, twice a week. I am still waiting to see how I will hatch. For months yet I will have to wear my plaster shell, I will actually have to begin university inside it, a newfangled version of the pale lady cursed with isolation:

But who hath seen her wave her hand?
Or at the casement seen her stand?
Or is she known in all the land,
The Lady of Shalott?

Ah well, I have always turned heads.

I will be very fair, they tell me, allergic to sunlight, my skin frail as ancient manuscripts that crumble into ash if touched. Dues to pay: for loving too warmly the hungry touch of young men's hands and of ocean and sun on my golden (though still chaste) flesh, I must get it to a nunnery. I will cloister it with high-necked dresses and long sleeves and wide-brimmed hats. This can be done elegantly. I shall think of myself as Ophelia, pale with doom. I have decided to be mysterious and desirable and infinitely remote. (*I am half sick of shadows, said the Lady of Shalott...*) I have decided to exist as my own literary commentary. I have decided that I will still be beautiful, though tragic.

I will be very fair, they tell me, allergic to sunlight, my skin frail as ancient manuscripts that crumble into ash if touched.

To believe otherwise....

I do not know how to believe otherwise – unthinkable as adjusting to a surgical change of gender.

We always meant to enrol together, Christina, Wendy, and I. Medicine, law, and literature. Strange how things turn out. Strange to sign up alone.

Alone. A word that sneaks up on me, causing breathing problems. Words and objects are becoming unreliable, turning unpredictably vicious. Street lamps, for instance.

But I still turn heads. I am not ordinary. No. Never.

Freshmen, freshwomen, and one fresh egg, I joke.

Fortunately they visualize *me*, me as I was, inside the egg. That me and this me: beauty and the beast. They are in awe of me.

She hath no loyal knight and true, the Lady of Shalott, though formerly the boys would follow, tongues lolling, as if I were in heat; the same boys who now stand shocked, coughing with embarrassment, who reach out nervously to shake my hand.

The night terrors have changed since I came home.

I dream that at the witching hour someone comes into my room with surgical scissors. "It's time," a voice says, and I see that I am in an amphitheatre. From the gallery hundreds of people watch, their faces pressed up against my comic little life, as my mask is cut away. My convulsions begin, my breathing goes into arrest.

From the gallery hundreds of people watch, their faces pressed up against my comic little life, as my mask is cut away.

"Please!" I gasp. "Please, leave it on. I'm used to it. I don't mind it. I *like* it!"

The cutting goes on inexorably until I am hatched.

A roar of laughter jangles from the gallery like doomsday bells, re-echoing and multiplying infinitely, a mirrored corridor of endless sound.

My mother has sobbed to Dr. Simon that I accuse her of laughing at me. I cannot forgive my dreams for spilling over in this improper way, for slopping their mess into other lives.

I tell Dr. Simon nothing.

Of course it was sheer defiance to use the subway when I could have taken taxis, but that is what I decided to do. I bought my tokens with aggressive nonchalance. I nodded to people with my egg head, I smiled through my mouth hole. Every morning I challenged my life, my bitter enemy: Try to defeat me!

I have made up my mind to be beautiful no matter what I look like. On this point I will not yield.

On the train I read for my philosophy course, an absorbing subject. I have been pondering such questions as fate, and how we shape it after our prevailing whim – as benign, as vicious, as random. I have been pondering democracy and how the subway, the great equalizer, is possibly its leading institution.

This happened one day: a group of schoolboys, half a dozen twelve-year-olds, began snickering at me. That is all. Snickering behind their hands.

If only it had been malicious, a calculated insult. If only I could have sent out in advance wallet photographs of my other self, along with pocket handkerchiefs.... If I could have stood like thunder, my frog disguise splitting in two, and said: behold, the princess!

There was no mistaking their guilt, their attempts to stifle the embarrassed spurts of merriment.

At that moment – even as I observed with supernatural clarity the subway map over their heads, the advertisement for H&R Block and for what to do about aching feet, the mole on one boy's ear lobe, the undone muddy shoe-laces of another – at that moment I remembered what had happened. The unbearable banality of it, that I had been hiding with such terror from myself.

If only I could have sent out in advance wallet photographs of my other self, along with pocket handkerchiefs.... If I could have stood like thunder, my frog disguise splitting in two, and said: behold, the princess!

The lake, the picnic table, the coals on the barbecue, the steaks that were still not sizzling.

"I think we should swim while we're waiting," Christina had said. "Why is it taking so long, I wonder?"

"Wendy didn't put enough starter fluid on the coals."

Her plaintive voice: "I'm sorry. I was sure I had plenty."

"Well, obviously you didn't. Squirt some more on."

"She can't do that, Cilla. It's dangerous once the coals are smouldering. Anyway, I want to swim."

"The boys will be here and the food won't be ready and we'll just have to admit...."

Wendy pleading: "I'll do it, Cilla. If I stand back, it should be okay, shouldn't it?"

"Nonsense!" Christina the Good inevitably restraining and comforting. "Who cares what the boys say? Let's swim first."

Such a child, Wendy. We were moon and sun to her. She did not shift her gaze from me, still pleading mutely.

Coward! my eyes scorned.

I seem to see it again in slow motion: the jerk of Wendy's arm, the can of starter fluid, and a long crystal arc hissing in below the steaks.

And then there was a great ball of fire, like the plaything of some wanton child-giant, which bounced lightly into the air and swallowed us up.

I remember bellowing like a gored bull at the snickering subway boys. Windows shattered under my outrage. Wheels and tracks beckoned with their hideous promises. All this extravagance I remember with horrid clarity. It was martyrdom I was frantic for. Tragedy. Significance.

"A monster should look monstrous, of course," I told Dr. Simon. "I'm sure I had it coming."

"This is quite an orgy." (How I hate that insufferable therapeutic gentleness!) "The devil incarnate herself."

"That's right. Were you hoping for soap opera? Tears, remorse, throwing myself at Wendy's feet?"

"No. I'm not sure even you could do anything for Wendy now."

I bridled at that. "If I smiled at her and asked her nicely, she would walk into the burning. If I took her hand she could walk right out of her twilight."

"She knows she is alone."

"So?" I said, fighting to breathe. "So? We're both alone. Who can be more alone than a freak locked inside a mask? Nobody even knows what I look like. And that's fine by me. I'll manage."

"And when the mask is removed?"

"I don't think a monster like me should be let loose on the world, do you? Scattering my kisses of death? I think I'll stay veiled. It's safer for all concerned."

"The mask is coming off next week, Cilla. There'll be nowhere to hide."

In the dream the world is on fire, glowing phantasmagoria flickering by me like the tattered frames of an old black-and-white movie. The Italian widow and the boys on the subway are laughing without a sound. Christina is standing transfigured, transparent with flame. Was she beautiful? We always thought so. We took it for granted. (Not in the same way that I am. Was. But just in that way...people looked at her with pleasure. At me with

I remember bellowing like a gored bull at the snickering subway boys. Windows shattered under my outrage. Wheels and tracks beckoned with their hideous promises.

awe or envy, perhaps. But at Christina with simple pleasure.) There's Wendy, floating in the flames. (Was Wendy beautiful? I never thought about it at all. Wendy was backdrop.)

I seem to have a moment of choice.

Christina has gone already, ascending from sight. Wendy is running earthward.

"Wendy!" I beg. "Wendy! Don't leave me!"

And she takes my hand.

In the dream the world is on fire, glowing phantasmagoria flickering by me like the tattered frames of an old black-and-white movie.

Today was my coming out.

I was afraid of the mirror, not wanting extraneous information. I have made up my mind that I am beautiful, a simple act of will.

My hair has been secretly growing inside its egg, soft as the down on a gestating chicken. I rake my fingers through it and toss it free. This is a different incarnation, a new adventure.

I hold my breath and look in the mirror. A stranger, someone I am just getting to know, stares back. This face, I think bravely, is an *interesting* face. When its eyes flash it will have a kind of aura more potent than before. And yet it is softer. Its scars caress it like ghostly ferns.

I touch them wonderingly, rather proudly.

I am on my way.

I am on my way to see Wendy.

"Don't leave me," I will say. "Dearest Wendy, don't leave me."

And then, I think, we will put our arms around each other. ▼

Being visible starts with seeing yourself as you really are. Pablo Picasso, *Girl Before a Mirror,* March 1932, oil on canvas (162.3 x 130.2 cm). Collection, The Museum of Modern Art, New York.

ACTIVITY 4 RESPONDING TO A STORY

1. In what way does this story remind you of an experience that you or someone you know has had? Describe it and discuss your feelings about it with a partner.
2. Reread the first two lines of "Golden Girl." Do you think this is an effective opening for this story? Why?
3. What do you think of Cilla's attitude toward the people around her before the accident, for example, Wendy, Christina, the Italian woman in the subway, and the people who admire her? Do you think she portrays them accurately?
4. Why does Dr. Simon say that Cilla is the only person who can help Wendy? Why do you think Cilla feels reluctant to do this?
5. How does Cilla choose to become visible?
6. Why is this story called "Golden Girl"? How does Cilla's sense of herself at the beginning of the story as "perfect" make it difficult for her to become visible?
7. At the end of "Golden Girl," Cilla resolves to talk to Wendy. Write the dialogue for their talk. Or, write a diary entry for Cilla in which she describes her meeting with Wendy.

END THOUGHTS

In this unit, you have considered the importance of becoming visible by expressing yourself. Using your reading, writing, group interaction, and viewing skills, you considered what happens when people choose to become visible. You have seen that the expression of your experience allows you to move from fear and vulnerability to a sense of strength that enables you to change the world around you. The choice of being visible is yours.

ACTIVITY 5 EXTENSION IDEAS

1. Watch a number of television programs. Analyze the secondary characters. How could they become more visible (more like the main characters)? Write a scene in which you show one of these characters increasing his or her visibility. With a partner, perform your scene for your class.
2. Make yourself and other people visible by writing humorous business cards. Your card might look like this:

Stephen "*THE SNAKE*" Lu FABRICATOR, FAST TALKER

3. Learn to analyze your own and others' handwriting by researching handwriting analysis. What does your handwriting reveal about you? How accurate a method of "reading" people is handwriting analysis?
4. Interview someone doing outreach work in your community (for example, a volunteer for the Meals on Wheels program or a literacy worker). Explore his or her reasons for doing this work. In what way is he or she concerned with being visible? Prepare a report on your findings and present them to your class.
5. Make a video self-portrait. Prepare a script in which you select details or scenes that will reveal your character. Consider including interviews with family and friends. Add music to your soundtrack that reveals something about your personality. Show your video to your class.

6. Create a short autobiography. Use these statements to get your ideas flowing:

   - My greatest achievement was...
   - My greatest loss was...
   - I have never felt happier than when...
   - I have never felt worse than when...
   - The funniest thing that ever happened to me was...
   - The most embarrassing thing that ever happened to me was...
   - The person who has influenced me the most is...
   - What is important to me is...
   - My future goals are...

   You may wish to write your autobiography chronologically or in another way that seems appropriate. Include photos and keepsakes to illustrate your narrative. You may wish to present your autobiography orally to the class.

7. In your journal, write about how we often form first impressions from a person's appearance. Just by looking at someone, we make assumptions about that person's personality, economic situation, marital status, and career. Can you recall an instance in which you formed conclusions about someone just by looking at that person, perhaps when you were riding on a bus or walking down the street? What first impression do you think someone would form about you based on your appearance?

8. Create a portrait of a friend or relative. You may wish to use photos, clippings from magazines, paint, or a video camera. Try to capture the person's personality in the portrait. When it is complete, show it to him or her to get a reaction. Does your friend or relative think it captures his or her individuality?

9. Do some historical research about a group of people, or an individual, who risked ostracism, or perhaps even their lives, to fight for something they believed in. For example, Galileo Galilei fought to establish his discovery that the planets revolve around the sun, not the earth.

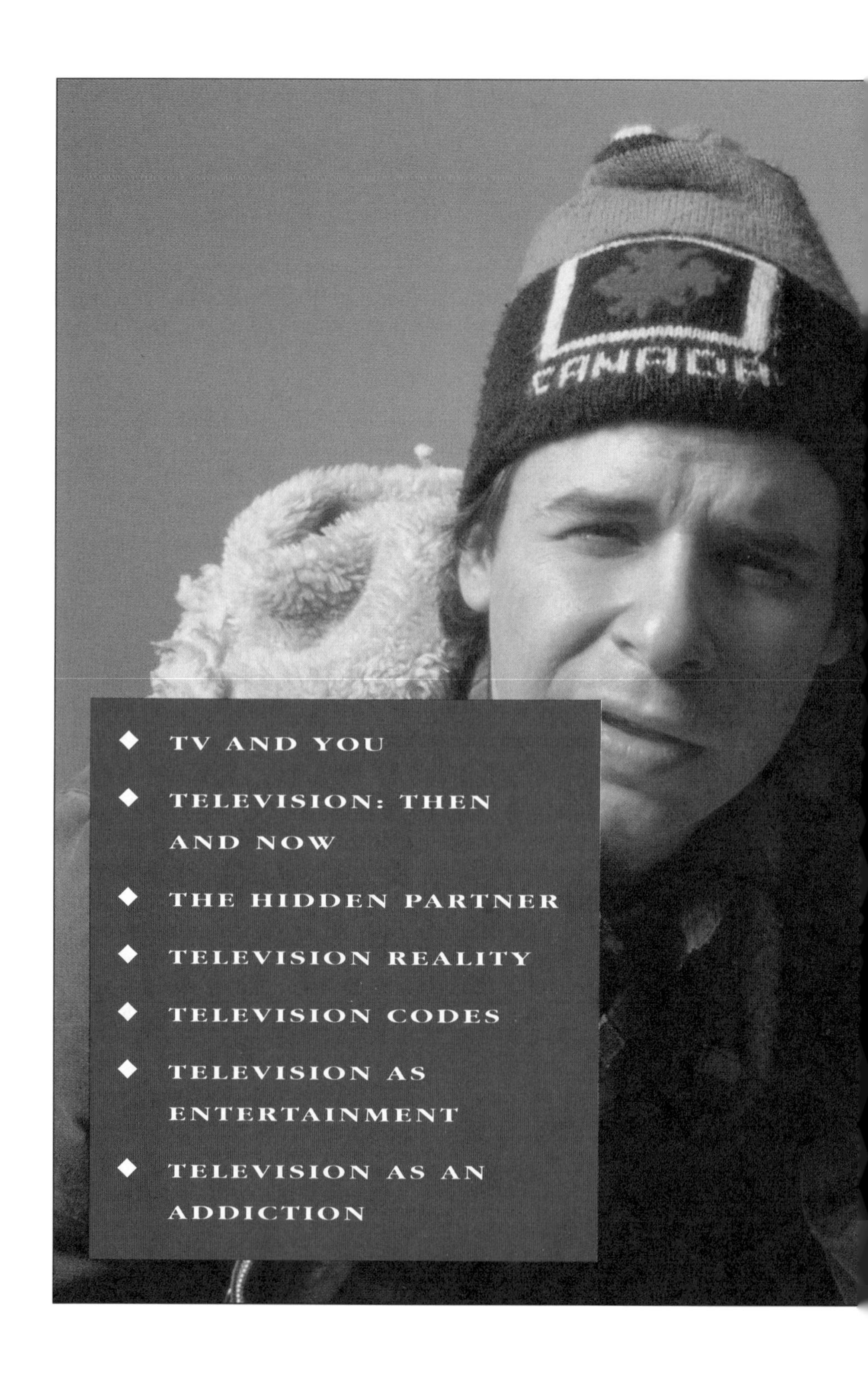

- TV AND YOU
- TELEVISION: THEN AND NOW
- THE HIDDEN PARTNER
- TELEVISION REALITY
- TELEVISION CODES
- TELEVISION AS ENTERTAINMENT
- TELEVISION AS AN ADDICTION

UNIT 4

TV WATCH

By the time you finish high school you will have spent more hours watching television than attending school. In fact, you will have spent more time watching TV than doing anything else except sleeping – if you are like the average student.

This unit invites you to examine the unexamined, to think critically about television and how it affects your life. This is not as easy as it seems. It has become such a natural part of our environment that it remains largely unexplored by those who consume it.

As you explore television in this unit, you will consider this question: Is what you see on television a reflection of what society is like? You will investigate television through a variety of activities, including an examination of past and present programs, the role of the audience in determining meaning, the construction of the television image, the ideas and values conveyed through programs, and the effects of television on your daily life.

TV AND YOU

ACTIVITY 1
THE TV YOU WATCH

These tasks will help you become more conscious of the way you use television:

1. Keep a log for one week of your personal viewing habits. Include the following information in each log entry: the day of the week, the time you turned on the TV set, what you watched, the time you turned it off.

2. Calculate the number of hours spent watching television each day, the total for the week, and the average number of hours a day for the week.

3. Make a note of your personal viewing habits. Use these questions as a guide: How often do you switch channels? Do you watch the commercials or do something else while they are on? Are you engaged in other activities while you watch television? Which times of day do you watch the most television? Who watches television with you? Do you talk to each other while you are watching television? What do you talk about?

4. Compare your use of television with that of other members of your family. What programs do they watch? How much time do they spend in front of the TV set? Who watches the most television? Who watches the least?

5. As a whole class, compile your log entries to create a profile of the viewing habits of all students in your class. What are the most popular programs? Is there a difference between the genders in terms of what and how much they watch?

6. Use the information you have collected in your surveys to have a debate on this topic: Be it resolved that parents should restrict the amount of television that their children watch.

These programs were popular in the 1950s.

The Burns and Allen Show

Father Knows Best

Dragnet

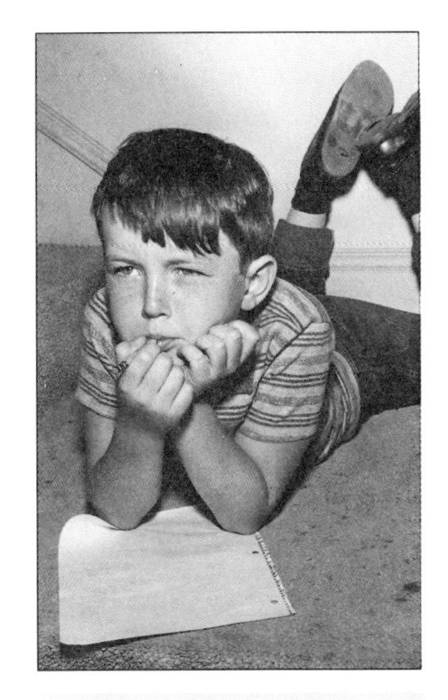

Leave It to Beaver

I Love Lucy

Wanted: Dead or Alive

TELEVISION: THEN AND NOW

In 1938 a total of 100 television sets were actually in use in all of North America. Today it is difficult to find a home without at least one television set. It seems hard to believe something that we now take for granted has had such a short history. The last fifty years have, however, brought incredible changes to both the technology and content of television. Several pages in this unit provide you with a pictorial overview of television from the 1950s to the present and offer suggestions for investigating the television programs of the past and the present. Note: You can see many of these programs as reruns or you may be able to rent them as video cassettes. Check with a local video store for a complete list.

ACTIVITY 2
TELEVISION THROUGH THE DECADES

To think about television of the past, divide into small groups. Each group will study one of the decades of television programming: the 1950s, 1960s, 1970s, 1980s.

1. Look carefully at the collage of popular television programs for your decade: 1950s – page 87, 1960s – page 89, 1970s – page 91, 1980s – page 93. On the basis of what you see, write down your impressions of the following:
   a) the kinds of programs that were most popular in this decade
   b) the ways in which men, women, and children were represented in these programs during the decade
   c) the values, interests, and concerns that were implicit in these programs
   d) historical and social factors that influenced the development of these programs

2. Now share with others in the class what you have learned about television in your decade.
   a) Each of the groups should send a member to every other group in the classroom. As a result, each new group will have as a member someone who has studied each of the decades.
   b) Group members will report to the new group what their first group found out about television. If there are two group members from one decade, these students will have to find a way to share the teaching duties.

Programs from the 1960s.

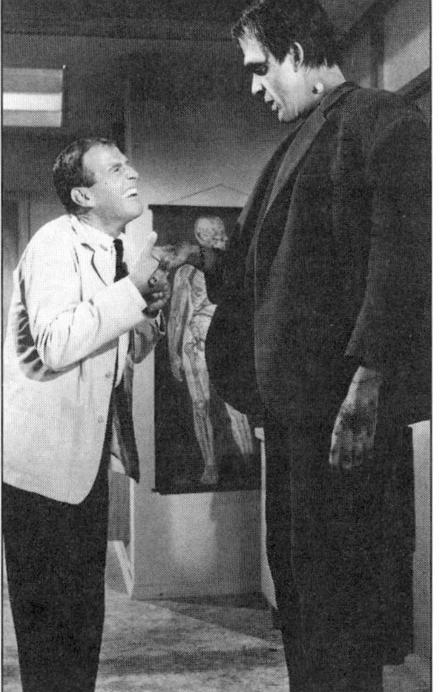

The Munsters

The Flintstones

Bonanza

Batman

The Beverly Hillbillies

ACTIVITY 3
TELEVISION RERUNS

If you have access to older television programs, either through your local video outlet or reruns on current television programming, you can study each decade by examining the actual TV programs. Form small groups and use the following questions to guide your look at the television programs.

1. Use these questions as guidelines to study the 1950s:
   a) From the early days of television to the present, comedies that focus on the family have been very popular. Among the early successes were such programs as *I Love Lucy*, *The Adventures of Ozzie and Harriet*, and *Father Knows Best*. Watch one or more of these family comedies. Describe the roles of the mother and father. What kinds of situations and problems arose? How were they resolved?
   b) Throughout the 1950s and early 1960s, westerns such as *Gunsmoke*, *Wagontrain*, *Rawhide*, and *Bonanza* dominated the airwaves. Watch some of these programs and prepare a report on the typical western hero. In what ways were westerns a reflection of the times? Why are they no longer as popular as they once were? Talk to some people who watched a lot of the westerns as children and discover whether the television cowboys influenced them as they grew up.
   c) Early Canadian television successes included such programs as *The Juliette Show*, *Front Page Challenge*, and *Don Messer's Jubilee*. Research the early days of the CBC. How did Canadian television get started? Compare early Canadian programs with their American counterparts.

2. Use these questions as guidelines to study the 1960s:
   a) Looking back at the television programs of the 1960s, you may observe that the themes of many TV programs had little connection with the reality of the average viewer's life. Programs such as *The Beverly Hillbillies*, *The Munsters*, *Batman*, *My Mother the Car*, and the first prime-time cartoon, *The Flintstones*, provided entertainment for millions. What do you think was the appeal of such programs? In what ways were these programs a reflection of what happened socially and culturally during the decade?
   b) A concept is a short description of a new series, its main characters, potential plots, setting, and audience appeal. The written concept for *Miami Vice*, for example, was as follows: *An exciting new drama with the look of the 80s...Exploring the teeming world of vice amid the sunshine, wealth, and waters of South Florida...narcotics, gun running, smuggling, gambling, pornography...and the personal lives of two cops who live on the edge and undercover....* Prepare a written concept for one of the 1960s series pictured on page 89.

The Waltons

The Jeffersons

Viewers watched these programs in the 1970s.

Chico and the Man

Hockey Night in Canada

Laverne and Shirley

3. Use these questions to study television of the '70s:
   a) The primarily white, middle-class look of television during the fifties and sixties began to change during the seventies with such programs as *All in the Family*, *The Jeffersons*, *The Flip Wilson Show*, *Chico and the Man*, and Canada's *King of Kensington* and *The Beachcombers*. Watch a program about an ethnic minority. Consider the roles played by the various characters, the situations and themes the programs explore, and the values they imply.
   b) Nostalgia was a characteristic of many popular programs of the 1970s. Programs such as *Happy Days* and *Laverne and Shirley* romanticized the 1950s. *Little House on the Prairie* did the same for pioneer days, as did *The Waltons* for the 1930s. What social and political events during this decade might explain the nostalgia for earlier times? Watch an episode from one of these programs. Describe what the characters do and say. What seems to be some of their major concerns? What messages do such programs give the viewer? What values do they suggest?
   c) Sports programs have always been popular fare for television. In Canada, *Hockey Night in Canada* has been consistently among the top-rated programs. One of the most-watched programs of the decade was the Canada-Russia hockey series in 1972. Why is hockey so important to Canadians? What values do sports programs convey to the viewers? What images of men and women do sports programs present?

4. Use these questions to study the '80s:
   a) Many of the programs of the eighties had a slick style conveyed through image and sound. Watch an episode from a popular comedy or drama series of the 1980s. What techniques give this program a unique look and sound?
   b) You might observe the changing role of women in television as you view such programs as *Moonlighting*, *Roseanne*, *Murder She Wrote*, *The Golden Girls*, *Street Legal*, and the *Oprah Winfrey Show*. View several shows featuring women to discover the roles played by women. Describe how women were presented in these programs. What do they do and say? How do they relate to men and children?
   c) A Canadian style of humour was exported to the United States through a program called *SCTV*. Analyze the humour in this television program. What makes people laugh at it? Do you see a difference in this style of humour in comparison with American humour? Explain.

SCTV

The Kids in the Hall

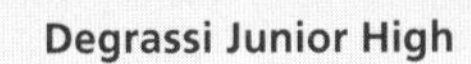

Degrassi Junior High

MuchWest

You may have watched some of these programs in the '80s.

The Oprah Winfrey Show

THE HIDDEN PARTNER

If someone asked you to list the people responsible for the creation of a television program, you would probably include the actors, the writers, the directors, the producers, perhaps even the "go-fers." One group missing from most lists, however, would be the audience. Yet without this hidden partner there is no television.

Even when you do think of the audience, a picture of a "couch potato" passively consuming hours and hours of TV may come to mind. People rarely think of the audience as engaged in anything active. In fact, the viewers, by switching a dial, make the ultimate decision whether a program lives or dies. The people who create television programs are very conscious of the role of the audience. Their success, after all, depends on whether they can deliver the right audience to the advertisers who pay for the program. They have good reason to know their audiences well.

How people react to television programs depends on many factors. Gender, age, education, social class, ethnic background, and economic status figure among the most significant. If you look over the television programs of the last four decades, you can identify programs that were aimed at specific audiences. In the activities that follow you will explore the role of this hidden partner in the world of television.

The image of a viewer glued to the television all day has become so vivid, we have termed this person a "couch potato."

ACTIVITY 4
THE ROLE OF THE AUDIENCE

1. Watch one of your favourite programs with your grandparents or someone of their generation. Afterwards, talk about your reactions. Ask them about their reactions to the program: what it made them think about, how it made them feel, what it reminded them of. Make notes on what they tell you. How do their reactions differ from yours? How do you account for these differences?
2. Look at the programs listed and illustrated on pages 87, 89, 91, and 93. What trends do you see? What kinds of programs were the most popular in each decade? Talk to some people who remember watching these programs. Ask them what made them popular. How do you account for the decline in interest of certain kinds of programs and the increasing interest in others? In what ways have audiences changed over the years?
3. Watch a program that you would not normally watch. Think about the assumptions that the creators make about their audience. How old are they? What do they like? What can you tell about their background? Look carefully at the products that are advertised during the program breaks. Who would buy these products and what can you tell about them from the commercials?
4. Len Masterman, a critic of the media, has said that a media text such as a television program offers us "positions from which we are asked to see experience in certain ways." To see what this means watch a television program and pretend that you are looking at each shot through the television camera. Where are you physically located in each shot? How do your locations change? How do your reactions as a viewer change according to the changes in position of the camera?

TELEVISION REALITY

People tend to believe pictures. After all, if the evidence is there in front of their eyes, it must be true, right? Because television consists of a series of pictures, people have a natural tendency to believe what is on the screen. But what is the reality of these images? The following activities invite you to explore the extent to which television reflects the world as you know it and the values and beliefs of the people who inhabit it.

ACTIVITY 5
THE ROLE OF IDEOLOGY

1. You often base your first impressions of people on their appearance – their physical characteristics, the way they do their hair, the clothes and accessories that they wear. These things give certain messages about what people value and believe to be important. Watch an episode from one of your favourite television programs. Make a list of the characters as they appear on the screen. Beside each name make a list of details that describe his or her physical appearance. In a third column list the messages or values that these physical details imply. Use the chart below as a model.

Character	Physical Detail	Implied Message

2. With a partner, watch a program with the sound turned off. Each of you pick a separate character and, while watching, describe what you see happening on the screen from the two points of view. Compare the two versions of the show. How do you account for the differences or similarities?

3. As you watch a popular television program, make a list of all the men and women as they appear on the screen. Beside each character make a note of his or her line of work, ethnic background, and social status. When you have finished watching, total the number of men, women, ethnic minorities, and social classes represented. Compared to the community in which you live, which groups are under-represented? Which ones are over-represented? What message does this representation give to the viewers?

4. Do the same exercise as in question 3 with one of the older television programs. How do your results differ from those you obtained in the above activity? To what do you attribute the difference or the lack of difference that you observed?

5. View this season's newest shows. To what extent do the stories, characters, settings, and situations reflect those found where you live. Which shows seem most realistic to you? Why?

The editor pieces together many segments to form a whole that is the television program.

TELEVISION CODES

When you watch a finished television product such as a commercial or an entire program, it looks like a single, complete whole. It is hard to believe that what you see on the screen is many bits and pieces that have been carefully sewn together to create the illusion of a seamless garment. As media critic Len Masterman has pointed out, "the processes of media production are, for the most part, actively concealed from the public." In television production these processes consist of several choices about the content of the various shots: the camera angles, kinds of shots, transitions, sound cues, and sequences used to present them. The following activities invite you to pose some questions about the construction of television programs.

ACTIVITY 6
THE PARTS OF THE WHOLE

1. Watch a two- to five-minute sequence of a television program. Make a note of each technical event, that is, each time a change occurs on screen. An example is provided below:
   - Long shot of a large ranch.
   - Soft violin music begins in the background.
   - Cut to a medium shot of horse and rider.
   - Music changes to trumpet solo.
   - Camera zooms to close-up of girl riding horse.
   - Fade out as music slows.

2. Do the same analysis of a two- to five-minute sequence from an older television show. What differences are evident in the number, kinds, and variety of technical events? What effects do these differences have on the audience?

3. Another set of choices has to do with the combination of the images shown on the screen and the words that accompany them.
   a) Look at the picture below and the two different voice overlays. Notice how the meaning you obtain from the picture varies according to the words that accompany it.
   b) In small groups, view a three- to five-minute segment from a television program. Cut the sound. Have each member of the group write out his or her version of the missing soundtrack. Afterwards compare the various versions. How does the message of what is conveyed on the screen change according to the words that accompany the pictures?

What impression does each voice overlay create?

"The police brutally attacked the student demonstrators."

"The police showed remarkable restraint in controlling the unruly mob."

4. Every television program contains a narrative sequence consisting of setting the scene, providing background information, introducing the main characters, setting up a problem or conflict, developing the situation, resolving the problem or conflict, and drawing a conclusion. The ways in which they are presented vary from one program to another. Pick a program and describe how each of the above procedures is accomplished.

5. To see how widespread the narrative elements mentioned in question 4 are on television, compare their use in a variety of programs. Have each member of your group watch a different kind of program and note how it presents each step. Compile your results in chart form like the following. How do you account for the similarities and the differences? How do you explain the widespread use of this sequence in such a wide range of television programming? To what extent is such a sequence an accurate reflection of what happens in real life?

	Police	Soap	Comedy	Commercial	News	Drama
setting the scene						
providing background						
introducing characters						
setting up problem/conflict						
developing situation						
resolving problem						
drawing conclusion						

TELEVISION AS ENTERTAINMENT

Most people have come to accept television as an entertaining part of their lives. The following article describes the role of television in the lives of one Canadian family. Before you read the article think for a few moments about the ways in which members of your family use television. Who watches what and how often?

Television can be an addiction. What activities can young people engage in instead of watching television?

FAMILY FUN

Catherine Dunphy

At last! A home-grown family that not only admits to watching television – and lots of it – but also is upfront about why.

"It's good entertainment," says Norm Graham.

> At last! A home-grown family that not only admits to watching television – and lots of it – but also is upfront about why.

He and his wife, Veda, have three children – Leigh-Anne, sixteen, Stephanie, twelve, and Ian, seven. They also have three televisions – a large twenty-eight-inch model in the basement family room of their Toronto home, one in the parents' bedroom and another in the breakfast nook.

How much TV do they watch? It boils down to this: When the family is home, the TV is on. The catch is that this is a family that doesn't hang around home. In winter, the girls skate four times a week and all day Saturday. In summer, Leigh-Anne works on her paddling and tennis skills; Ian plays T-Ball and lacrosse.

Norm, who works in a brokerage firm, rarely gets home before 7 PM and by then, he says, the kids have already turned on the television.

But his wife says he's the kind of guy "who has his right hand on the knob when he walks in the door."

Either way the television in the family room is usually on. Before dinner it's *Cheers* reruns and *Family Ties*, which all three children love. After dinner, it depends on who's home and what season it is. If the girls are skating, they won't be watching until after 9 PM; otherwise, they'll be watching by 7:30 PM.

This family adores movies and subscribes to pay TV's movie channel. On top of that they rent a couple of videos a week. Favorites? For Leigh-Anne it's *The Graduate* ("a classic"), Stephanie loves *Ferris Bueller's Day Off* and Ian see-saws between *The Goonies* and *Race For Your Life, Charlie Brown.*

They've all seen *Bull Durham*, steamy scenes included.

Says Veda: "I object more to the utterly stupid things on television like Pee-Wee Herman. To behave that stupidly is beneath people."

She says she stopped acting as a censor for what her children watch on TV the day she walked in on the girls watching the movie *Fame*. "Every second word was the 'f-word.' I turned it off and said to them, 'Why are you listening to this horrible language?' and the girls told me they hear much worse on the street every day."

She says she then turned the movie back on and left the room. "They can watch as long as they understand it's not acceptable to me."

"I still do a lot of educating with Ian, especially when he watches wrestling. I always tell him you can't knee drop somebody and survive. It's not real."

What she has stressed to the children – and, with Ian, continues to stress – is that television "is entertainment. It's not real. Actors who get shot in a movie get up, walk away and make another movie. But not if they were shot in real life."

Still, Ian declares his favorite show is *G.I. Joe*, "because there's lots of action and killing in it."

Veda interjects: "I still do a lot of educating with Ian, especially when he watches wrestling. I always tell him you can't knee drop somebody and survive. It's not real."

Because *G.I. Joe* is his favorite show, Ian owns several toy guns. "I vowed I would never give my child a gun," says Veda, "but he can play with it and then put it down. It's got no big secret, no big pull for him. That's the same with my kids and television. The kids have friends whose parents don't allow them to watch any TV or don't own one, and when they come over to the house they are glued to it. My kids can get up, shut it off in the middle of something and walk away."

She has decided television should not be used as a reward or punishment and its use should not be regulated. It simply is there, part of their home, in the same way as books or music are.

They all enjoy *The Nature of Things*, any of the National Geographic documentaries and *The Cosby Show* – except Stephanie, who says Vanessa, the second youngest Cosby kid, "bugs" her. "She's always grumbling."

They love *Degrassi Junior High* because of the show itself and because they know a couple of the actors in it.

The girls are not thrilled with *Growing Pains* but love *The*

Wonder Years. Even though lots of her friends love *21 Jump Street*, Stephanie adds, she doesn't. At school, the other kids talk about the true-life series *America's Most Wanted*, which she never watches either, she says.

Stephanie and Leigh-Anne do watch *Family Feud*, "because there's nothing else good on then." And when Stephanie is sick or has a day off school, she watches *The Price Is Right*: "I like the questions."

"He's the kind of guy who the first thing he does when he goes into a hotel room is turn on the television."

That's usually the only time during the day when the television is on, unless Ian is watching cartoons Saturday mornings or weekdays between 4 PM and 5 PM. That is his hour in front of the set, his mother says.

Veda loves *Roseanne*, is cool to *Murphy Brown*, and is a great fan of Thursday night TV. She watches *Cheers*, then *L.A. Law* (she hasn't missed an episode), then CTV's news. Veda expresses a cautious interest in CBC Newsworld, the national network's new all-news channel. Although she had yet to see it, she said the idea sounds intriguing because she likes her TV news "in short bits."

Veda says she prefers to watch TV on her own because Norm is a channel flipper.

"I hate commercials. I drive Veda crazy," he admits.

He is also a "TV sponge," according to his wife. "He's the kind of guy who the first thing he does when he goes into a hotel room is turn on the television. He's into trivia. He sucks it up as he reads the newspaper."

Norm says he always reads while he watches TV. One reason is that he reads four newspapers a day; the other is that if he's watching TV it's usually baseball. "If something does happen, they play it back fourteen times, so there's no way you miss anything."

Both Norm and Veda are sports fans. They subscribe to the pay TV sports channel, Norm for Jays or Expo baseball, and golf but never hockey; Veda for tennis or curling.

There was a time when both were hooked on *Hill Street Blues*, then on *St. Elsewhere*. This season, they started to watch – but never got hooked on – the blockbuster mini-series *War and Remembrance*.

"It's hard to sustain an interest over sixteen or whatever hours," says Norm. "And you have to commit four or five nights in a row. We don't want to do that."

Instead of watching the eleven o'clock news with his wife, he'll catch Johnny Carson or sometimes Arsenio Hall's show. "I'm a reader," he says. "I get my news from newspapers. Television is for entertainment."

Veda agrees. "It's entertainment, but it's also part of life," she says. She admits she fought having the set on so much when her eldest, Leigh-Anne, was young. "It wasn't part of my life as a child, so I thought it shouldn't be part of theirs."

Now she enjoys it and enjoys the fact that her children enjoy it as well.

"Television is here. It will be part of their life forever." ▼

ACTIVITY 7
TV IN THE FAMILY

1. Reread the article carefully and make a list of the family members, their favourite programs, how often they watch television, and their reactions to what they watch.
2. Pretend that your family's viewing habits had been the subject of the article. Make a list of the favourite programs of each member of your family and their reactions to them. Observe and record the viewing habits of your family members. How do your results compare with those described in the article?
3. Below are several statements made by the mother in the article. State whether you agree or disagree and why.
   a) "They [the children] can watch as long as they understand it's [bad language] not acceptable to me."
   b) "I vowed I would never give my child a gun...but he can play with it and then put it down. It's got no big secret, no big pull for him."
   c) "Television is here. It will be part of their life forever."
4. Other than watching television, how do members of the Graham family spend their spare time? How does this compare with your family? Calculate the approximate amount of time spent on various spare-time activities by members of your family, including watching television.

TELEVISION AS AN ADDICTION

How would you react if there were no television set in your house? How long would it be before you began to experience discomfort – a day, a week, a month? What would you do instead of watching television?

Some people have described television as an addiction. They argue that people become dependent on television just as they do on drugs. In her book *The Plug-In Drug,* Marie Winn describes the trance-like behaviour of children as they watch television:

> The child's facial expression is transformed. The jaw is relaxed and hangs open slightly; the tongue rests on the front teeth (if there are any). The eyes have a glazed, vacuous look. Considering the infinite varieties of children's personalities and behavior patterns, there is a remarkable sameness of expression among television-watching children. Occasionally they come out of the trance – when a commercial comes on, when the program ends, when they must go to the bathroom – but the obvious "snapping out" effect, as the face resumes a normal expression and the body returns to its normal state of semi-perpetual motion, only deepens the impression that the mental state of young children watching television is trance-like. There is certainly little indication that they are active and alert mentally.

The next time you have an opportunity to observe young children watching television, see if the above description is accurate.

The following story is a graphic illustration of addiction. It presents the conflict between a father and a son, each of whom has his own dependency. Before you read it think about any confrontations about television that you have had with your parents or guardian. What were they about? How did they get resolved?

Before television was invented there was no danger of it becoming an obsession, but people did not have the advantage of instant visual communication.

In the days before television

Viewers choose TV programs for two reasons: the style and the content. Which reason is more important for you?

HOOKED

John Cheever

Nailles walked through the dining room, crossed the dark hall to the living room where Tony was watching a show. The tube was the only light, shifting and submarine, and with the noise of the rain outside the room seemed like some cavern in the sea.

> The tube was the only light, shifting and submarine, and with the noise of the rain outside the room seemed like some cavern in the sea.

"Do you have any homework?" Nailles asked.

"A little," Tony said.

"Well I think you'd better do it before you watch television," Nailles said. On the tube some cartoon figures were dancing a jig.

"I'll just watch to the end of this show," Tony said. "Then I'll do my homework."

"I think you'd better do your homework now," Nailles said.

"But Mummy said I could see this show," Tony said.

"How long has it been," said Nailles, "that you've asked permission to watch television?" He knew that in dealing with his son sarcasm would only multiply their misunderstandings but he was tired and headstrong. "You never ask permission. You come home at half past three, pull your chair up in front of the set and watch until supper. After supper you settle down in front of that damned engine and stay there until nine. If you don't do your homework how can you expect to get passing marks in school?"

"I learn a lot of things on television," Tony said shyly. "I learn about geography and animals and the stars."

"What are you learning now?" Nailles asked.

The cartoon figures were having a tug of war. A large bird cut the rope with his beak and all the figures fell down.

"This is different," Tony said. "This isn't educational. Some of it is."

"Oh leave him alone, Eliot, leave him alone," Nellie called from the kitchen. Her voice was soft and clear. Nailles wandered back into the kitchen.

"But don't you think," he asked, "that from half past three to nine with a brief interlude for supper is too much time to spend in front of a television set?"

"It is a lot of time," Nellie said, "but it's terribly important to him right now and I think he'll grow out of it."

"I know it's terribly important," Nailles said. "I realize that. When I took him Christmas shopping he wasn't interested in anything but getting back to the set. He didn't care about buying presents for you or his cousins or his aunts and uncles. All he wanted to do was to get back to the set. He was just like an addict. I mean he had withdrawal symptoms. It was just like me at cocktail hour but I'm thirty-four years old and I try to ration my liquor and my cigarettes."

"He was just like an addict. I mean he had withdrawal symptoms. It was just like me at cocktail hour but I'm thirty-four years old and I try to ration my liquor and my cigarettes."

"He isn't quite old enough to start rationing things," Nellie said.

"He won't go coasting, he won't play ball, he won't do his homework, he won't even take a walk because he might miss a program."

"I think he'll grow out of it," Nellie said.

"But you don't grow out of an addiction. You have to make some exertion or have someone make an exertion for you. You just don't outgrow serious addictions."

He went back across the dark hall with its shifty submarine lights and outside the noise of rain. On the tube a man with a lisp, dressed in a clown suit, was urging his friends to have Mummy buy them a streamlined, battery-operated doll carriage. He turned on a light and saw how absorbed his son was in the lisping clown.

"Now I've been talking with your mother," he said, "and we've decided that we have to do something about your television time." (The clown was replaced by the cartoon of an elephant and a tiger dancing the waltz.) "I think an hour a day is plenty and I'll leave it up to you to decide which hour you want."

Tony had been threatened before but either his mother's intervention or Nailles's forgetfulness had saved him. At the thought of how barren, painful, and meaningless the hours after school would be the boy began to cry.

"Now crying isn't going to do any good," Nailles said. The elephant and the tiger were joined by some other animals in their waltz.

"Skip it," Tony said. "It isn't your business."

"You're my son," Nailles said, "and it's my business to see you do at least what's expected of you. You were tutored last summer in order to get promoted and if your marks don't improve you won't be promoted this year. Don't you think it's my business to see that you get promoted? If you had your way you wouldn't even go to school. You'd wake up in the morning, turn on the set and watch it until bedtime."

At the thought of how barren, painful, and meaningless the hours after school would be the boy began to cry.

"Oh please skip it, please leave me alone," Tony said. He turned off the set, went into the hall and started to climb the stairs.

"You come back here, Sonny," Nailles shouted. "You come back here at once or I'll come and get you."

"Oh please don't roar at him," Nellie asked, coming out of the kitchen. "I'm cooking veal birds and they smell nice and I was feeling good and happy that you'd come home and now everything is beginning to seem awful."

"I was feeling good too," Nailles said, "but we have a problem here and we can't evade it just because the veal birds smell good."

He went to the foot of the stairs and shouted: "You come down here, Sonny, you come down here this instant or you won't have any television for a month. Do you hear me? You come down here at once or you won't have any television for a month."

The boy came slowly down the stairs. "Now you come here and sit down," Nailles said, "and we'll talk this over. I've said that you can have an hour each day and all you have to do is to tell me which hour you want."

"I don't know," Tony said. "I like the four-o'clock show and the six-o'clock show and the seven-o'clock show..."

"You mean you can't confine yourself to an hour, is that it?"

"I don't know," Tony said.

"I guess you'd better make me a drink," Nellie said. "Scotch and soda."

Nailles made a drink and returned to Tony. "Well if you can't decide," Nailles said, "I'm going to decide for you. First I'm going to make sure that you do your homework before you turn on the set."

"I don't get home until half past three," Tony said, "and sometimes the bus is late and if I do my homework I'll miss the four-o'clock show."

"If I sat down to drink at half past three and drank steadily until nine I'd expect someone to give me some help."

"That's just too bad," Nailles said, "that's just too bad."

"Oh leave him alone," Nellie said. "Please leave him alone. He's had enough for tonight."

"It isn't tonight we're talking about, it's every single night in the year including Saturdays, Sundays and holidays. Since no one around here seems able to reach any sort of agreement I'm going to make a decision myself. I'm going to throw that damned thing out the back door."

"Oh no, Daddy, no," Tony cried. "Please don't do that. Please, please, please. I'll try. I'll try to do better."

"You've been trying for months without any success," Nailles said. "You keep saying that you'll try to cut down and all you do is watch more and more. Your intentions may have been good but there haven't been any noticeable results. Out it goes."

"Oh please don't, Eliot," Nellie cried. "Please don't. He loves his television. Can't you see that he loves it?"

"I know that he loves it," Nailles said. "That's why I'm going to throw it out the door. I love my gin and I love my cigarettes but this is the fourteenth cigarette I've had today and this is only my fourth drink. If I sat down to drink at half past three and drank steadily until nine I'd expect someone to give me some help." He unplugged the television set with a yank and picked the box up in his arms. The box was heavy for his strength, and an awkward size, and in order to carry it he had to arch his back a little like a pregnant woman. With the cord trailing behind him he started for the kitchen door.

"Oh, Daddy, Daddy," Tony cried. "Don't, don't, don't" and he fell to his knees with his hands joined in a conventional, supplicatory position that he might have learned from watching some melodrama on the box.

"Eliot, Eliot," Nellie screamed. "Don't, don't. You'll be sorry, Eliot. You'll be sorry."

...He fell to his knees with his hands joined in a conventional, supplicatory position that he might have learned from watching some melodrama on the box.

Tony ran to his mother and she took him in her arms. They were both crying.

"I'm not doing this because I want to," Nailles shouted. "After all I like watching football and baseball when I'm home and I paid for the damned thing. I'm not doing this because I want to. I'm doing this because I have to."

"Don't look, don't look," Nellie said to Tony and she pressed his face into her skirts.

The back door was shut and Nailles had to put the box on the floor to open it. The rain sounded loudly in the yard. Then, straining, he picked up the box again, kicked open the screen door and fired the television out into the dark. It landed on a cement paving and broke with the rich, glassy music of an automobile collision. Nellie led Tony up the stairs to her bedroom, where she threw herself onto the bed, sobbing. Tony joined her. Nailles closed the kitchen door on the noise of the rain and poured another drink. Fifth, he said. ▼

Sometimes it takes drastic measures to break an addiction. What do you think of Nailles's actions?

ACTIVITY 8
TV JUNKIE

1. What thoughts and feelings came to mind as you were reading the story? Did the story remind you of a discussion you have had with your parents or guardian about your television viewing habits? Briefly describe what was said and done.
2. What connections does the author make between the child's addiction to television and the father's addiction to alcohol? In what ways are they similar? What are the effects of the addiction in each case? Do you think the parallel drawn between the addictions is fair? Explain.
3. What is your opinion of the role each character plays? Why do you think the author portrayed the characters this way?
4. Briefly describe the differences between the father's and the mother's reactions to their child's viewing habits.
5. If you have children, do you plan to place any restrictions on their viewing habits? If so, what will they be? If not, why will you not impose any?
6. Now that Nailles has destroyed the television set, what do you think will happen next?

END THOUGHTS

In this unit, you have become increasingly conscious of the ways in which television influences you, the viewer. The next time you watch a program, think about your reactions to what is happening on the screen and the techniques that have been used to create these reactions. Think also about the influence of television on your life in general: if and how it affects the choices you make, the way you use your time, and the relationships you have.

ACTIVITY 9
EXTENSION IDEAS

1. Pretend that the members of your community have decided to turn off their television sets for a week. Plan the publicity campaign that would be used to inform the public, enlist their support, and provide them with alternatives to television.
2. You are a member of a Parliamentary Committee that has been assigned the task of investigating the effects of television on the lives of Canadians. Make a list of the various fictional people you would call as witnesses to your commission. In groups, work out what each expert would say. Role-play the investigation.
3. Prepare a videotape that shows the same content presented in different ways using various kinds of shots, camera angles, transitions from one shot to the next, sound cues, and so on.
4. Using a weekly television guide, survey the programs between 7:30 and 11:00 PM to find out the following:
   a) How many programs have male lead characters? How many have female leads?
   b) What are the occupations of the characters in each show?
   c) How many shows have families in them? Who makes up these families?
   d) What is the ethnic background of the characters?
   e) Where do they live?

   Discuss the extent to which the results of the survey reflect the people in your community.
5. Imagine that Norm Graham from "Family Fun" and Nailles from "Hooked" meet to talk about television and children. Write the dialogue that might occur and perform it before an audience.

◆ AT THE MOVIES
◆ A MODERN QUEST
◆ A CLASSIC QUEST

UNIT 5

QUESTS

The search for a particular objective is the basis of many of the movies, music videos, and television programs you watch and the stories and novels you read. The search, or quest, is one of the most common elements in literature. Greek and Roman literature and medieval romances often focus on a quest. Writers and artists have been reinterpreting this classic theme up to the present.

In this unit, you will think about reworkings of the quest theme that you are familiar with as well as read and respond to a short story and a poem.

AT THE MOVIES

Literary sources have been a basis for movies since the early days of the film industry. Many films are adaptations of novels or short stories. Others explore common literary themes or story types.

You have probably seen movies that tell the story of a journey. The characters are often involved in some form of quest or search which may lead to funny – or frightening – adventures. In the next activity, you will have the opportunity to reflect on your viewing experiences.

The character of the Tramp, created and played by Charlie Chaplin, was constantly in search of new and unusual experiences.

The movie *Stand By Me*, directed by Rob Reiner, features four young boys on an unusual quest. The movie is an adaptation of the short story "The Body" by Stephen King.

Many adventure and fantasy films stereotype female characters as damsels in distress. In the film *The Wizard of Oz*, the female lead succeeds in her quest on her own.

In the Canadian movie *Goin' Down the Road*, two down-on-their-luck Newfoundlanders unsuccessfully quest for "greener grass" in the big city.

ACTIVITY 1 YOUR EXPERIENCES

1. Look at the movie stills above and on page 116. What do the stills tell you about the characters? about the story line? If you have seen any of the movies, consider if the still for it reflects your impression of the movie.

2. a) Form a small group. Brainstorm a list of movies, television programs, songs, novels, and short stories that feature a quest.
   b) Talk about the items on this list with your group. Are there any common patterns in the descriptions of these items? If so, how are they similar? In what ways do they differ?

3. As a group, discuss why you think the quest is such a popular theme. What advantages do movies have over novels and short stories in telling the story of a journey? what disadvantages? Support your responses with examples from your experience.
4. If possible, arrange to see a film that features a quest. You could see a contemporary film such as *Stand By Me* or a classic such as *The Gold Rush* or *The Wizard of Oz*. Describe how the movie follows the common patterns of a quest.

A MODERN QUEST

Many stories, old and new, follow the quest theme. There are several different kinds of quests: looking for adventure, searching for an object, or trying to find meaning in life. This last type is called a psychological quest.

The short story "Run" is a modern quest story. The narrator, fifteen-year-old Peter, has become discouraged with his life so he sets out on a quest to make sense of it. As you read, you will find out why he acts as he does – and how he tries to find meaning in his life.

Some of the objects and symbolism that Daphne Odjig presents in her painting *The Indian in Transition* represent obstacles Peter must face on his quest to find meaning in his life.

RUN

Barry Milliken

"Uhnee-peesh mah?" my mother asks. She has been watching me since I came downstairs, and now that I have eaten, she knows that I'm going.

"Up the road," I say. That is all I tell her because that is all I know. She doesn't say anything for a minute, just stands by the noisy old wash machine looking grumpy and feeding wet clothes into the wringer. Her hair is tied by a rubber band at the back, but many strands are loose and hang like little droopy antennas beside her face. I see many lines that weren't there before my father died. In her eyes there is a sadness that makes me mad when I see it, just like everything seems to do lately. I know what she is going to say next, and I turn away as she does.

Her hair is tied by a rubber band at the back, but many strands are loose and hang like little droopy antennas beside her face. I see many lines that weren't there before my father died.

"When you gonna be back?"

For a minute I stand like that, with my back to her, feeling suddenly like I want to cry. But I am fifteen, so I will not.

"Peter?"

A loud bump, and then my sister's laughing comes from above me. The mad feeling gets worse. I shrug my shoulders.

"Are you going to Budge's?" I shrug again and hear her sigh; I know that some of the sadness in her eyes is because of me.

Finally, I turn halfway around and nod.

She goes to the cupboard, and, from the edge of my vision, I see her reach up to the top shelf. My sister's baby starts to cry in his high chair. My mother comes to me and holds out her hand. Without looking up, I take the thing and shove it into my back pocket.

"Don't forget," she says. I turn and go, feeling her eyes on me. As I reach the front door, I think I hear her say my name, but when I turn, she has gone into the kitchen and I hear the high chair bang as she lifts the baby from it.

Out on the porch, I can see without looking, the mess of beer bottles and cigarette butts around me on the floor. After the washing, and after the baby is cleaned up, my mother will come like a servant woman and clean up this mess my sister and her friends made last night. Her and Tucker.

Above me, the clouds look like blankets, dark and light, a big unmade bed. In front of the house is Tuck's car, which sits exactly as he left it yesterday about four o'clock. That's when he and my sister's friends arrived. All around it the ground is bare and oily, littered with tools, flattened old cigarette packages, beer bottles from other days and yesterday. The trunk and one door are open. On a table beside the car there is part of a carburetor and beside this Sacha, our cat, is sprawled. As I come down the porch steps, she gets up yawning and stretching. A car comes along the road and stops in a big cloud of dust. It backs up, then comes up our laneway with the wheels spinning, throwing dirt and stones behind it and sending Sacha running. I recognize who it is before the car comes to a stop about three feet from Tuck's. They are two of his friends, Manny and Sly. One look and I know they have been drinking all night. Manny's eyes are only half open as he tilts his head out the window.

All around it the ground is bare and oily, littered with tools, flattened old cigarette packages, beer bottles from other days and yesterday.

"Hey Pee-pee," he says and leans his head back on the seat. His mouth is twisted into a half-smile, and he looks about ready to pass out.

"C'mere."

When I go up beside the car, he lifts his arm and lets it rest along the top of the door. In his hand is a half-full bottle of beer.

"Wanna drink?"

I say no and stare at a tattoo he has put on his arm himself, the shape of a star with letters at the points. With his head still back, he squints up at me.

"Where's Tuck?"

I look out towards the lake and shrug my shoulders.

"Sleeping, I guess," I say.

He repeats the word "sleeping" so softly I can hardly hear it. His eyes close, and for a minute I think he is gone, but then, in a voice louder and harder, he says:

"Don't you know?"

His eyes half open and fix on me. There is white stuff around the corners of his mouth.

"Nope," I say, and bend forward, letting a gob of spit fall to the ground beside the car. For a minute again his eyes close and he says nothing, then when I glance down I see a little smile has come to his face.

"Hey, Pee-pee, I hear you're a fast runner."

His smile gets bigger. "'Nother Longboat, I hear."

I shrug and say nothing. Sly laughs from his side of the car, and Manny rolls his head to look at him.

"I hear he's 'nother Longboat," he says again.

They laugh harder. I turn and walk away and see the black shape of my dog back along the tree-line. He stops and looks up when I whistle and comes towards me as I start to trot along the path leading south from home. Manny calls out something, and Sly's laughing reaches me like high, strange barking, pushing me faster. Boog comes jumping through the high grass and reaches the road the same time as me. There is dust and pieces of dry grass on his black fur. Once free of the grass, he leaps high beside me, then runs ahead. He will stop and sniff around a tree or pole until I pass, then run on again. He was a present from my father for my tenth birthday. Now he's the best friend I have.

Manny calls out something, and Sly's laughing reaches me like high, strange barking, pushing me faster.

At first as I run, the road feels hard; I hear my feet on the gravel which lies along both sides. There are bumps in the middle where I never go except to cross, and now I find the smooth part which lies just beside the gravel. My feet under me go faster; the air hits harder, cleaning me, crashing away the sound behind me.

Because it is Sunday morning, there is no one around and no cars in sight. The lake on my right doesn't sparkle the way it does when the sun is out, but it doesn't matter. I fall into a good pace, and I know that soon nothing will matter. The ground lies out flat and straight, my feet flash under me, and I am filled with something that washes everything else away. It is a power that makes me know that when I run I am strong, and there is nobody who is better. That's the way it has been since the first time the strangeness happened nearly two years ago when I had just turned fourteen.

People were just starting to notice how fast and far I could run, although I hadn't yet raced against Simon Cloud, who was known to be the fastest runner on the reserve.

An older boy bet me that I couldn't run from his place, out to the highway and back, in less than an hour. I told him I had no money to bet, but I knew, too, that I hesitated because I wasn't sure I could do it. The distance he talked about was four and a half miles each way. I had never gone more than six miles without a rest, and never against a clock. I also knew that my mother wouldn't want me getting into something like that. Nine miles without a rest. It scared me alright. But the more I thought about it, the more I wanted to try it.

Nine miles without rest. It scared me alright. But the more I thought about it, the more I wanted to try it.

Carman Fisher was there, and rather than see a good bet go down the drain, he covered the other boy's money, then told me that if I could do it, I'd get ten dollars.

It was very hot that day, and fifteen minutes after I started I was wishing that I had put it off till evening. But I found a pace that I knew I could keep until at least the halfway point, and although it seemed like an hour before I reached the highway, someone yelled as I started back that twenty-four minutes were gone.

I had done better than I thought, but now as I ran the sun seemed like a torch that hung too close above me, the road stonier than I ever remembered it. I knew that it was because I was afraid. Please God, I said inside, don't let me fail and shame myself. Don't let it happen that they laugh at me.

But, as I ran, my arms and legs went away from me and became only things I saw faintly, at the edges of my vision. My breath became a useless noise that flew in and out of my open mouth. Sweat flew from me and into my eyes, until I had to close them. *Please*, I said again. Then ahead of me the road blurred and a brightness flashed that seemed to go into me like a shock, and suddenly, not as much in vision, but in feeling as strong as the flash of light had been, my father was there, around me, in me. The tiredness was gone, the road and the air helped me again. But more than that was the joy I felt that my father had come back to me.

All I knew about Carman Fisher before I made that run was that he was about three years older than me, he had a car, and he worked at the lumberyard in town. After that day, he'd honk his horn if he passed me on the road, or sometimes he'd stop and talk a little.

After he was gone, we couldn't seem to talk, but instead, as if like dogs, we each took our sorrow to a different part of the house, not willing to share it.

One day he asked if I'd like to go for a ride. I felt important and honoured to be considered a friend by someone who was working and had his own car. We went to the beach where he met some people he knew – older kids, like him. When they offered him a beer, he said, "I hope you got one for my fast buddy here. We're gonna be watchin' him in the Olympics one day." Everybody laughed, but Carman looked at me and winked as if to say, "you'll show 'em."

After that I didn't see him for a long time, then I heard he had found a job in the city and was living there.

It was then that the trouble at home started. When my father died, he took something that had made everything good for our family. After he was gone, we couldn't seem to talk, but instead, as if like dogs, we each took our sorrow to a different part of the house, not willing to share it.

My sister quit school and started going with Tuck, who is a good-for-nothing drunk. The next thing I knew, he was living with us and sharing my sister's bed every night. She had a child one year after my father died. The boy is a symbol of the shame she has brought to our family. He cries and messes, and it is my mother who sees to him, and cooks the meals, and cleans up.

"We need the money Glenda gives me," she says. "You want us to live on welfare?"

I want to tell her that it wouldn't be any worse to have that shame than it is to have the shame of living the way we are. At least then she'd be able to tell them to get out. But of course I don't say it, because I know she wouldn't do it. That's the real shame. She has let it happen. She has betrayed my father. And that's why I have to go. Now, as I run, I have decided. I will do what has been in the back of my mind to do for a long time. It's a good day for running and I have a good start. Almost fifty miles to the city, almost two marathons.

Something I remember, too, makes me more excited. A while ago I saw Carman when he was back for a week-end, and though I didn't write it down, I remember his address because he joked about it.

"Just think of thirteen turtles walking down the road," he said. That was it, 13 Turtlewalk Road.

Now that I have decided to go, I want to save all the time and distance I can. Two miles along the lake road, I turn east following a creek that winds through the bush. Though the path is rocky in parts and I have to watch my step, most of it is smooth and wide.

Boog runs past me and disappears into the bush up ahead. Seeing him makes me sad, because I know how hard it's going to be to leave him behind. I tried to think of some way I could take him with me, but I know that he would never be happy in the city. Then I remembered Aunt Budge once saying that if she had a dog she would want it to be like Boog. He'll be happy there, because he likes her too.

Out of the bush and onto a dirt road that takes me to her place, I notice that something isn't right. My wind? My stride?

Before I can think any more about it, I am there, and as I go up the lane, I see that her car is gone. Boog circles the house, barking loudly. Although I want to see her before I go, I'm relieved that she's gone to church. I know it would be hard not to let her talk me out of it. This way is sneaky, but at least I'll be gone.

Although I want to see her before I go, I'm relieved that she's gone to church. I know it would be hard not to let her talk me out of it. This way is sneaky, but at least I'll be gone.

Her back door is padlocked, so I look in the shed for what I need. Because there are no windows, I leave the door open and Boog comes in to sniff around. I find a piece of cardboard, but there is no rope. After watching him for a minute, I know what I have to do, although it's not what I wanted. He comes like a black ghost out of the darkness when I call. Already, as I bend to say goodbye, my throat is tight, my eyes full of tears. I say no words, but circle his neck with my arms. As if starting to know what is happening, he whimpers. I tell him to stay, then go to the door. When I turn to close it, he takes a step towards me, confused. Quickly I close and hook it, then stand for a minute listening. He knows I'm still here and waits quietly to see what game we're playing. For the first time since deciding to go, I am unsure, and for a while longer I stand. Am I really doing this – locking Boog up in a shed so I can run away? It seems wrong. But then I think about home, and it's enough to get me moving again. I dig in my pockets for the pencil stub I keep, and come across what my mother gave me for Aunt Budge. It's a photograph of my parents that must have been taken just before my father died, one that I haven't seen before. They stand beside my father's car, my father looking at the camera, my mother looking at him. Aunt Budge probably took the picture. It looks as if she has just called to my father, because the camera has caught him with a look that he hardly ever had – serious, maybe even sad. My mother, too, is caught with a faint smile and brightness in her eyes, her hand in mid-air, just above my father's arm. Suddenly I can't look any longer. I stand, jamming the picture back into my pocket and start to print a message on the cardboard. My hand shakes, the pencil barely shows up, but it will do. Boog whimpers in the shed, then barks.

I stand, jamming the picture back into my pocket and start to print a message on the cardboard. My hand shakes, the pencil barely shows up, but it will do.

Aunt Budge, left because I have to. Can't take home any longer. Boog is yours now. I'll be with a friend – don't worry. Love Peter.

I fold it and wedge it in beside the door-handle, then, after glancing again towards the shed, I trot back down the laneway to the road, hearing Boog bark and rattle the door as he jumps against it.

The highway is good to run on, like the track at school, my feet barely seem to touch it as I go. But after awhile, I start to have the feeling again that something is wrong. I have only come about four miles, and my breathing already is too hard and quick. Another mile. I concentrate on what Mr. Quinto, my track coach, teaches me, *use your mind to beat the distance. Distract yourself from the tiredness.* I see myself in the last miles before the city, still strong and sure in my stride, still with the power. I try to bring it back, to feel it come into me now, but it won't. There is only the pain of going on. Six miles, but it feels like sixty. I go on until the highway becomes a haze. I see the photograph again: my father looking straight at me; the great love in my mother's eyes as she looks at him. Great love where there is only sadness now. My body burns; my feet pound as I make them go. ▼

ACTIVITY 2
PETER'S LIFE

1. Rank the following items. At the top of your list, note the item you think Peter would value most. Continue your list until you have noted the item he would value least. Explain why you chose this order.
   a) a new trail bike
   b) a secure, harmonious family life
   c) a case of beer
   d) his Native Indian heritage
   e) his dog, Boog

2. Rank the items listed below. Begin with the person you believe has had the greatest impact on Peter's life and end with the person who has had the least impact. Why do you choose this order?
   a) his father
   b) his mother
   c) his Aunt Budge
   d) his sister and Tucker
   e) people such as Manny and Sly
   f) Carman Fisher

3. Which of the following items do you believe caused Peter's unhappiness and his need to run away from home? Why?
   a) his sister living with Tucker and having a baby
   b) life on his reserve
   c) the death of his father
   d) the drinking of the young people around him
   e) his own need for peace and security
   f) his mother's inability to take charge of the family life
4. What is your opinion of the drinking that occurs among the young men whom Peter meets: Sly and Manny, Tucker, Carman Fisher? How do you think Peter would answer this question?
5. What are the positive aspects of life on a reserve that are shown in this short story?

ACTIVITY 3 PETER'S QUEST

1. How does the story "Run" illustrate the quest theme?
2. Peter writes this explanation to his aunt for running away: "Aunt Budge, left because I have to. Can't take home any longer."
   a) What is your opinion of his decision to leave?
   b) Why did Peter leave the note with his aunt, and not his mother?
3. What alternatives, besides leaving home, could Peter choose to make sense of his life?
4. What is your opinion of the title "Run"? What other titles might work for this story?
5. How would Peter's mother tell the story of what happened to her family? How would she react to Peter's leaving home?
6. The story ends with this sentence: "My body burns; my feet pound as I make them go." Continue the story. What happens to Peter?

A CLASSIC QUEST

"The face that launched a thousand ships."
– *Christopher Marlowe*
Helen was so beautiful that Paris stole her away from the Greek king. In retaliation, the Greeks set out for Troy in their battleships.

"Whatever it is, I fear Greeks even when they bring gifts."
– *Virgil*
The Trojans should have feared the Greeks' gift of a horse.

Greek and Roman literature and medieval romances often focussed on a quest. Writers and other artists have been reinterpreting these classic tales up to the present. The following poem by Alfred, Lord Tennyson, written in the nineteenth century, was inspired by the ninth- or eighth-century B.C. Greek poet Homer. He is attributed with writing the epic poems *Iliad* and, its sequel, *Odyssey*.

Iliad tells the story of the fall of the city of Troy. As Homer explains, the war between Troy and the confederated Greek states started because Prince Paris of Troy had carried off the Greek queen, Helen.

The battle finally ended after ten years when the Greeks came up with an ingenious plan. They built a huge monument in the form of a horse and hid some soldiers in it. They then placed it outside Troy's city gates. Thinking the horse was a gift or sacrifice, the Trojans pulled the horse into the city. When night fell, the Greek soldiers stole out of their hiding place, opened the gates, and let the rest of the Greek soldiers in. That night, Troy was defeated.

One of the Greek heroes in this battle was Odysseus. The poem *Odyssey* by Homer is set after the fall of Troy and tells of Odysseus's sea voyage home from the Trojan wars. It describes how the gods made Odysseus's return difficult by obstructing his progress with monsters, giants, and tempestuous weather. After several years, he finally made his way back to Ithaca where his wife, Penelope, and his son, Telemachus, were waiting for him.

Penelope spent many years ruling Ithaca while Odysseus was away. She worked hard, unsure whether her husband were dead or alive. It was the custom at this time for Greek women to remarry when their husband died. For this reason, many suitors came to Penelope's court, trying to force her to marry. None of these men were suitable because they were greedy, selfish, and cruel. Penelope used her wits to ward them off.

The British poet Tennyson used Homer's story of *Odyssey* to write about Odysseus in Ithaca. He called his poem "Ulysses," which is the Latin version of the name Odysseus. Tennyson's poem deals with how the hero must have felt to return home after so many years of adventure.

ULYSSES

Alfred, Lord Tennyson

It little profits that an idle king,
By this still hearth, among these barren crags,
Matched with an aged wife, I mete and dole
Unequal laws unto a savage race,
That hoard, and sleep, and feed, and know not me.
I cannot rest from travel: I will drink
Life to the lees: all times I have enjoyed
Greatly, have suffered greatly, both with those
That loved me, and alone; on shore, and when
Through scudding drifts the rainy Hyades
Vexed the dim sea: I am become a name:
For always roaming with a hungry heart
Much have I seen and known: cities of men
And manners, climates, councils, governments,
Myself not least, but honored of them all;
And drunk delight of battle with my peers,
Far on the ringing plains of windy Troy.
I am part of all that I have met;
Yet all experience is an arch wherethrough
Gleams that untravelled world whose margin fades
For ever and for ever when I move.
How dull it is to pause, to make an end,
To rust unburnished, not to shine in use!
As though to breathe were life! Life piled on life
Were all too little, and of one to me
Little remains: but every hour is saved
From the eternal silence, something more,
A bringer of new things; and vile it were
For some three suns to store and hoard myself,
And this gray spirit yearning in desire
To follow knowledge like a sinking star,
Beyond the utmost bound of human thought.

There is my son, mine own Telemachus,
To whom I leave the sceptre and the isle –
Well-loved of me, discerning to fulfil
This labor, by slow prudence to make mild
A rugged people, and through soft degrees
Subdue them to the useful and the good.
Most blameless is he, centred in the sphere
Of common duties, decent not to fail
In offices of tenderness, and pay
Meet adoration to my household gods,
When I am gone. He works his work, I mine.

There lies the port; the vessel puffs her sail:
There gloom the dark broad seas. My mariners,
Souls that have toiled, and wrought, and thought with me –
That ever with a frolic welcome took
The thunder and the sunshine, and opposed
Free hearts, free foreheads – you and I are old;
Old age hath yet his honor and his toil.
Death closes all: but something ere the end,
Some work of noble note, may yet be done,
Not unbecoming men that strove with gods.
The lights begin to twinkle from the rocks:
The long day wanes: the slow moon climbs: the deep
Moans round with many voices. Come, my friends,
'Tis not too late to seek a newer world.
Push off, and sitting well in order smite
The sounding furrows; for my purpose holds
To sail beyond the sunset, and the baths
Of all the western stars, until I die.
It may be that the gulfs will wash us down:
It may be we shall touch the Happy Isles
And see the great Achilles, whom we knew.
Though much is taken, much abides; and though
We are not that strength which in old days
Moved earth and heaven, that which we are, we are;

One equal temper of heroic hearts,
Made weak by time and fate, but strong in will
To strive, to seek, to find, and not to yield.

ACTIVITY 4
RESPONDING TO THE POEM

1. Ulysses has decided to continue to travel and leaves the task of ruling his country to his son, Telemachus. In the role of Telemachus, write an account of what happens once Ulysses leaves. Write in poetry or prose.
2. Think ahead to the years when you will be elderly like Ulysses. Write a journal entry describing your feelings about travel and adventure at that point in your life. How are they the same as, or different from, how you feel now?

END THOUGHTS

In this unit, you have examined various reworkings of the quest theme. Use your new understanding of common elements and story patterns to look critically at the movies, television programs, and music videos you watch and the stories, novels, and poems you read.

ACTIVITY 5
EXTENSION IDEAS

1. Many famous travellers are profiled in history and literature. With a partner, brainstorm a list of well-known travellers and explorers. Choose one of the people on your list. In your school or community library, research his or her journeys. Present to your class an account of the individual's adventures.
2. Use the *Oxford Companion to English Literature* in your school or community library to learn more about quests. If you are interested in a particular work mentioned, find a version of it to read.
3. Choose a character from an adventure film you have seen that you would like to interview. Generate a series of questions you would like to ask about this person's adventures as the character, or experiences on the set. You might want to role-play the interview with a partner or present an audiotape or videotape recording to the class.

◆ TECHNOLOGY TODAY
◆ ROBOTS
◆ TOUCHING THE PAST
◆ A PLANNING MODEL

UNIT 6

TECHNOLOGY

The Age of Technology! Is this what historians will call the world you live in? Technology affects everyone; it touches all aspects of life. To succeed in today's world, you must be literate, a person who has mastered the skills of reading and writing. You must also be technologically literate. What exactly is a technologically literate person? Such a person not only uses technological advances but examines them critically. To provide you with an opportunity to think about technological literacy, this unit will prompt you to consider such questions as these: What will I need to learn and do to be technologically literate? Am I prepared for the era of technology? Will I be a user of technology? Can I recognize whether technology is enhancing or destroying the quality of human life? As you seek answers to questions such as these, you will apply your critical-thinking ability.

TECHNOLOGY TODAY

You might think about technological change in the context of the twentieth century, 100 years, which is not long at all in the wider sweep of history. At the beginning of this century, your grandparents or great-grandparents witnessed the invention of the radio and the car. Toward the middle of the century, they heard about airplanes and the possibility of air travel. Then in the 1950s, they saw television for the first time, in black and white only. The 1980s brought about the personal computer. Each of these changes has had a major impact upon individual people, and upon society. Questions you might ask yourself are: What good have these changes brought about and has society lost anything of value as a consequence? To gain more insight about issues posed by technological advances, read the article "Here Comes the Future." As you read this article, try to develop a better understanding of the nature of technology and its place in your world.

What do these photos of a light-weight plane and a heat-generated visual of a future space plane suggest about technological changes in the twentieth century?

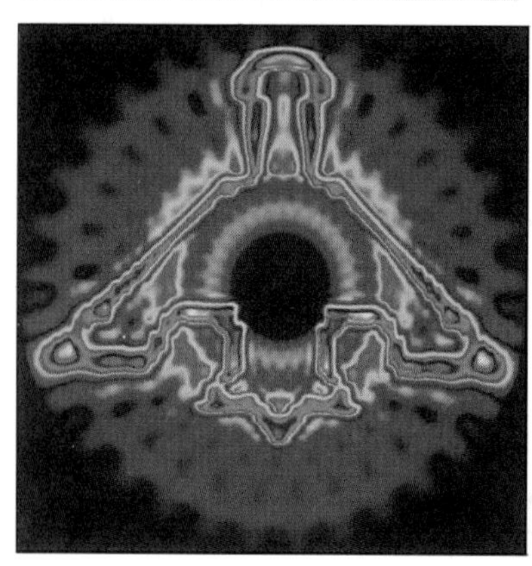

HERE COMES THE FUTURE

The Royal Bank Reporter

Banking at midnight, watching yesterday's TV special today, microwaving dinner, phoning home from the car: these are no-big-deal activities for many Canadians today. But what we now accept as commonplace would have seemed like science fiction twenty years ago.

> ...What we now accept as commonplace would have seemed like science fiction twenty years ago.

We are living in a revolutionary time – an age in which technology is rapidly changing both what we do and, especially, how we do it. Who would have believed even ten years ago that the majority of Canadian homes today would be equipped with cable television, microwave ovens and video cassette recorders (VCRs)? But as they say in show business, you ain't seen nothing yet. Imagine this: shopping at a supermarket without cash; phoning your stove from your car and telling it to start cooking dinner; carrying a computer the size of a chequebook (or a voice-activated portable phone no bigger than a pencil). No, this isn't a science-fiction scenario; rather, it's a preview of what is in store for us in the 1990s, thanks to modern technology.

High-tech devices started to become familiar household furniture in the 1980s. In the 1990s, the trend will gather even more momentum. It should be remembered that technology is not an invincible force that drives forward with a will of its own. The ongoing incorporation of new technology into our everyday lives is happening because we, as consumers, want the convenience, comfort and excitement that high-tech products can provide. Technology, which is perhaps best defined as "the means employed to provide objects and services necessary for human sustenance and comfort," is a tool humans use to create useful servants for society generally.

Although technology has always been a necessary force in human existence, what sets our society apart is the rapidity with which technological achievements have entered our lives. One single invention in 1971 is at the heart of the sudden, momentous change: the microchip – a piece of silicon no bigger than a thumbtack that can count, memorize, recognize symbols, store vast amounts of information and respond to instructions. The development and application of micro-technology led to smaller and less expensive electronic products; as a consequence, powerful and reliable computerized gadgets and machines came within the grasp of ordinary people for the first time in the 1980s.

One single invention in 1971 is at the heart of the sudden, momentous change: the microchip – a piece of silicon no bigger than a thumbtack that can count, memorize, recognize symbols, store vast amounts of information and respond to instructions.

As more and more people are discovering each day, new technology is one instance in which familiarity does not breed contempt. Quite the reverse: just a taste of high-tech wizardry makes one thirsty for more. And now, in a decade that will lead us into the twenty-first century, more is what we are in for.

Social changes are fuelling the high-tech revolution. The last decade saw the emergence of the dual-income couple as the family norm; as more women continue to enter the labor force, as they inevitably will, two-career families will become even more dominant. The new-style family has less time to cope with many of the necessities and chores of daily life, such as shopping, house cleaning, bill paying and banking. As a result, demand for the convenient efficiency offered by high-tech products and services will increase.

Some other social changes will also keep the fires of technological innovation well stoked. The ever-expanding ranks of older Canadians will seek out high-tech conveniences for their homes to help them achieve their goal of independent living. And last but certainly not least are the children of the 1970s and 1980s – the "computer-comfortable kids," as social forecaster John Naisbitt dubbed them – for whom electronic devices are a way of life. As the first full-fledged high-tech generation grows older, it will expect widely applied technology as a matter of course. ▼

ACTIVITY 1 UNDER-STANDING TECHNOLOGY

Use the information in the article to answer these questions:

1. a) Quote in your notebook the definition of technology given in the article and then explain it in your own words.
   b) Do you agree with this definition? Should some part of it be deleted? Should something be added?
2. Brainstorm to create a personal list of social changes you believe are having a major impact on the high-tech revolution.
3. Yours is a generation of "computer-comfortable kids." What does this mean and how will it affect technological change?
4. Name at least five ways in which you use or are affected by technology today.
5. What technological invention has been most important to you? How has it influenced or affected you?
6. What would you like to see invented in the near future that would be of great help to make your life more comfortable or exciting? Describe the effects this invention might have on your life.

The videotex terminal enables a person to bank, shop, and access a databank of information at home.

ROBOTS

What view of the technology of the future would be complete without some mention of robots? The word *robot* comes from the Czech word *robota* meaning "forced labour." The word was first used in a 1923 play by Czechoslovakian playwright Karel Capek entitled *R.U.R.* (which stands for Rossum's Universal Robots and refers to the robot manufacturing company in the play). Capek's play is about a future world in which robots revolt against their human rulers.

The following skit by Jane V. Miller is also about robots. As you read it you might consider what sort of relationship Miller's robots have with humans.

Robots have been depicted in many different ways in movies and on television.

ROBOTS FOR SALE

Jane V. Miller

Characters SALES CLERK
CUSTOMER
ROBOT HOUSEKEEPER
ENTERTAINMENT ROBOT
FIX-IT ROBOT
MEDICAL ROBOT
EXECUTIVE ROBOT
OTHER ROBOTS

SETTING
A store where many kinds of robots are for sale. NOTE: *This may be indicated with chairs and table at front of classroom and signs reading:* CASH REBATES FOR OLD ROBOTS, ASK ABOUT OUR LIBERAL TRADE-IN POLICY FOR OLD MODELS, ROBOT SHOWROOM, WE SPECIALIZE IN REHABILITATED ROBOTS, LOWEST PRICES FOR NEW AND USED MODELS – MECHANICAL WONDER WORKERS, *etc.*

AT CURTAIN RISE
All ROBOTS, *except* MEDICAL ROBOT *and* EXECUTIVE ROBOT, *are seated on chairs in a row.* SALES CLERK *is dusting them.*

SALES CLERK
Business certainly has been quiet. In fact, there isn't any business. I haven't sold a single robot all week. (CUSTOMER *enters.*) But wait – here's someone now. (*To* CUSTOMER) Hello. May I help you?

CUSTOMER
Yes. I want to buy a robot housekeeper.

CLERK
(*Going to* ROBOT HOUSEKEEPER) Step this way, please. Here's our latest and best model. (*Pushes buttons on* ROBOT's *back.* ROBOT *stands and pantomimes actions as* CLERK *describes them.*)

You can see that this robot does everything – it washes dishes...sweeps the floor...hangs pictures...dusts furniture... (ROBOT *starts to move faster and faster.*) It polishes silverware...irons clothes...does the washing...(ROBOT *begins to slow up, performing actions in slow motion. Finally, it stops moving. Head and body hang forward with arms hanging almost to floor.*)

CUSTOMER
It moved too fast, and now it's exhausted. It didn't last very long, did it?

CLERK (*Flustered*)
Well...ah...(Gets idea) That's really part of our demonstration. Our robots are very adaptable and easy to repair. The power pack probably needs recharging. Our Fix-It Robot can take care of that. (Goes to FIX-IT ROBOT, *pushes buttons.* FIX-IT ROBOT *stands and goes to* ROBOT HOUSEKEEPER.) The Fix-It Robot can fix anything and everything: a lawnmower, a car, a jumbo jet, your food processor. It will have the Housekeeping Robot in perfect condition in no time. (*Pushes more buttons on* FIX-IT ROBOT's *back. With large screwdriver,* FIX-IT ROBOT *begins to poke and prod* ROBOT HOUSEKEEPER, *who makes grinding and whirring noises and begins to move arms and legs.*)

CUSTOMER
It's beginning to move again!

CLERK
It is amazing, isn't it? (FIX-IT ROBOT *helps other* ROBOT to feet. ROBOT HOUSEKEEPER's *head is tilted to one side, right arm pointing up, left arm pointing over right shoulder. It stands bent over and walks about jerkily, going backward and forward.*)

CUSTOMER
That Robot Housekeeper's still not right. Somehow I don't think your Fix-It Robot fixed it.

CLERK
No, I just think the Robot Housekeeper isn't quite broken in. It

needs a couple of weeks to get the bugs out, and then you have to bring it in for a five-hundred mile check-up and oil change. But remember, after all, no one is perfect. (CLERK *helps* ROBOT HOUSEKEEPER *to chair where it sits.*)

CUSTOMER
I really don't think it's quite what I'm looking for.

CLERK
Sh-h-h! This robot is very sensitive. We don't want to hurt its feelings.

CUSTOMER (*Going to* ENTERTAINMENT ROBOT)
What does this robot do?

CLERK (*Enthusiastically*)
That's the Super-Deluxe Entertainment Robot, our latest model – a complete home entertainment center in a new, beautifully designed robot. Let me demonstrate. (*Pushes buttons on* ROBOT's back.) First, some music. This robot can sing a wide selection of songs. Just name your favourite song. (ROBOT *gets up, walks to center.*)

CUSTOMER
Can it sing "Over the Rainbow"?

CLERK
Of course. That's easy. (*Pushes buttons.* ROBOT *spreads arms wide, sings a few bars of "Over the Rainbow" offkey, in scratchy voice.*)

CUSTOMER
(*Hands over ears*): Stop! Stop! That's terrible.

CLERK
It sounds fine to me – of course, it needs a little tuning. But don't we all? (*Pushes button*) Now, how about some dancing? What would you like to see? Tap dance? Ballet? Disco? Or an old-fashioned waltz? You name it – our Entertainment Robot can do it.

CUSTOMER
How about a waltz? (*Waltz music may be played.* ENTERTAINMENT ROBOT *grabs* CUSTOMER *and starts whirling* CUSTOMER *around stage in a waltz with increasing speed.*) Help! Help! Stop this thing! Let me go! (CLERK *runs after them, frantically pushing buttons. Suddenly,* ENTERTAINMENT ROBOT *stands rigid, and* CUSTOMER *falls to floor.*)

CLERK
Are you all right?

CUSTOMER
I guess so. (*Gets to feet, rubs his arm*) No bones broken. (*Points to* ENTERTAINMENT ROBOT) I'd like to enter that model in a dance marathon. It would be a sure winner. (*Rubs leg*)

CLERK
Do you feel all right? We have a new experimental robot in the back room – a Medical Robot. Shall I get it?

CUSTOMER
(*Edging away*): Uh...no, thanks.

CLERK
It knows all the latest wonder cures. It can do physical therapy, psychoanalysis, acupuncture, remove warts and bunions, perform major surgery – with or without anesthesia. (MEDICAL ROBOT *enters. It wears white coat and reflector on forehead, has stethoscope hanging around neck, and carries hammer, saw, chisel, etc.*)

CUSTOMER
(*Drawing back*): No never mind! I feel fine. (*Limping toward exit*) I never felt better in my life! Goodbye. (*Exits*)

CLERK
I wonder what's the matter with him? (*Dejected*) Another sale lost. I'm afraid I'm never going to be a success in this robot business. (EXECUTIVE ROBOT *enters, carrying briefcase.*)

EXECUTIVE ROBOT
(*In flat, mechanical voice*): I...want...to...talk...to...you.

CLERK
(*Looking* EXECUTIVE ROBOT *over*): I've never seen a robot like this. It must be the very newest model. A V.I.P. executive type with a briefcase.

EXECUTIVE ROBOT
I…have…a…message…for…you…from…Mr. Thing.

CLERK
Mr. Thing, Mr. Charles C. Thing? The owner of the store? You must be his own important, personal message-carrying robot. Tell me, what's the message?

EXECUTIVE ROBOT
In…recognition…of…your…long…service…to…the…company…

CLERK (*Eagerly*):
Yes, yes?

EXECUTIVE ROBOT
Effective…at…once.…You…are…fired. (EXECUTIVE ROBOT *goes to other* ROBOTS, *and all shake hands. Then all* ROBOTS *stand and start to pantomime their various jobs as* CLERK *dejectedly walks to door.*)

CLERK
(*Turning*): By the way, may I use your name and model number for a reference?

ROBOTS (*Together*)
Don't…call…us.…We'll…call…you. (*Curtain*)

THE END

ACTIVITY 2
ROBOTS AND US

1. The author of "Robots for Sale" suggests: "Many different robot roles can be added to this skit, and students will be able to think of other activities the robots might perform, or lines they might say." In small groups, expand or completely change "Robots for Sale" using this suggestion.
2. Using either the original version of the play or the version you created in the above activity, write a brief explanation of the nature of the relationship between humans and technology in the play.
3. Create a visual display on the subject of robots. Possible themes you might consider are:
   - robots of the past, present, and future
   - benefits and dangers of having robots
   - the depiction of robots in film and television

TOUCHING THE PAST

Since the late 1700s when the Industrial Revolution began in Britain, many writers have expressed their opinion that industrialization has brought about social problems. During the early years of the Industrial Revolution, many people lived in terrible conditions. Industry was more concerned with technological advances than the welfare of workers and their families. William Blake's poem, written at the beginning of the nineteenth century, is set during the Industrial Revolution.

Technological changes today have their roots in the Industrial Revolution. The chimney sweeps pictured here look much like those of the late 1700s.

THE CHIMNEY SWEEPER

William Blake

When my mother died I was very young,
And my father sold me while yet my tongue
Could scarcely cry "'weep! 'weep! 'weep! 'weep!"
So your chimneys I sweep, and in soot I sleep.

There's little Tom Dacre, who cried when his head,
That curled like a lamb's back, was shaved: so I said
"Hush Tom! never mind it, for when your head's bare
You know that the soot cannot spoil your white hair."

And so he was quiet, and that very night,
As Tom was a-sleeping, he had such a sight!
That thousands of sweepers, Dick, Joe, Ned, and Jack,
Were all of them locked up in coffins of black.

And by came an Angel who had a bright key,
And he opened the coffins and set them all free;
Then down a green plain leaping, laughing, they run,
And wash in a river, and shine in the sun.

Then naked and white, all their bags left behind,
They rise upon clouds and sport in the wind;
And the Angel told Tom, if he'd be a good boy,
He'd have God for his father, and never want joy.

And so Tom awoke; and we rose in the dark,
And got with our bags and our brushes to work.
Though the morning was cold, Tom was happy and warm:
So if all do their duty they need not fear harm.

ACTIVITY 3
THE SWEEPER'S LIFE

1. As a small group or whole class, talk about the world of the chimney sweeps. What do you think their working conditions were like?
2. Are you aware of any people today who live a kind of life that is similar to that of the young chimney sweeps? What can be done to improve their life?
3. Use this structured group-response technique to think about Blake's poem:
   a) Form groups of about five people and have one person read the poem aloud to the group.
   b) Start with the person to the left of the reader. Go around the group, with each person making a statement in response to this poem. No one is allowed to interrupt the speaker.
   c) If you can't think of anything to say when it's your turn, you could read the poem aloud one more time, or a part of it.
   d) After the last reader has had a chance to make his or her comment, hold a group discussion in which you consider the responses that were made. Do you agree with these responses? What other ideas might you add to someone's response? Let your discussion of these responses lead wherever it goes.
4. Working on your own, think about Blake's poem. What is it saying about humans and technological advances? In what ways has the condition that humanity finds itself in changed since Blake wrote his poem? Write in your notebook a summary of your thoughts.

The word *technology* has different meanings for different people. What is your definition?

A PLANNING MODEL

To be a good user of technology, you should be able to examine technological innovations critically to assess their benefits and their liabilities. You need to think through the technological advances to decide what to do about them. To do this review of a technological change, you might use a plan of action. To develop a plan of action, you need a problem-solving model. This section will introduce you to the steps in a two-stage planning model.

1-3-6-All Procedure

Step One: Working on Your Own

In this stage you brainstorm by yourself. On file cards or on small pieces of paper, you write down your goal, idea, need, or concern – whatever it is that you need to make a decision about. Each of these is written on a separate file card or sheet of paper.

After you have written out your ideas, arrange them in order from best liked or most important to least liked or least important.

"I think we're beginning to chip away at the stigma."

The controversial issue of nuclear power will have to be handled with an action plan that attends to all its advantages and disadvantages.

Step Two: Working in Groups of Three

You now form groups of three, with each person bringing the file cards that he or she has developed individually. Share your cards.

In the group discussion, each person clarifies and explains his or her ideas. Similar ideas are combined and put on one file card. After the group has shared, discussed, clarified, and explained all ideas on the file cards, the group arranges all the file cards in order from best liked to least liked. At the end of this step, the group of three will have developed one set of file cards, arranged in order of preference.

Step Three: Working in Groups of Six

Two groups of three now form one group of six students and repeat the procedures for Step Two. Again, ideas are shared, clarified, and explained within the group. Similar ideas are combined and placed on one file card.

Through agreement of all six group members, file cards are arranged so that there is one set, arranged in order from best-liked to least-liked ideas.

Step Four: Working as a Class

List the ideas from all of the groups of six on the chalkboard and have a class discussion.

The result of the discussion will be a list of ideas in order from the best liked to the least liked.

To solve problems such as this one, you need to form a plan for making decisions.

Plan of Action

At this stage of the decision-making process, you need to answer questions like these:

- What do you want to do with your idea?
- How do you want to carry out your solution or idea?
- When do you want to carry it out?
- Who is going to carry it out?

The following is an example of a plan of action. As a result of advances in technology, you can get soft drinks in disposable cans. People like these cans. They are convenient. People like the feel of them. They like the cans better than bottles. As a result, many more people buy drinks in cans than bottles. As with many technological changes, there are problems with the drink cans: littering and waste of metal resources. The following action plan outlines the way Central High School dealt with its problem with disposable drink cans.

The Problem: Disposable Drink Cans

Students purchasing canned drinks at school are littering by throwing the cans away, leaving them in the halls, in classrooms, on the school grounds, and in the parking lot. This littering makes for several problems:

- The premises are unattractive.
- Teachers, caretakers, and administrators complain about the problem.
- The littering is environmentally wasteful since the cans could be recycled.

The Solution: The 1-3-6-All Model

Step One: Working Alone

Pearce listed on file cards three separate ideas to solve the problem. He set them in order of preference:

1. Place containers for cans only throughout the school.
2. Have the caretakers collect the cans at lunch and after school.
3. Eliminate canned drinks from the cafeteria.

Step Two: Working in Groups of Three

Here are the four ideas that Pearce, Gertrude, and Chan listed on their file cards in order of preference:

1. Have a school club or team place brightly decorated containers for canned drinks around the school, indicating they are collecting cans to be recycled as a fundraiser.
2. Suggest that the caretakers collect the cans and take them to the recycling depot and use the money for their coffee fund.
3. Have an anti-litter poster campaign in the school.
4. Write an article for the school newsletter explaining the need to recycle cans.

Step Three: Working in Groups of Six

When the groups of three joined to form a group of six, they decided on two ideas:

1. Have the School Council collect the cans, recycle them, and use the project as a fundraiser for the school.
2. Make students aware through newspaper articles and posters in the cafeteria of the ecological importance of recycling drink cans.

Step Four: Consensus

After discussion of several ideas presented by the groups of six, the class adopted the two ideas suggested in Step Three.

A Plan of Action

In completing the 1-3-6-All process, the class reached a decision – the first step in a plan of action. Now they had to complete the action plan.

1. *What do you want to do with your plan of action?*

The class decided to appoint a committee of three to approach the School Council about the problem and the two possible solutions they had developed.

2. *How do you want to carry out your solution or idea?*

As a class project, they decided to write a brief for the School Council, the school, and the community about the problem and the benefits of recycling. This brief would be presented to the School Council by the committee of three.

3. *When do you want to carry out your solution or idea?*

The class gave themselves a two-week deadline to prepare the brief to be presented to the School Council.

4. *Who is going to carry out your solution or idea?*

While the class hoped that the School Council would adopt the idea, they agreed that they would serve on committees formed by the School Council to carry out the project, and would volunteer as a class to make posters for the School Council explaining the project to the school as a whole.

A PLAN OF ACTION

Stage One: The 1-3-6-All Procedure

Step One:	Working on Your Own
Step Two:	Working in Groups of Three
Step Three:	Working in Groups of Six
Step Four:	Working as a Class

Stage Two: A Plan of Action

You need to make four decisions:

Decision One:	What do you want to do with your solution or idea?
Decision Two:	How do you want to carry it out?
Decision Three:	When do you want to carry it out?
Decision Four:	Who is going to carry it out?

ACTIVITY 4 DEVELOPING AN ACTION PLAN

Select an issue in your school or community and develop *A Plan of Action*, using the model presented in the infobox. You should look for issues that are related to technological change. Here are two examples of such concerns that might be applicable to your school or community.

1. Are students in your school concerned about the fact that computer usage is making people think they are only "numbers"? Develop a plan of action to balance computer use with personal feelings.
   Hint: Students are assigned numbers and everything is done by that number.

2. Develop a plan of action to persuade students who are spending an excessive amount of time on video games to channel their efforts into more productive activities.
   Hint: You don't expect these people to quit playing video games altogether.

END THOUGHTS

This unit has outlined some of the issues surrounding technological advances. You have looked at what these changes might be and how they affect you, personally, and society, in general. The activities in this unit have encouraged you to explore this topic and to find out what you think about it. You have also practised using a decision-making action plan to consider a technological issue. You should be able to use this decision-making model to solve almost any problem.

The issue of the impact of technological change is complex. Technological changes have many consequences, some good, some bad. Writer Alexander Ross has a promising view of the future and the impact of technological change. Ross said, "Any new technology – and especially electronic technology – is not merely an assortment of things that can be abolished with an axe. It is a process, a system, a new part of ourselves. You cannot destroy it. You can only learn to use this new technology to live abundantly and wisely and well."

ACTIVITY 5 EXTENSION IDEAS

1. Form groups of three to five to discuss the impact of technological change upon schools. Present a report to your class in which you outline what a classroom might be like in the next century.
2. Get together with a small group. Talk about this statement: *Technology both shapes and is shaped by society.* Summarize your discussion and prepare a group essay on this topic which can be read by other members of your class.
3. As a small group talk about this problem: *Who has the responsibility to form the public policy that controls technological change?* Be prepared to lead a class discussion on this issue.
4. Find a social issue that is related to advances in science, such as genetic engineering. Read about this issue and talk about it with others. Report your findings to your class so that class members will be informed about this issue. They should know what the issue is and have a chance to make up their minds what they think about it.
5. As a small group, think of a problem that your class or school has. Then use the 1-3-6-All problem-solving technique to come up with a plan of action to deal with this problem.
6. Watch several television programs or modern movies. Look specifically at how these productions treat the issue of technology. Prepare a report which you could give to your class.
7. For a period of two weeks, watch for articles in newspapers and magazines about technology and society. Make a bulletin-board display of these articles.
8. Read several science-fiction short stories. Prepare a book talk to give to your class or a small group about the message about technology that you find in these stories.

NORTHLAND
◆ LOOKING AT MASKS
◆ PAINTING A MASK
◆ MASKS AROUND THE WORLD

UNIT 7

MASKS

Masks are intriguing because they serve some interesting purposes. When you put on a mask, you do one of many things: transform your character, hide your identity, or protect yourself. Everyone has worn a mask at some point in life. When was the last time you wore a mask? How did it feel to have a mask on in that situation?

By responding to the works of various artists, you will explore many types of masks and how they are significant to those who create, wear, and encounter them.

LOOKING AT MASKS

Masks have been worn in many different cultures over the centuries. No matter what culture or time period it is from, the visual impact of a mask is often dramatic. Even though you might know very little about the cultural or historical significance of a mask, you can still understand a great deal about it by considering its effect on you. In the next section, you will have the opportunity to examine your reaction to various masks.

ACTIVITY 1
YOUR THOUGHTS

1. In a small group, brainstorm a list of masks that people wear. Consider masks worn to protect as well as masks worn to disguise. How do you feel when you encounter someone wearing a mask? Does your reaction depend on the situation? Explain your response.
2. Together, brainstorm a list of movies, songs, plays, short stories, comics, and television programs featuring characters that wear masks. Why do the characters wear masks? How does the mask affect your perception of the character?
3. In your group, discuss your own experiences wearing masks. On what occasions have you worn masks? Did wearing a mask affect your actions and feelings?

This African mask comes from the Niabwe tribe of the Ivory Coast. It is used to appease evil spirits.

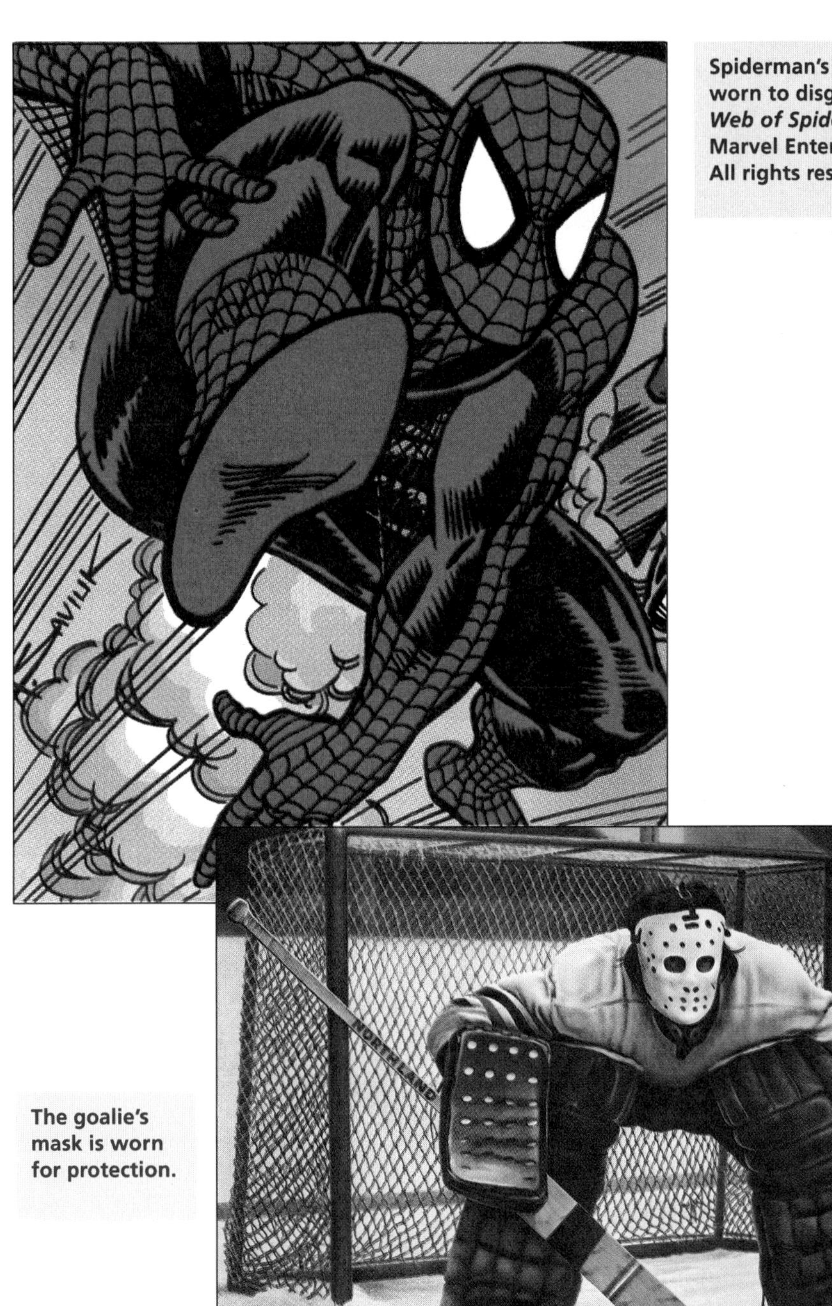

Spiderman's distinctive mask is worn to disguise and frighten. From *Web of Spiderman*: TM & © 1990 Marvel Entertainment Group, Inc. All rights reserved.

The goalie's mask is worn for protection.

This illustration shows a Roman actor trying on a mask.

Some of the characters in this dramatic scene are puppets and some are actors wearing masks.

ACTIVITY 2
COMPARING VISUAL REPRESEN-TATIONS

1. Study the masks on pages 156, 157, and on this page. In what ways are the masks alike? In what ways do they differ?
2. Jot down some notes describing your reaction to each of the masks. Support your opinion by referring to details in the picture. In your response, consider the design elements of colour, shape, size, and composition as well as the characters and setting represented.
3. Compare your observations with those of other people in the class. Are any of their observations similar to your own? If so, in what ways? If not, how do they differ? How do you account for the similarities and the differences?
4. In a journal entry, summarize your thoughts on the masks .

PAINTING A MASK

So far in the unit you have explored different types of masks and where you have encountered them in your life. Also, you have begun to explore your responses to visual representations of masks. In this section, you will practise your ability to analyze a painting by viewing and responding to Alfred Pellan's *Evasion*. As you discuss your reactions in a group, you will form a collaborative response.

***Evasion* by Alfred Pellan, 1949.**

ACTIVITY 3
RESPONDING TO A PAINTING

1. Examine the class's reactions to the painting *Evasion* by Alfred Pellan on page 159. See the *Collaborative Response to a Painting* infobox below.
   a) On your own, organize your thoughts in a chart. Think about your response to each component of the painting – the colours, textures, shapes, design, content – and the overall effect it has on you.
   b) Form groups and take turns describing your personal responses to the painting.
   c) Discuss and compare each other's responses.
   d) Form a collaborative response.
   e) Report your collaborative response to the class.

Collaborative Response to a Painting

1. Create a chart. On the left-hand side, summarize the various components of the painting. On the right-hand side, use pictures or words to record your thoughts, feelings, memories, and associations that the various elements evoke.
2. Form groups of four or five with one person acting as a scribe. Describe in turn your personal responses to the painting. All ideas are welcome and the speaker should not be interrupted.
3. Freely discuss the responses. Your teacher may also add some comments.
4. Bring together the various comments into a collaborative response to the painting. The scribe records this group response.
5. Each group presents its collaborative response to the class.
6. All students and your teacher join in a free discussion about what they have heard.

MASKS AROUND THE WORLD

Among the many different types of masks, some are used, or have been used, by specific cultures. Masks may appear at celebrations that are part of a culture's tradition; during festivals, parties, and during holidays. Or, there may be a more serious use for a mask, as part of a religious ritual or ceremony. To understand the significance of masks in various cultures and faiths, you must learn how and why they are used. This section allows you to explore the use of masks during a cultural or religious occasion.

The Haida Indians on the northwest coast of Canada create masks, totem poles, and sculptures of various animals such as the raven, the beaver, the dog, and the bear. The Haida consider these animals to be ancestral spirits. By wearing a mask in a ceremony, the performer is temporarily identified with the protecting spirit.

ACTIVITY 4
MASKED EVENTS

1. In a group of four or five, brainstorm some cultural or religious events that contain the use of masks, such as an ancient Egyptian burial or Hallowe'en. Perhaps you or someone you know has participated in a modern occasion that includes masks. Discuss what you know about the function and purpose of the mask in each of these events.
2. On your own, choose one of the occasions that your group discussed in number 1. Research at the library to discover more about the use of masks during the event. Also, phone or write to the appropriate cultural centre, religious organization, or museum to request more information.
3. Report your findings to the class. Either prepare a written report or present your report to the class. Include photos of the masks and, if possible, bring in a mask to show the class during your presentation.

END THOUGHTS

In this unit, you have examined various types of masks and the different ways in which artists approach masks. Write a personal statement in which you explore your own feelings about masks. Use the following statement openers to help organize your thoughts:

- The wearing of masks means to me...
- The removal of masks means to me...
- My feelings when I wear a mask are...

ACTIVITY 5
EXTENSION IDEAS

1. Interview someone who wears a mask for protection as part of a job, for example, a goalie, a welder, a surgeon. Focus on this person's feelings about putting on a mask to work. Share your insights with the class.
2. Watch a classic film that features a masked character such as *Phantom of the Opera*, *The Elephant Man*, *Batman*. Write a review of the film.
3. Create a mask or a series of masks from papier mâché. You might want to use your masks in a theatrical performance or display them for the class.

4. Write the script for a short play featuring physical masks or masks that hide thoughts or feelings. You may want to stage the play in the classroom or videotape the performance to show to an audience.
5. Read Margaret Laurence's short story "The Mask of the Bear." It can be found in Laurence's book *A Bird in the House*. In what ways do the characters in this story wear masks? Prepare a book report that answers this question.
6. Research the significance of the use of masks for Hallowe'en. Why do people wear masks on this day? Write a research report to share what you found out.
7. Go to a store that sells masks for costumes parties. What types of masks are popular now? Ask someone who works at the store what masks were popular last year. Can you think of reasons for the shifting popularity of different types of masks? Report your discoveries to the class.
8. Get information about working as a fantasy character at an amusement park or as a clown. Call someone at an amusement park who hires and trains people to be fantasy characters, or call a clown association or agency. What is it like for someone to wear a costume all day? How does this person create a personality for the character he or she portrays? How does he or she maintain the illusion of the character?

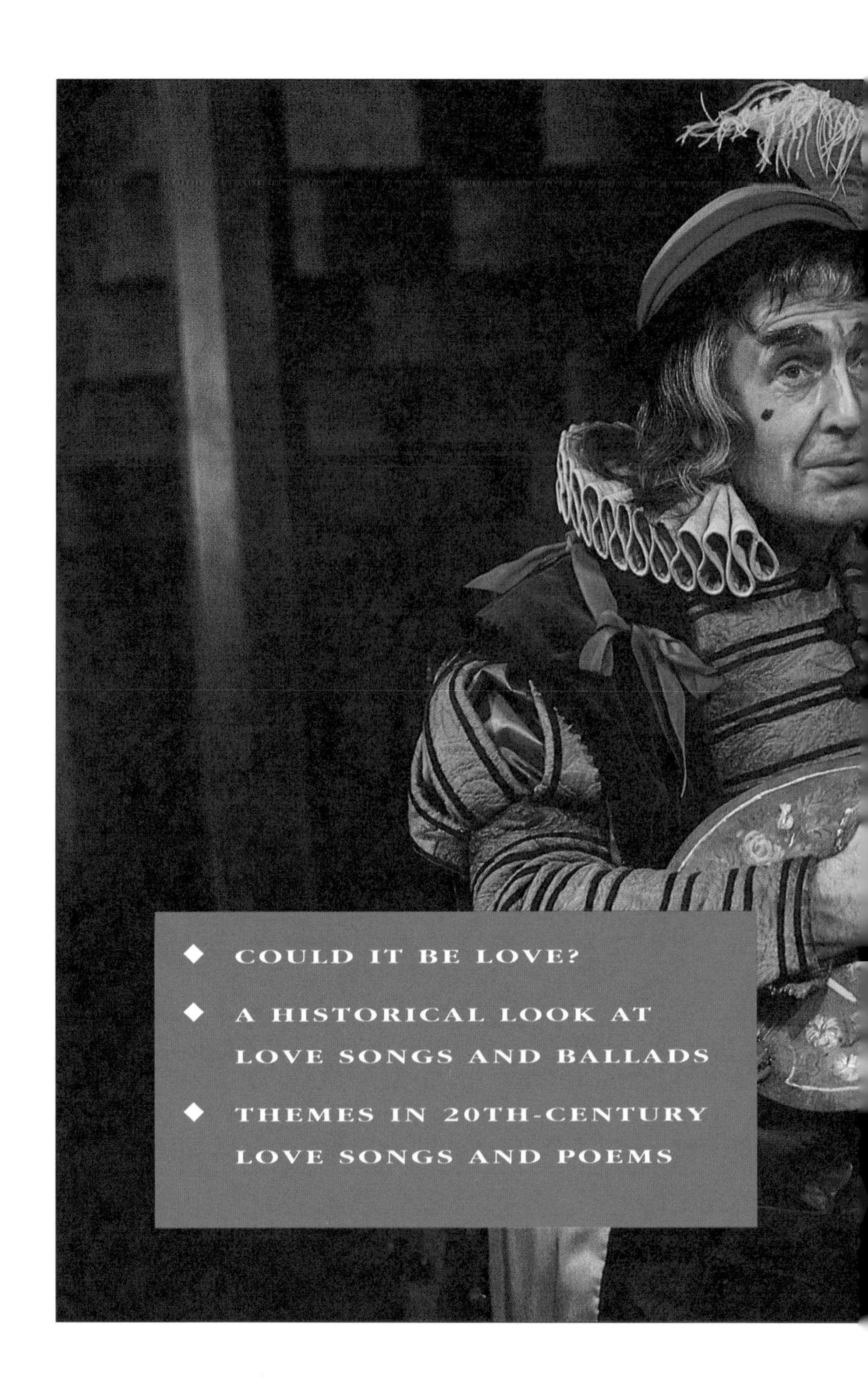
◆ COULD IT BE LOVE?
◆ A HISTORICAL LOOK AT LOVE SONGS AND BALLADS
◆ THEMES IN 20TH-CENTURY LOVE SONGS AND POEMS

UNIT 8

LOVE SONGS, LOVE POEMS

Each generation believes it is the first to discover the true meaning of love and to write the music, songs, and poetry to express it. Song writers and poets from every culture have explored various aspects of love.

In this unit, you will have the opportunity to read and respond to poetic expressions of love from different periods of English literature as well as explore your own thoughts and feelings on the subject.

COULD IT BE LOVE?

ACTIVITY 1
YOUR THOUGHTS

1. In a journal entry, record your thoughts on love. Is it possible for ideal love to be realized? Why or why not?
2. Many love poems and songs use similar means to describe feelings of love or the attributes of a loved one. With a partner or in a small group, brainstorm a list of clichés found in popular love songs, poems, or music videos.

The two following poems express different attitudes toward love. The first poem, "How Do I Love Thee?," was written in the nineteenth century and the second one, "First Person Demonstrative," was written in the twentieth century.

HOW DO I LOVE THEE?

(from *Sonnets from the Portuguese*)
Elizabeth Barrett Browning

How do I love thee? Let me count the ways.
I love thee to the depth and breadth and height
My soul can reach, when feeling out of sight
For the ends of Being and ideal Grace.
I love thee to the level of every day's
Most quiet need, by sun and candlelight.
I love thee freely, as men strive for Right;
I love thee purely, as they turn from Praise;
I love thee with the passion put to use
In my old griefs, and with my childhood's faith;
I love thee with a love I seemed to lose
With my lost saints, – I love thee with the breath,
Smiles, tears, of all my life! – and if God choose,
I shall but love thee better after death.

FIRST PERSON DEMONSTRATIVE

Phyllis Gotlieb

I'd rather
heave half a brick than say
I love you, though I do
I'd rather
crawl in a hole than call you
darling, though you are
I'd rather
wrench off an arm than hug you though
it's what I long to do
I'd rather
gather a posy of poison ivy than
ask if you love me

so if my
hair doesn't stand on end it's because
I never tease it
and if my
heart isn't in my mouth it's because
it knows its place
and if I
don't take a bite of your ear it's because
gristle gripes my guts
and if you
miss the message better get new
glasses and read it twice

Like writers, artists express the feeling of love in unique ways.

ACTIVITY 2 RESPONDING TO POETRY

1. How did you feel after reading "How Do I Love Thee?" How did you feel after reading "First Person Demonstrative"? Which poem do you like better? Why? Which do you think is the more appealing poem?
2. "How Do I Love Thee?" and "First Person Demonstrative" both are poetic expressions of love. With a partner or in a small group, compare the thoughts and feelings of the two poets. How do the poems differ? How are they similar? Does this comparison change your feelings toward either of the poems?

A HISTORICAL LOOK AT LOVE SONGS AND BALLADS

In the Middle Ages in Europe, minstrels or troubadours wandered from place to place in search of an audience. They would perform love songs, folk songs, and popular ballads of the time, at local inns or at a court. Their songs were often about actual recent events, with the result that local news was spread from community to community. Many of these traditional ballads have survived, but the exact details of the events they describe remain a mystery. Refer to the infobox on page 00 for a list of the features of a ballad. Many of the ballads tell of love, often love that goes astray. The following ballad is an example of a traditional love ballad.

The ancient Greeks celebrated many different aspects of love in poetry and song.They set poetic words to the music of a lyre, a stringed instrument, giving us the modern word *lyrics* and the phrases *song lyrics* and *lyric poetry*.

The sound is amplified and the strings are electrified, but singers still need lyrics with music – and audiences still enjoy love songs.

THE DEMON LOVER

Anonymous

"O where have you been, my long, long love,
    This long seven years and mair*?" — *more*
"O I'm come to seek my former vows
    Ye granted me before."

"O hold your tongue of your former vows,
    For they will breed sad strife;
O hold your tongue of your former vows,
    For I am become a wife."

He turned him right and round about
    And the tear blinded he ee*: — *eye*
"I wad never have trodden on Irish ground,
    If it had not been for thee.

"I might have had a king's daughter,
    Far, far beyond the sea;
I might have had a king's daughter,
    Had it not been for love o' thee."

"If ye might have had a king's daughter,
    Yer sel' ye had to blame;
Ye might have taken the king's daughter,
    For ye kend* that I was nane*. — *knew, none*

"If I was to leave my husband dear,
    And my two babes also,
O what have you to take me to,
    If with you I should go?"

"I have seven ships upon the sea –
    The eighth brought me to land –
With four-and-twenty bold mariners,

And music on every hand."

She has taken up her two little babes,
Kissed them baith* cheek and chin: *both*
"O fair ye weel*, my ain* two babes, *farewell, own*
For I'll never see you again."

She set her foot upon the ship,
No mariners could she behold;
But the sails were o' the taffetie*, *fine material*
And the masts o' the beaten gold.

She had not sailed a league, a league,
A league but barely three,
When dismal grew his countenance,
And drulie* grew his ee. *bothered*

They had not sailed a league, a league,
A league but barely three,
Until she espied his cloven foot,
And she wept right bitterly.

"O hold your tongue of your weeping," says he,
"Of your weeping now and let me be;
I will show you how the lilies grow
On the banks of Italy."

"O what hills are yon, yon pleasant hills,
That the sun shines sweetly on?"
"O yon are the hills of heaven," he said,
"Where you will never win."

"O whaten a mountain is yon," she said,
"All so dreary wi' frost and snow?"
"O yon is the mountain of hell," he cried,
Where you and I will go."

He strack the tap-mast wi' his hand,
    The fore-mast wi' his knee,
And he brake that gallant ship in twain,
    And sank her in the sea.

ACTIVITY 3
A LOVE BALLAD

1. a) Tell the story of "The Demon Lover" to another student, in your own words. Together, decide upon any details that may not appear in the ballad. Share your interpretation of the ballad with your classmates.
   b) Does this love ballad remind you of any other song lyrics you have heard, poems or stories you have read, or films or plays you have seen? If so, how is it similar? How does it differ?
2. This ballad, like many ballads of its time, takes a particular attitude toward women and how they were supposed to behave. What does this ballad tell us about the perceived role of women in medieval society?
3. With a group or partner, prepare an oral reading of this ballad. You will have to decide who will read which lines, what tone of voice to use, and what mood you will be trying to convey. You may want to share your presentation with the class.

INFO BOX

Features of a Ballad

Refer to this list to recognize a ballad, or to write one. "A Red, Red Rose" by Robert Burns on page 174 is a good example.

- Deals with highly emotional theme – tragic love or the exploits of warriors
- Well-adapted to music
- Four-line stanzas
- Second and fourth lines rhyme (abcb)
- Rhyming lines are eight syllables long
- Other lines are six syllables long

Many of William Shakespeare's plays, even his tragedies, contain songs. The theatre of his time attempted to satisfy the tastes of all members of the audience, including those who liked a rousing drinking song and those who preferred a tender love song. In his play *Twelfth Night*, Shakespeare included the following song with a message to young lovers that is still popular with writers of love songs today.

Shakespeare included songs in his plays to suit the tastes of his audience.

O MISTRESS MINE

from *Twelfth Night*, Act II, scene iii

William Shakespeare

O mistress mine! where are you roaming?
O! stay and hear; your true love's coming,
That can sing both high and low.
Trip no further, pretty sweeting;
Journey's end in lovers' meeting,
Every wise man's son doth know.

What is love? 'tis not hereafter;
Present mirth hath present laughter;
What's to come is still unsure:
In delay there lies no plenty;
Then come kiss me, sweet and twenty,
Youth's a stuff will not endure.

ACTIVITY 4
A LOVE SONG

1. Choose a word or phrase that you think is the most important in "O Mistress Mine." Why do you think it is important?
2. What feeling do you get from the song? What has contributed to this mood?
3. What tone does Shakespeare create? How are the mood and the tone related?

Robert Burns (1759-96), a popular poet from Scotland, lives again each January 25th, when millions around the world celebrate his poetry. In his poetry, Burns expresses his concern for people of the working class. He is also one of the first poets to question the treatment of women and children in society. Robbie Burns is best remembered for his love poetry. The following selection is one of his better-known ballads.

A RED, RED ROSE

Robert Burns

My love is like a red, red rose,
  That's newly sprung in June;
My love is like the melodie
  That's sweetly play'd in tune.

So fair art thou, my bonnie lass,
  so deep in love am I;
And I will love thee still, my dear,
  Till a' the seas gang dry.

Till a' the seas gang dry, my dear,
  And the rocks melt wi' the sun;
And I will love thee still, my dear,
  While the sands o' life shall run.

And fare thee well, my only love!
  And fare thee well awhile!
And I will come again, my love,
  Tho' it were ten thousand mile!

Lady with a Lute **by Thomas Wilmar Dewing, 1880.**

Christina Georgina Rossetti (1830-94) is a well-known poet of the Victorian period. She was acclaimed for her poetic skill and distinctive style. Some recurrent themes in her poetry are of unhappy, delayed, or frustrated love. "A Birthday," one of her best-known poems, has a more positive theme.

A BIRTHDAY

Christina Rossetti

My heart is like a singing bird
    Whose nest is in a watered shoot;
My heart is like an apple tree
    Whose boughs are bent with thickset fruit;

My heart is like a rainbow shell
    That paddles in a halcyon sea;
My heart is gladder than all these
    Because my love is come to me.

Raise me a dais of silk and down;
    Hang it with vair and purple dyes;
Carve it in doves, and pomegranates,
    And peacocks with a hundred eyes;
Work it in gold and silver grapes,
    In leaves, and silver fleurs-de-lys;
Because the birthday of my life
    Is come, my love is come to me.

This painting of a woman playing a harp is from the fifteenth century.

ACTIVITY 5 METAPHORS OF LOVE

1. Burns and Rossetti both use a common literary technique, the metaphor, to describe feelings of love. Identify and discuss with a partner the similarities and the differences between the two poems.
2. What effect does the repetition of the phrases create in the poems? Do you like the effect that is created? Why or why not?
3. Choose your own personal metaphor for describing love. Write a poem, song, or prose passage or create a collage of images which incorporates your metaphor for love.

THEMES IN 20TH-CENTURY LOVE SONGS AND POETRY

A frequent theme in poetry and love songs is the difficulty of saying goodbye – as lovers part for the summer, a school term, the duration of a war, or a lifetime. The following song expresses a young man's feelings about the end of a relationship.

I GET ALONG WITHOUT YOU VERY WELL

Hoagy Carmichael

I get along without you very well,
Of course I do,
Except when soft rains fall and drip from leaves,
Then I recall the thrill of being sheltered in your arms,
Of course I do,
But I get along without you very well.

I've forgotten you, just like I should,
Of course I have,
Except to hear your name or someone's laugh that is the same
But I've forgotten you just like I should.
What a guy! What a fool am I
To think my breaking heart could kid the moon;
What's in store: Should I phone once more?
No it's best that I stick to my tune.

I get along without you very well,
Of course I do,
Except perhaps in spring, but I should never think of spring
For that would surely break my heart in two.

Music provides a way of expressing a range of powerful emotions. Even when the writer is experiencing deep personal pain, a song can emerge. In 1939, a young Toronto singer named Ruth Lowe, suddenly widowed, wrote the following song.

Lowe's song "I'll Never Smile Again" became a hit when it was recorded by the Tommy Dorsey band featuring the young and wildly popular singer Frank Sinatra.

I'LL NEVER SMILE AGAIN

Ruth Lowe

You loved me in the past,
But our romance didn't last.
You thrilled me with your kiss, darling.
Now, I promise this:

I'll never smile again
Until I smile at you.
I'll never laugh again.
What good would it do?

For tears would fill my eyes;
My heart would realize
That our romance is through.

I'll never love again.
I'm so in love with you.
I'll never thrill again to someone new.

Within my heart,
I know I will never start to smile again
Until I smile at you.

Amy Lowell (1874-1925), an American poet, wrote "The Taxi." This poem exemplifies her style of writing in free verse using visual images.

THE TAXI

Amy Lowell

When I go away from you
The world beats dead
Like a slackened drum.
I call loud for you against the jutted stars
And shout into the ridges of the wind.
Streets coming fast,
One after the other,
Wedge you away from me,
And the lamps of the city prick my eyes
So that I can no longer see your face.
Why should I leave you,
To wound myself upon the sharp edges of the night?

ACTIVITY 6
LOVE HURTS

1. "I Get Along Without You Very Well," "I'll Never Smile Again," and "The Taxi" offer different poetic responses to ending a love relationship. In a small group, compare these songs and poems. What thoughts and feelings were each of the writers trying to express? Which one do you think is the most effective?
2. In a journal entry, record your feelings about the songs and poem you read.
3. a) If you were to make a music video for "I'll Never Smile Again," what might it look like? Create a storyboard for the video.
   b) If possible, shoot your video. Read the lyrics and choose suitable background music or play a recording of the song. Present your video to an audience.
   c) If you don't have access to video equipment, get together with a small group and compare the storyboards you prepared for your video. Critique each other's work. Choose one of the storyboards to present to the class.
4. Create a visual image, such as a photograph, an illustration, or a collage, to express your feelings about "The Taxi."

END THOUGHTS

There is music and poetry around you – defining you, challenging you, helping you express your emotions, allowing you to grow. Words and music together, that powerful combination of poetry, melody, rhythm, and harmony, help you express your thoughts and feelings in a unique way. Take a few minutes to write a journal entry explaining how a song, poem, music video, movie, play, or television program has helped you to better understand the concept of love.

Tracy Chapman sings ballads with modern political and social themes.

ACTIVITY 7
EXTENSION IDEAS

1. Find an anthology in your class, school, or community library that contains traditional ballads. Read to find out about these ballads. Prepare a presentation for your class in which you talk about and read ballads.
2. How much does it cost to record a new song? What does it cost to make an album? What is involved technically in producing a single? an album? How much does it cost? Arrange an interview with someone in the recording industry. Present your findings either orally or in writing to a partner or small group.
3. Compare your interpretation of the lyrics of your favourite song with the video of the same song. How are they similar? How do they differ? Record your observations in your notebook or compare your observations to a partner's.

4. Arrange to interview someone of your parents' or grandparents' generation. What songs or poems were important to them when they were younger? Can they remember the words? What did they like about these poems or songs? Why are they memorable? What personal memories come to mind when they think of them? Tape-record the interview or write it in the form of a short essay or report and give a copy for comment to the person you interviewed. (See Unit 14 for help with essay writing.)

5. With a small group of three to five people, create a radio show which will play your group's favourite music around one particular theme.
   a) Choose someone in the group to be the announcer. Write the script which the announcer will use to provide the continuity between songs. Include ads if you wish.
   b) Tape a five-, ten-, or fifteen-minute radio show featuring your group's songs or cuts from them.
   c) Play the tape for another small group, or for the class as a whole.

6. Try a "love rap." Can you celebrate your love, or that of someone you know, in rap? Perform your rap for a small group or the whole class. If you prefer, rap another topic. Use published poems or songs – or write your own.

7. Write your own song lyrics or lyric poem. Model your lyrics on one of those found in this unit, or on the lyrics of a song or poem you like. Try to imitate the form of the poem which is your model. Or, create your own lyrics without using a model. Read your lyrics to a partner, post them on the bulletin board, set them to music and tape-record them, or publish in some other way.

8. Interview a much younger person and a much older person about their musical tastes. Note their preferences in your notebook. Note ways in which their opinions are similar or different. What kinds of music are important to each person? Prepare a short report on your findings to present to your class.

9. Although love is a popular and enduring topic, it is not the only subject that poets and song writers choose to write about. In a small group, decide on a theme and collect poems and song lyrics on that theme. Prepare an illustrated book to present your selections and theme.

Read
◆ CANADA'S LITERACY PROBLEM
◆ CHILDREN'S LITERATURE
◆ THE JOYS OF LITERACY
◆ ROCK AND ROLL READING
© MARCI LIPMAN FOR CAN

UNIT 9

THE ROOTS OF LITERACY

The need for high levels of literacy in our society is more important than ever before. New technological developments result in changes in the workplace. New, more sophisticated technology often requires superior reading skills. Moreover, much of the information you need for your daily life is presented in print form. For example, instructions, labels, signs, application forms, government and legal documents all require strong reading skills.

In this unit, you will have the opportunity to read, think, talk, and write about print literacy, its importance in society, and its development through childhood experience. You will also reflect on how reading enriches your life.

CANADA'S LITERACY PROBLEM

One in five Canadians is functionally illiterate. While these individuals may recognize a few words, they are unable to read dense text such as an application form or the directions on a label. Such an inability to read or write causes serious problems both for individuals and for society. The following article by June Callwood examines Canada's literacy problem.

The graphics company headed by Marci Lipman (*here with a young friend*) designed these T-shirts to promote literacy.

WHY CANADA HAS TO BEAT ITS LITERACY PROBLEM

June Callwood

Carole Boudrias shuddered when she remembers the time she almost swallowed Drano because she thought it was Bromo. Even more painful to recall is the time she mistook adult pain-killers for the child-size dose and made her feverish child much sicker.

Carole Boudrias shudders when she remembers the time she almost swallowed Drano because she thought it was Bromo.

"When you can't read," she explains, "it's like being in prison. You can't travel very far from where you live because you can't read street signs. You have to shop for food but you don't know what's in most of the packages. You stick to the ones in a glass jar or with a picture on the label. You can't look for bargains because you can't understand a sign that says 'Reduced.' I would ask the clerk where is something and the clerk would say, aisle five. Only I couldn't read aisle five. I'd pretend that I was confused so they'd lead me right to the shelf."

Carole Boudrias is able to read now, at last. She's a thirty-three-year-old single parent who lives with her five children in a handsome townhouse on Toronto's harbourfront and holds a steady job. But her struggle with illiteracy is all too vivid in her memory. "You can't get a job," she says earnestly. "You can't open a bank account. You have to depend on other people. You feel you don't belong. You can't help your children. You can't help yourself."

Six years ago when her oldest child started school, the boy floundered. Because he had been raised in a household without books, print was strange to him. He would point to a word in his reader, that classic, endearingly silly *Dick and Jane*, and ask his mother what it was. She was as baffled as he, so he'd check with his teacher the next day and that evening would proudly read the new word to this mother. She began to absorb the shape of the words he identified. She found she could recognize them even days later.

That was astonishing. As a child she had been labelled mentally retarded and confined to "opportunity classes" where reading wasn't taught. She grew up believing that she wasn't intelligent enough to learn. Nevertheless, she *was* learning. The vocabulary of words she could read in her son's reader was growing. She began to think maybe the experts were wrong. Then, one miraculous day, she realized she was learning to read even faster than her son was.

As a child she had been labelled mentally retarded and confined to "opportunity classes" where reading wasn't taught.

"My son was my first teacher," she grins. She had never allowed herself to believe that it was possible that she could learn to read. She hadn't even tried: no one whose life is made up of poverty and failed relationships is ready to take on, voluntarily, the potential for another defeat, another kick in the self-esteem. She hesitated a long time but the evidence was persuasive – she was beginning to read. Her welfare worker had always been kind, so she summoned the nerve to ask her where she could find help.

That lead her to Beat the Street, a program that helps people who are illiterate for all the reasons that befall sad children: unrecognized learning disabilities, emotional stress, too many schools, scorn and belittling, terror, bad teachers. She was linked with a volunteer tutor, and they came to admire each other deeply.

"Now I can read, I can read books, anything. I can write. In English *and* French."

Carole Boudrias has written a book, *The Struggle for Survival*, which tells of her tortured childhood lacerated with incest and violence, and her triumphant recovery from illiteracy. Last summer she was the poet laureate of the annual golf tournament hosted by Peter Gzowski, the beloved and respected heart of CBC Radio's *Morningside*. He has befriended the cause of literacy in Canada and over the past four years has raised a quarter of a million dollars for Frontier College, one of the first organizations in the country to tackle the problem of illiteracy.

"Learning to read," Carole Boudrias says quietly, "was like a second birth, this time with my eyes open. Before I could read, I was a blind person."

Canada has nearly five million adult citizens who are described as functionally illiterate, which means that they can recognize a few words, such as washroom signs and exits, but they can't read dense print at all. They can't decipher directions, for instance, or application forms, or warnings on labels. The world of newspapers, posters, advertising, books, menus, banking, recipes, and instructions-for-assembly that literate people take for granted is barred to them; they live a life of bluff, anxiety, embarrassment, and isolation.

"Learning to read," Carole Boudrias says quietly, "was like a second birth, this time with my eyes open. Before I could read, I was a blind person."

A good many Canadians are as profoundly illiterate as Carole Boudrias was. People who meet illiterate adults are struck by the similarity of their textural experience. All of them liken the inability to read and write with being disabled or chained in a prison. Edwin Newman, a U.S. broadcaster who writes about language, calls illiteracy "death in life."

The sense of being caged and blinded is not morbid fantasy. People who can't read may be able to walk freely but they can't go far. Subway stops rarely have pictures to guide them and the destinations bannered across the front of buses and streetcars are meaningless. If they ask for directions, well-intentioned people tell them, "Go along Main Street to Elm and turn left." Consequently, they must travel by taxi or stay home, though they usually are the poorest of the poor.

Almost every job, even simple manual labour such as street-cleaning, requires an ability to read. Personnel managers don't take kindly to people who can't fill out an application, or when asked, can't spell their own addresses.

The divide between the literate and illiterate has never been wider. In this half of the century North America has become a world of forms and documents and instructions, written warnings, posted rules, leaflets, and vital information circulated in brochures. Two generations ago, illiteracy was prevalent but not such a great disadvantage. Someone functionally illiterate could fake it through an entire lifetime and still hold a good job. Employment skills were acquired by watching someone else; apprenticeship was the accepted teacher, not two years in a community college.

Today inability to read is a ticket to social segregation and economic oblivion. A poignant example is the skilled house-painter who turned up one day in the crowded quarters of the East End Literacy Program in Toronto. He said he wanted to read. The counsellor asked him, as all applicants are asked, what he wanted to read. "Directions on paint cans," he answered promptly. "I'm losing jobs. I can't read how to mix the colours."

To pay for goods, she would hold out a handful of money and let the cashier take what was needed – and perhaps more, she never knew.

Many who are illiterate can't read numbers. When they are paid, they don't know if they are being cheated. Because she couldn't fill out bank deposit slips, Carole Boudrias used to cash her welfare cheque in a storefront outlet which clips poor people sharply for no-frills service. To pay for goods, she would hold out a handful of money and let the cashier take what was needed – and perhaps more, she never knew. Once she would have been short-changed $50 she could ill afford if a stranger who witnessed the transaction hadn't protested.

The common emotional characteristic of people who can't read is depression and self-dislike. All feel at fault for their situation; with few exceptions, they went through school with bright little girls exactly their age who leaped to their feet to recite and smart little boys who did multiplication in their heads. Everyone else in the world, it seemed, could learn with ease; for them, even C-A-T looked a meaningless scribble. Teachers called them stupid; worse, so did other children.

"Stupid" may just be the cruellest word in the language. It consumes confidence, on which the ability to learn relies. Seven-year-olds having trouble with reading will frolic at recess with an edge of glee; eleven-year-olds who can't read have bitter faces and scarred souls.

Loss of hope for oneself is a descent into desolation without end. It causes men to rage in fury and women to wound themselves. People who can't read come readily to view themselves as worthless junk, and many feel they must grab what they can out of life and run. Canada's prisons are full of young men who can't read. The Elizabeth Fry Society estimates that close to ninety per cent of the women in Kingston's infamous prison for women are illiterate.

Because Canada has five million people who can't read, the political shape of the country and the priorities of governments are not influenced greatly by the needs of the poor. Since illiterates are effectively disenfranchised, the political agenda is written by the more powerful. Candidates rarely find it advantageous to uphold the causes that matter most to Canada's illiterates – an end to homelessness and the need for food banks, welfare payments that meet the poverty line, and better educational and job-training opportunities. Few votes would follow any politician with such a crusade. The electorate that can't read won't be there to ruffle the complacent on election day.

Loss of hope for oneself is a descent into desolation without end. It causes men to rage in fury and women to wound themselves.

Their silence costs this country severely. Education is free in Canada because it was recognized that democracy isn't healthy unless all citizens understand current events and issues. Five million Canadians can't do that. Voters, most of them literate, choose candidates who help their interests; those who don't vote, many of them illiterate, by default get a government that does not need to know they exist.

The result is a kind of apartheid. The government has lopsided representation, which results in decisions which further alienate and discourage the unrepresented. The gap between the haves and have-nots in Canada is already greater than at any time in this century, and widening. Urban apartment houses are the work places of crack dealers, the streets are increasingly unsafe, and households have installed electronic security systems. The poor, if asked, would have better answers than guard dogs. The best, most lasting responses to crime and addiction and violence are literacy programs, coupled with job training and full employment.

Schools are in disgrace, with a failure rate of fully one-third of all high school students. A soup company with such a record would be out of business in a day. The educational system has managed to exacerbate the class differences which are developing in this country. Canada's millions of illiterates went through school the required number of years, give or take time-out for truancy, illness, running away from abuse, and confinement in detention homes. These human discards, identified promptly in the first years of elementary schools, will ever after drift around disconsolately. They are surplus people, spare parts for which society has no use. Unless there is a war.

Carole Boudrias is working on a project, Moms in Motion, to help young mothers to get off welfare rolls. She says to them, "What do you want?" They reply, "To go back to school."

Another chance. Five million Canadians need another chance. Maybe they can become literate, maybe they can become healed and whole. What a lovely goal for the 1990s. ▼

Reading can be a shared experience.

ACTIVITY 1 RESPONDING TO AN ARTICLE

1. Write a journal entry in which you examine your feelings and thoughts about the article. Were you aware of the problems of illiteracy before you read this article? Did the article remind you of anyone you know, stories you have read, or anecdotes you have heard? If so, you might want to refer to these in your journal entry.
2. Form a small group. Discuss your reactions to the article. How did you feel after reading about the problems faced by Canada's functionally illiterate? How did you feel about Carole Boudrias's accomplishments? How would you feel if you were unable to read or write?
3. In your group, sum up June Callwood's perspective on the literacy problem in Canada. What are her major concerns? Explain with specific reference to the text.
4. Continue working in groups to discuss the meaning and significance of the following ideas that Callwood presents in her article:
   - "The divide between the literate and illiterate has never been wider. In this half of the century North America has become a world of forms and documents and instructions, written warnings, posted rules, leaflets, and vital information circulated in brochures."
   - "Today inability to read is a ticket to social segregation and economic oblivion."
   - "Because Canada has five million people who can't read, the political shape of the country and the priorities of governments are not influenced greatly by the needs of the poor."
   - "The gap between the haves and have-nots in Canada is already greater than at any time in this century, and widening."
   - "These human discards [people who can't read], identified promptly in the first years of elementary schools, will ever after drift around disconsolately. They are surplus people, spare parts for which society has no use. Unless there is a war."
5. Do you agree with Callwood's arguments? Why or why not?
6. What do you think should be done to alleviate the problems of illiteracy? In your group, brainstorm a list of ways to promote literacy in your school and in your community.

CHILDREN'S LITERATURE

It has been said that literacy begins in the home. Children who come from families where reading is a frequent and natural activity for everyone tend to be readers.

It is important to remember that children's literature is serious literature. While the language and stories may seem simple, the art of writing good children's literature is as complex as that of writing good adult literature. Sometimes a work of literature can be equally appropriate and appealing to both adults and children. The following excerpt from a guide to children's books written by well-known Canadian journalist Michele Landsberg points out some aspects of the value of children's literature.

READ Canada is a program of Frontier College aimed at developing literacy in children.

Books were far more than an amusement in my childhood; they were my other lives, and the visible existence I now lead in the workaday world was touched and transformed by them forever. The spell was never broken; all through my adult life, children's literature has given me unabated pleasure. It's like those huge blackball candies we used to buy: the longer you rolled one around inside your cheek, the more splendid and various were the colours revealed. As my own children grew, the books I had loved and the books I discovered through and for them took on ever-new colours and shades of meaning, and confirmed my belief that a child's life without books read for pleasure is a child's life deprived.

ACTIVITY 2
REFLECTING ON YOUR EXPERIENCES

1. Think back to your own childhood. Did you enjoy reading or being read to?
2. Do you still remember favourite stories, poems, or books from your childhood? If so, why do you think you remember them?
3. What do you remember of your childhood reading habits such as a weekly trip to the library or reading at bedtime?
4. What are your reading habits like today? How are they similar to or different from your reading habits as a child?
5. Write a journal entry describing your thoughts about reading.

Many people have memories of their parents or guardian reading them a bedtime story.

THE AMAZING BONE

· WILLIAM STEIG ·

It was a brilliant day, and instead of going straight home from school, Pearl dawdled. She watched the grownups in town at their grownup work, things she might someday be doing.

She saw the street cleaners sweeping the streets and she looked in at the bakery on Parsnip Lane and saw the bakers taking hot loaves of pumpernickel out of the oven and powdering crullers with sugar dust.

On Cobble Road she stopped at Maltby's barn and stood gawking as the old gaffers pitched their ringing horseshoes and spat tobacco juice.

...Spring was so bright and beautiful, the warm air touched her so tenderly, she could almost feel herself changing into a flower.

Later she sat on the ground in the forest between school and home, and spring was so bright and beautiful, the warm air touched her so tenderly, she could almost feel herself changing into a flower. Her light dress felt like petals.

"I love everything," she heard herself say.

"So do I," a voice answered.

Pearl straightened up and looked around. No one was there. "Where are you?" she asked.

"Look down," came the answer. Pearl looked down. "I'm the bone in the violets near the tree by the rock on your right."

Pearl stared at a small bone. "You talk?" she murmured.

"In any language," said the bone. "¿Habla español? Rezumiesh popolsku? Sprechen sie Deutsch? And I can imitate any sound there is." The bone made the sounds of a trumpet calling soldiers to arms. Then it sounded like wind blowing, then like pattering rain. Then it snored, then sneezed.

Pearl couldn't believe what she was hearing. "You're a bone," she said. "How come you can sneeze?"

"I don't know," the bone replied. "I didn't make the world."

"May I take you home with me, wonderful bone?" Pearl asked.

"You certainly may," said the bone. "I've been alone a long time. A year ago, come August, I fell out of a witch's basket. I could have yelled after her as she walked on, but I didn't want to be her bone any longer. She ate snails cooked in garlic at every meal and was always complaining about her rheumatism and asking nosy questions. I'd be happier with someone young and lively like you."

Pearl picked the bone up and gently put it in her purse. She left the purse open, so they could continue their talk, and started home, forgetting her schoolbooks on the grass. She was eager to show this bone to her parents, and she could guess what would happen when she did. She would tell about the talking bone, her mother would say "You're only imagining it," her father would agree, and then the bone would flabbergast them both by talking.

> "... I didn't want to be her bone any longer. She ate snails cooked in garlic at every meal and was always complaining about her rheumatism and asking nosy questions."

The spring green sparkled in the spring light. Tree toads were trilling. "It's the kind of wonderful day," said Pearl, "when wonderful things happen – like my finding you."

"Like *my* finding *you*!" the bone answered. And it began to whistle a walking tune that made the going very pleasant.

But not for long. Who should rush out from in back of a boulder and spoil everything but three highway robbers with pistols and daggers. Pearl couldn't tell what breed of animal they were, because they wore cloaks and Halloween masks, but they were fierce and spoke in chilling voices.

"Hand over the purse!" one commanded. Pearl would have gladly surrendered the purse, just to be rid of them, but not with the bone in it.

"You can't have my purse," she said, surprised at her own boldness.

"What's in it?" said another robber, pointing his gun at Pearl's head.

"I'm in it!" the bone growled. And it began to hiss like a snake and roar like a lion.

The robbers didn't wait around to hear the rest, in case there was any more. They fled so fast you couldn't tell which way they'd gone. It made Pearl laugh. The bone, too.

They continued on their way, joking about what had just happened and chatting about this and that. But it wasn't long before a fox stepped forth from behind a tree and barred their path. He wore a sprig of lilac in his lapel, he carried a cane, and he was grinning so the whole world could see his sharp white teeth.

"Hold everything," he said. Pearl froze. "You're exactly what

I've been longing for," he went on. "Young, plump, and tender. You will be my main course at dinner tonight." And he seized Pearl in a tight embrace.

"Unhand her, you villain," the bone screamed, "or I'll bite your ears off!"

"Who is that speaking?" asked the surprised fox.

"A ravenous crocodile who dotes on fresh fox chops, that's who!" answered the bone.

He wore a sprig of lilac in his lapel, he carried a cane, and he was grinning so the whole world could see his sharp white teeth.

The wily fox was not as easily duped as the robbers. He saw no dangerous crocodile. He peered into Pearl's purse, where the sounds seemed to be coming from, and pulled out the bone. "As I live and flourish!" he exclaimed. "A talking bone. I've always wanted to own something of this sort." And he put the bone in his pocket, where it roared and ranted to no avail.

Pushing Pearl along, the fox set out for his hideaway. Pearl's sobs were so pitiful the fox couldn't help feeling a little sorry for her, but he was determined she would be his dinner.

"Please, Mr. Fox," Pearl whimpered, "may I have my bone back, at least until I have to die?"

"Oh, all right," said the fox, disgusted with himself for being so softhearted, and he handed her the bone, which she put back in her purse.

"You must let this beautiful young creature go on living," the bone yelled. "Have you no shame, sir!"

The fox laughed. "Why should I be ashamed? I can't help being the way I am. I didn't make the world."

The bone commenced to revile the fox. "You coward!" it sneered. "You worm, you odoriferous wretch!"

These expletives were annoying. "Shut up, or I'll eat you," the fox snarled. "It would be amusing to gnaw on a bone that talks...and screams with pain."

The bone kept quiet the rest of the way, and so did Pearl.

When they arrived at the fox's hideaway, he shoved Pearl, with her bone, into an empty room and locked the door. Pearl sat on the floor and stared at the walls.

"I know how you feel," the bone whispered.

"I'm only just beginning to live," Pearl whispered back. "I don't want it to end."

"I know," said the bone.

"Isn't there something we can do?" Pearl asked.

"I wish I could think of something," said the bone, "but I can't. I feel miserable."

"Shut up, or I'll eat you," the fox snarled. "It would be amusing to gnaw on a bone that talks...and screams with pain."

"What's *that*?" Pearl asked. She'd heard some sounds from the kitchen.

"He's sharpening a knife," the bone whispered.

"Oh, my goodness!" Pearl sobbed. "And what's *that*?"

"Sounds like wood being put into a stove," answered the bone.

"I hope it won't all take too long," said Pearl. She could smell vinegar and oil. The fox was preparing a salad to go with his meal. Pearl hugged the bone to her breast. "Bone, say something to comfort me."

"You are very dear to me," said the bone.

"Oh, how dear you are to me!" Pearl replied. She could hear a key in the lock and was unable to get another word out of her throat or turn her eyes toward the door.

"Be brave," the bone whispered. Pearl could only tremble.

She was dragged into the kitchen, where she could see flames in the open stove.

"I regret having to do this to you," sighed the fox. "It's nothing personal."

"Yibbam!" said the bone suddenly, without knowing why he said it.

"What was that?" said the fox, standing stock-still.

"Yibbam sibibble!" the bone intoned. "Jibrakken sibibble digray!" And something quite unexpected took place. The fox grew several inches shorter.

"Alabam chinook beboppit gebozzle!" the bone continued, and miraculously the fox was the size of a rabbit. No one could believe what was happening, not Pearl, not the fox, not even the bone, whose words were making it happen.

"Adoonis ishgoolak keebokkin yibapp!" it went on. The fox, clothes and all, was now the size of a mouse.

"Scrabboonit!" the bone ordered, and the mouse – that is, the minuscule fox – scurried away and into a hole.

"I didn't know you could do magic!" Pearl breathlessly exclaimed.

No one could believe what was happening, not Pearl, not the fox, not even the bone, whose words were making it happen.

"Neither did I," said the bone.

"Well, what made you say those words?"

"I wish I knew," the bone said. "They just came to me, I *had* to say them. I must have picked them up somehow, hanging around with that witch."

"You're an amazing bone," said Pearl, "and this is a day I won't ever forget!"

It was dark when they reached Pearl's house. The moment the door swung open she was in her mother's arms, and right after that in her father's.

"Where on earth have you been?" they both wanted to know. "We were frazzled with worry."

Pearl didn't know what to say first. She held up the bone. "This bone," she said, "can talk!" And just as she had expected, her mother said, "A talking bone? Why, Pearl, it's only your imagination." And her father said something similar. And also as Pearl had expected, the bone astonished them both by remarking, "You have an exceptional daughter."

Before her parents had a chance to get over their shock, Pearl began telling the story of her day's adventure, and the bone helped out. It was all too much for Pearl's parents. Until they got used to it.

The bone stayed on and became part of the family. It was given an honored place in a silver tray on the mantelpiece. Pearl always took it to bed when she retired, and the two chatterboxes whispered together until late in the night. Sometimes the bone put Pearl to sleep by singing, or by imitating soft harp music.

Anyone who happened to be alone in the house always had the bone to converse with. And they all had music whenever they wanted it, and sometimes even when they didn't. ▼

ACTIVITY 3
RESPONDING TO A CHILDREN'S STORY

1. Discuss your reactions to *The Amazing Bone* with a partner.
   a) What did you like about the story? What did you dislike?
   b) Was the author able to capture your interest? If so, explain how. If not, why not?
2. Do you think children would enjoy this story? Why or why not?
3. What do you think the theme of the story is?
4. Why do you think the author chose the characters of Pearl and the bone for his story?
5. Does this story remind you of any other children's literature you have read or had read to you? Describe the similarities and the differences.
6. How does this story differ from young adult and adult fiction you have read? How is it similar?
7. Prepare and practise a reading of *The Amazing Bone* for a younger sibling, friend, neighbour, or relative. Refer to the infobox *How to Read Aloud to Children* below for some tips.

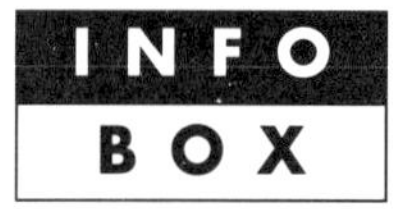

How to Read Aloud to Children

- Choose a story that you enjoy because your interest and enthusiasm will affect the children.
- Read the story silently several times. Concentrate on the mood, pictures, and images you want to create.
- Practise reading aloud until you know the characters and situations so well that you can picture them. Don't memorize the words, but have the ideas and the plot firmly in your mind.
- Get your timing right. Pause before the important words. Emphasize certain words and ideas. Build to a climax.
- Change your voice. Speak in a whisper at times. Make it loud and thundering at other times.

THE JOYS OF LITERACY

Reading and writing have become necessary survival skills in our society. Yet the *joys* of reading can far surpass the practical benefits of being able to read and write. Reading literature helps us to learn about ourselves and others and the world we live in. And reading can become a source of ideas for our own writing. In the following interview, well-known Canadian author Robertson Davies shares some of his thoughts on the joys of literacy.

The READ Canada Celebrity Reading Team includes such people as Mila Mulroney, Mark Osborne, Kevin Lowe, and Denise Donlon. The idea behind Celebrity Reading is simple. Children are influenced by people who are prominent in the media. If a celebrity – local or national – reads to them and shows them that reading is a good thing to do, chances are children will hear the message in a way they never have before.

Often they are clever at concealing the fact that the world of print is closed to them. That is a very dangerous kind of illiteracy.

A CHAT ABOUT LITERACY

Robertson Davies

Writer: So we're going to talk about literacy, are we? What do you think the word means?

Student: Being able to read and write; isn't that it?

Writer: That's it, certainly. But literacy is one of those words that means different things to different people. For instance, if I say that somebody is illiterate, what do you think I mean?

Student: That they can't read and write. Or not very much.

Writer: There, you see? Already you have made a qualification when you say, "not very much." There are hundreds of thousands of people who would be very cross if you called them illiterate, but it is true that they can't read and write very much. People who can't read and write at all are not numerous in a country like Canada. Most people can write their names, and they know what signs that say STOP and GO mean, and perhaps even DANGER. But they can't read the directions on a bottle of medicine, for instance, or the handbook that comes with the car they are driving. Often they are clever at concealing the fact that the world of print is closed to them. That is a very dangerous kind of illiteracy.

Student: How many kinds of literacy do you suppose there are?

Writer: Suppose we say three. There is the kind we have just been talking about – being shut off from everything that requires understanding of even quite simple things that are written down. Of course that really only applies in a country like ours, where the written word is so important. There were millions of people in the past, and there are millions now, who do not live in what we might call the Verbal World. A hundred and fifty years ago you could be an efficient farmer or blacksmith without being able to read or write. You were a valuable person and you knew your job thoroughly. You could get somebody else to do any reading or writing you needed. But now we live in a world where that is impossible. Though there are other parts of the world – Central Africa, for instance – where reading and writing count for very little – it would be wrong to say that people who do not belong to our Verbal World are stupid. Millions of those people want to join the Verbal World, and CODE helps them. But we are talking about our world, right here, which is very much part of the Verbal World.

Student: But you said there were three kinds of literacy. What is Number Two?

Do you want to join the adult world knowing your job and the daily news, and nothing else?

Writer: Number Two takes in all the people who can read and write, have no trouble with medicine bottles or books of directions, and may be skilled in technical work of some complexity. They read the newspapers; sometimes they read magazines. They don't pay much attention to books, unless the books are concerned with their work. Some of them are professional people who read and understand complicated books about law, and medicine, and insurance, and all kinds of business. They have fair-sized vocabularies and their grammar is pretty good, but not precise. No doubt about it, they are literate, in the Number Two sense of the word.

Student: What's Number Three, then? It seems to me you have been talking about everybody that matters.

Writer: The whole idea of literacy is filled with shady areas that overlap. The Number Two people can read anything that concerns them. But consider yourself, as an example. Do you want to join the adult world knowing your job and the daily news, and nothing else?

Student: I'm not sure I understand. What else is there?

Writer: What you have just asked me is the kind of question Socrates used to ask people when he wanted to make them think. I am sure you know what else there is that is involved in literacy. Do you know who Socrates was?

Student: Vaguely. He was a Greek philosopher, wasn't he?

Writer: Yes, and like you he pretended not to understand what people said in order to make them clarify their thinking. To a tremendous extent thinking is a matter of language.

Student: Yes, but everybody has language. Even the Number One people you talked about have language.

Writer: Not to the same degree that the Number Two people have language. And the Number Three people have language in a degree that the Number Ones and the Number Twos do not have it, because they can use it to extend their personal knowledge in a way that goes far beyond the others. They can use language to ask hard questions, and explore kinds of thinking that the Number Ones and the Number Twos never bother their heads about. They can define things accurately and they can discuss things intelligently about which strict accuracy is impossible. They are the people who enlarge human knowledge – perhaps only their own knowledge, or perhaps the knowledge of the whole world.

...Anybody can see that slavery is wrong. Imagine owning somebody else, and buying and selling another person just as you pleased.

Student: Give me an example.

Writer: There you are, being Socratic again. Well – here's an example. Suppose you become a doctor, a healer. Are you going to be content with what you have learned in medical school, and never venture beyond it? I hope not. I hope you would be one of those who perpetually question what you have learned and look for new approaches to medicine. If nobody had ever done that we would still be treating tuberculosis by hanging bags of herbs around the necks of sick people, because that was what our teacher had told us.

Student: But that's thinking. What has that got to do with literacy? When I think of literacy I think about having to read books I am told to read in school – books that tell stories, or poems that don't even do that. I don't see how that teaches you to think.

Writer: Yes you do. Those books have taught you to think: What good is all this stuff? What does it tell me? That's thinking.

Student: In my class we have to read *Huckleberry Finn.* It's a pretty good book, but what does it teach me? What is there in *Huckleberry Finn* that is any good to me?

Writer: It teaches you a lot about the value of independent thought. Huck was a simple boy – a Number One, in fact, but an unusual Number One because he thought that slavery was wrong, and that black people have rights just as much as white people. That wasn't the kind of thinking he met with among the people around him, and he supposed he was a very wicked boy because he thought differently. But do you think he was wicked?

Student: Oh no. He was right. Everybody knows that. I mean, anybody can see that slavery is wrong. Imagine owning somebody else, and buying and selling another person just as you pleased.

Writer: Not everybody knew that was wrong in Huck's time and a lot of people don't know it now. But you know it, and at least, in part, you have learned it from *Huckleberry Finn.* You are standing on Huck's shoulders, so you can see farther and clearer than he did. Now, about poetry –

Splendour and beauty are the things that have lifted mankind out of the mud. And you don't want to stay in the mud.

Student: I don't see the use of poetry at all. Just a tangle of words.

Writer: Wait a minute. When I was about your age I had to memorize a poem that didn't mean much to me. It went like this:

> It is not growing like a tree
> In bulk, doth make Man better be;
> Or standing long an oak, three hundred year,
> To fall a log at last, dry, bald and sere:
> A lily of a day
> Is fairer far in May,
> Although it fall and die that night
> It was the plant and flower of light:
> In small proportions we just beauty see;
> And in short measure life may perfect be.

You see, I have remembered that for more than sixty years, and what it says – *That it isn't how long you live but how well you live* – is extremely important, and it has taken me a lifetime to understand all the poet meant.

Student: But why not say it just the way you said it? Why all the words?

Writer: Because my version lacks the splendour and beauty of the poem. And without splendour and beauty, what is the good of life?

Student: I don't get it.

Writer: But you will. The questions you have been asking tell me that you will. And that's what the Third Degree of literacy means. Splendour and beauty are the things that have lifted mankind out of the mud. And you don't want to stay in the mud. ▼

ACTIVITY 4
A WRITER'S PERSPECTIVE

1. Summarize Davies's views on the levels of literacy.
2. Refer to the examples that Davies uses to support his arguments. Why do you think he chose these particular examples? Do they make his point more effective for the student interviewer? for the reader?
3. Do you agree with Davies that the third level of literacy is important? Why or why not?
4. Do you enjoy reading outside of what is required for school? Why or why not? Have Davies's arguments affected your thinking? Why or why not?

ROCK 'N' ROLL READING

Denise Donlon, producer of *The New Music* "Rock 'n' Roll and Reading" show, interviewed a number of contemporary musicians about the link between their music and their reading habits. It may seem obvious that musicians are generally literate people. They work with words in writing lyrics, they are required to read complicated business transactions, and they have lots of time to read when on tour. Perhaps what you didn't realize (or maybe you did) is how often their music is influenced by what they read.

Musical Literary References

The Grapes of Wrath took their name from the 1939 John Steinbeck novel of the same name.

Tanita Tikaram: "I think the important thing about reading is, especially if you start reading when you are quite young, that you have a ready-made sense of using words. When I write I don't have to think about structure or sense, because I've read so much it all falls into place."

Bruce Cockburn's album *Big Circumstance* acknowledges the poet e.e. cummings.

Peter Townsend, owner of Book Publishing Co. and Bookshop: "I started by loving just books, which is really strange, because I started loving records before I loved music."

Songs Inspired by Reading

Blue Rodeo's *Love and Understanding* was inspired by the book *Rolling Thunder* by Doug Boyd.

Melissa Etheridge: "I've discovered a Canadian female writer Anne Cameron. She's of Indian heritage. Her books are very spiritual. I'm rediscovering a lot about the Canadian heritage and especially about the Indian heritage. You learn about one view of history in school. Then you see it from the other side and it really opens up your mind. I really enjoy her writing for that reason."

Murray McLauchlan: "The first thing I realized about reading, the most amazing thing I realized – it hit me like a ton of bricks – was you were talking to dead people, which I think is absolutely bizarre. People could have been dead for centuries and you were hearing their words exactly as they occurred in their own head as they wrote them."

Writers and Musicians

Iron Maiden's Bruce Dickinson's first novel *The Adventures of Lord Iffy Boatrace* was published in 1990.

ACTIVITY 5
A MUSICAL PERSPECTIVE

1. Study the photos, captions, and quotes from "Rock 'n' Roll and Reading." Are you surprised by the use of direct literary references in contemporary music? Why or why not? Are you surprised that songs and lyrics are inspired by reading? Why or why not?
2. Can you think of other literary references in the names of musical groups, in the titles or lyrics of their songs, or the images of their videos? Brainstorm a list with a partner.
3. Does knowing the source of the inspiration make the music more interesting to you? Why or why not? Are you interested in reading the book that inspired it? Why or why not?
4. Have you ever been affected by something you read? For example, did it change your ideas on a particular issue or did you want to learn more about a particular subject? In a journal entry, write about a book that affected you personally.
5. Prepare a set of interview questions for one of your favourite music artists to learn more about his or her reading habits and thoughts on literacy. Role-play the interview with a partner. If possible, videotape your interview.

END THOUGHTS

In this unit, you have read, thought, talked, and written about the importance of being print literate in our society. You have looked at the idea that literacy is rooted in childhood experience. As well, you explored the joys of literacy in your own life.

ACTIVITY 6
EXTENSION IDEAS

1. Invite a speaker to your classroom to talk about some of the issues related to the questions you want to ask about literacy. This speaker could be someone involved with CODE, READ Canada, or a community literacy program, a writer, a librarian, or a musician.
2. Write a letter to new parents encouraging them to understand the importance of reading to their children. Find a new parent and send him or her your letter. Ask for a response to your letter and report to your class what happened.
3. Create a collage of newspaper and magazine clippings, words, and pictures related to the theme of literacy. Display your collage in your classroom.

4. Listen to a small child telling you a story. Transcribe the story in his or her own words. Type it up, using a word processor. Work with the child to illustrate the story that he or she is telling.
5. With a partner discuss this statement: "Schools and teachers can work to develop literacy, but parents and families must first build strong roots on which literacy and a love of language, storytelling, and storymaking will grow." Agree or disagree with this statement, giving specific examples as proof. Turn your discussion into a joint report to be presented to your class.
6. Working with a partner, study the issue of adult literacy in your community. How big a problem is it? What is being done to promote literacy? What else needs to be done? What can you do to help? Prepare a joint report on this topic to share with your class or write as an editorial for the school newspaper.
7. Spend an hour or so reading in the children's section of your local library. Choose one story you think would be most appealing to children and share it with a small group of children.
8. Complete a study of children's picture books. Look at the illustrations in several books and note the various styles used. Write a report that you can share with your class.
9. View the movie version of a children's book such as *Huckleberry Finn* or *Anne of Green Gables*. Then read the book. Write a report to compare the book with the movie. Share your thoughts with your class or a small group.

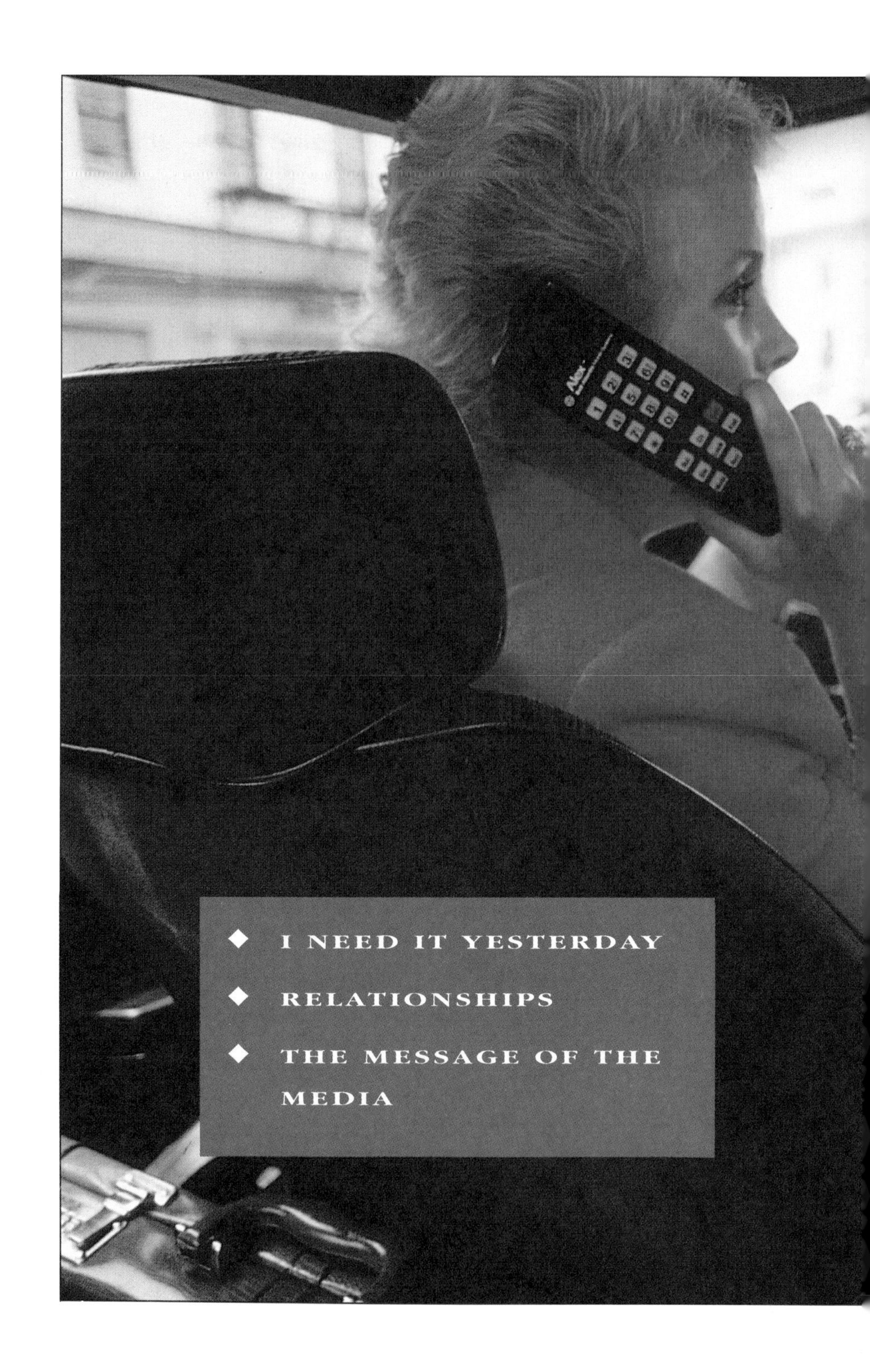
◆ I NEED IT YESTERDAY
◆ RELATIONSHIPS
◆ THE MESSAGE OF THE MEDIA

UNIT 10

INSTANT COMMUNICATIONS

Communications technology – including cellular phones, fax machines, computers, videotapes, and satellite dishes – has radically increased the speed with which people communicate and receive information. But in what other ways have these new technologies altered how they communicate? How does "instant communication" affect you?

In this unit, you will use your listening, speaking, writing, and non-verbal skills to consider recent technological innovations and how you might use them. You will explore the effect "instant communication" might have on your relationships with other people. And you will examine the role of the media in shaping your ability to communicate.

I NEED IT YESTERDAY

Today, communicating with other people can occur with rapid speed and with few geographical boundaries. For example, an advertising company can send a fax of an ad design to a client in Japan, receive a faxed approval within minutes, and be able to meet a newspaper printer's deadline. You can use your home video equipment to send a "videogram" to a friend and appear almost in-the-flesh each time she plays the tape on her VCR – even though you are 2000 kilometres apart.

Langdon Winner is a writer who argues that instant communication has a hidden cost. Read his article on page 213 and think about why he believes we should approach this technology with caution.

Cellular car phones are a way of using time more efficiently. The question is whether it is safe to drive while talking on the phone.

This computer reads pages of a book for visually impaired people. With this technology, they are no longer limited to braille books and "talking book" tapes.

By attaching the telephone receiver to this computer, a deaf person can type in messages that will appear on a small screen at the other end of the line and on his or her own screen.

THE ELECTRONIC BEEHIVE

Langdon Winner

It was about a year ago that someone first asked for my fax number. What an embarrassment it was to confess that I didn't have one. Since then, without my ever having chosen it, faxing has subtly forced its way into my daily routine. Faxes come in and faxes go out with a digitized urgency that whispers "no time to spare."

> Corners of our lives once sheltered from direct technological intervention are now bombarded by the demands of incoming and outgoing messages.

The fax machine is, of course, just one weapon in the bulging arsenal of electronic communication tools. Telephone answering machines, beepers, cellular phones, laptop computers and other electronic wonders all promise to save time and make us more productive. But these benefits, if they ever materialize, come at a cost. Corners of our lives once sheltered from direct technological intervention are now bombarded by the demands of incoming and outgoing messages.

Society is beginning to look like a vast electronic beehive, in which information processing in search of economic gain overshadows other personal and social goods. Restaurants, for example, used to be havens where one could sit down for a peaceful meal and quiet conversation. But in our larger cities, many customers now take cellular phones to their tables, handling calls just as they would back at the office. Does this mean we will have to get used to public spaces – shops, taverns, theaters, galleries – filled with people chattering on portable communication systems? Would you prefer the phoning or non-phoning section?

The automobile is undergoing a similar transformation. Drivers once used their road time to talk to passengers, listen to music, gaze at the scenery – or just think. But cellular phones and car fax machines have made such moments seem woefully unproductive. How much more efficient it is to sail down the highway in a multimedia center, making deals, checking the stock market, or updating one's calendar. Says a Los Angeles entertainment executive quoted in the *Wall Street Journal*: "I can't drive and enjoy the radio. I have to be on the phone."

Throughout the twentieth century, each new labor-saving device has encouraged us to think we'd soon be liberated from toil, free to move on to more creative and enjoyable pursuits. Such dreams have always been frustrated. Yes, our available time expands, but much of it is absorbed by the frenetic interactions that our new machines encourage and our working lives demand.

How much more efficient it is to sail down the highway in a multimedia center, making deals, checking the stock market, or updating one's calendar.

A standard that seems to be winning credibility is that if a message *can* move quickly, it *must* move quickly. Information that could just as well have come by U.S. mail arrives in seconds. In December I received a number of faxes, including some from overseas, wishing me a "Merry Christmas and Happy New Year." A friend recently sent out letters to a group of philosophers asking for ideas for a conference to be held two years from now. Of the sixteen who responded, fifteen did so by fax. The philosophers, of all people, would do well to ponder: What's our hurry?

As this fashion spreads, high-tech gadgets that at first seemed optional end up being compulsory. If technologies make it possible to reach you, then you have an obligation to remain accessible. People get annoyed if they sense that you are disconnected from the electronic pulse even for a short time. The desire to do things faster and faster eventually destroys the possibility that we might work without haste.

Yet quality takes time. Our embrace of high-tech gadgetry could turn life into a series of rushed encounters and clipped exchanges, producing ideas of diminishing depth. In our enthusiasm for electronic immediacy, we should take care to preserve the quiet places in our lives where genuine productivity and satisfaction dwell. ▼

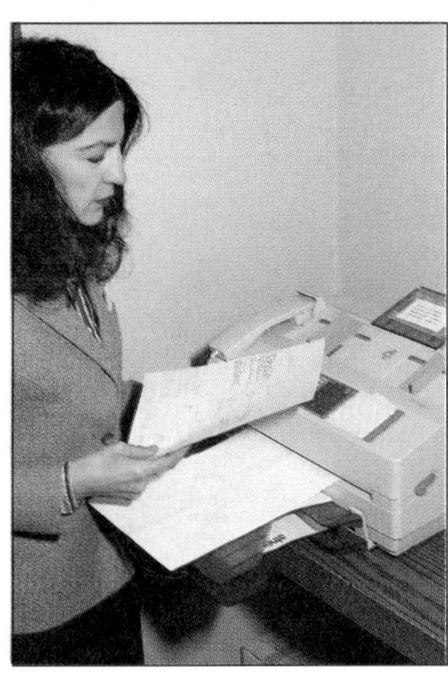

These devices replace activities and tasks that were commonplace before the "computer age." What did people do before they had each of these items?

This ad presents an image of what advantages you have when you are "plugged in" to communications technology.

ACTIVITY 1 FASTER AND BETTER?

1. Examine the photographs on this page and page 212. Brainstorm a list of communications devices available in society today. Then write a paragraph in which you examine how you might benefit from using these devices. Be sure to contrast how they would be useful to you with how you would have to cope without them.

2. According to Winner, "Our embrace of high-tech gadgetry could turn life into a series of rushed encounters and clipped exchanges, producing ideas of diminishing depth." What examples does he give to support this statement? Write a paragraph in which you explain why you either agree or disagree.

RELATIONSHIPS

Whether you use a telephone, fax machine, or meet face-to-face, communicating with others requires skill and practice. Some people feel that technological devices can both help and hinder effective listening and speaking skills, as well as the ability to view non-verbal behaviours. Read the following story about the relationship between a mother and daughter. Why does the narrator find it difficult to communicate with her mother? How does she overcome this problem?

Radio and television shows such as Dr. Ruth Westheimer's, in which people receive advice about their relationships, are immensely popular.

AMANDA AND THE WOUNDED BIRDS

Colby Rodowsky

...There was my mother's voice coming out of our kitchen radio, sounding slightly frantic and giving those first callers more than they bargained for...

It's not that my mother doesn't understand, because she does. In fact, she understands so well, and so much, and so single-mindedly, that half the time she goes around with a glazed look in her eyes and forgets to get her hair cut, and go to the dentist, and that we're almost out of toilet paper or tuna fish.

She makes her living understanding, which may make more sense when I tell you that my mother is Dr. Emma Hart. Now, if that doesn't help, then probably, like me until my consciousness was raised, you've always thought of radio as the place to hear the Top Forty or sometimes the weather report when you're heading for the shore on a summer Friday afternoon. But just try twiddling the dial and you'll find her, way over to the left on the band, next to the country and western station.

Maybe what I should do is go back a little and explain. You see, my mother is a psychotherapist, which means that she counsels people and tries to help them find ways of dealing with their problems. She's also a widow. My father died when I was a baby, and sometimes I try to imagine what it must have been like for her, taking care of a baby alone and trying to establish a practice all at the same time. One thing I'm sure of is that knowing Mom, she handled it gracefully, and stoically, and with that funny way she has of biting her lower lip so that for all her hanging-in-there attitude she still looks like a ten-year-old kid – the kind you want to do something for because she's not always whining or sniffling. I guess you'd have to say that as much as possible my mother is in charge of her own life, which is the way she tries to get the people who call in to her on the radio to be.

The way the radio program got started was that several years ago the producer was looking for something to put on in the late afternoon when people were mostly fixing dinner or driving carpool or just sitting with their feet up. It wasn't exactly prime time. Then he remembered how he'd heard Mom speak at a dinner once and had thought at the time that putting someone like her on radio would be a real public service. Besides, the ratings couldn't be any lower than they had been for the Handy Home Fixit show he'd had on before. Anyway, he tracked her down, arranged for a test, and then Mom was on the air.

I never will forget that first show. I mean, there was my mother's voice coming out of our kitchen radio, sounding slightly frantic and giving those first callers more than they bargained for: I guess she was afraid if she let them off the line there wouldn't *be* any more. That day even the producer called with a question. And the boy in the studio who went for coffee. But mom hung in there, and calls continued to come in, and then they started backing up, and it wasn't long before people opened by saying, "I didn't think I'd *ever* get through to you." After only a month on the air the Emma Hart Show went from one hour to two; and the way I figured it, a lot of people were eating dinner later than they ever had before. Including us.

...Once I referred to one of her callers as a fractured canary and almost started World War III.

Mom really cared about the people who telephoned her, and almost right from the beginning she was calling them her "wounded birds." Not on the air, of course, and *never* to anyone but me. I got used to her looking up in the middle of dinner or from watching the late news on TV and saying, "I hope my wounded bird with the abusive husband will get herself into counseling" or "The wounded bird with those children who walk all over her had better learn to assert herself before it's too late." And *I* sure learned not to joke around: once I referred to one of her callers as a fractured canary and almost started World War III.

Not long after this, things really started to happen. First, Mom's show was moved to a better time slot. Then it was syndicated, so that she wasn't just on the air here but in a bunch of other cities, too. The way "Doonesbury" and "Dick Tracy" are in a bunch of newspapers. Now, I have to say that for the most part my mother's pretty cool about things, but the day she found out that the Emma Hart Show was being syndicated she just about flipped. She called me from the studio and told me to meet her at the Terrace Garden for dinner, to be sure and get spiffed up because we were going all out.

During dinner Mom spent a lot of time staring into the candlelight and smiling to herself. Finally she said, "Just think of all those people who'll be listening now." And let me tell you, I *was* thinking about them, and it worried me a lot. I mean, the way I saw it, there were going to be even more problems: more victims who were downtrodden or misunderstood. More stories about people who had been abused or who had kids on drugs or dropping out, or ne'er-do-well relatives moving in. But when I tried to say that, Mom was suddenly all attention. "Don't be silly, Amanda. It's the same amount of time and the same number of calls – you'll hardly notice any difference. Only now I'll have wounded birds in Phoenix and Pittsburgh and Philadelphia."

Sometimes I felt that life was nothing but a revolving door: Mom going out while I was coming in.

In one way she was right: the show sounded pretty much the same. (Except that *I* found out that when your husband/lover/friend walks out on you it hurts as much in Peoria as it does in Perth Amboy.)

In another way she was wrong: she was busier than she had ever been before, what with traveling and lecturing and doing guest shows from other cities. For a while there, it was as if I was spending as much time at my best friend Terri's as I was at my own home. Then eventually Mom decided I could stay at our place when she had to be out of town, as long as Terri stayed there with me, which wasn't as good or as bad as it sounds, because Terri lives right across the street and her mother has X-ray eyes. I mean, we can hardly manage to reach for our favorite breakfast of Twinkies and Oreo ice cream with an orange juice chaser before her mother is on the telephone telling us to eat cornflakes instead – and to wash the dishes.

Sometimes I felt that life was nothing but a revolving door: Mom going out while I was coming in. I know there are some kids who would've thought I was lucky, but the thing about my mother is that she's okay. And I wanted to see more of her. Besides that, I needed to talk to her. I don't know why, but all of a sudden it seemed that things were piling up around me. No major crises, you understand. Nothing that would exactly stop traffic.

I'll give you an example.

Take my friend Terri. I have a terrible feeling that she has a secret crush on my boyfriend Josh. If she does, it would be a disaster, because how could we really be friends anymore? But then again how could Terri and I *not* be friends? I'm not sure *why* I think this, unless it's because she gets quiet and acts bored when I talk about him a lot – the way you do when you don't want to let on about liking someone. I mean she couldn't *really* be bored. Could she?

Then there's Miss Spellman, my English teacher, who has this really atrocious breath and is forever leaning into people as she reads poetry in class. Imagine somebody breathing garbage fumes on you as she recites Emily Dickinson. If something doesn't happen soon I may never like poetry again.

Now, maybe these aren't world problems, any more than the incident with the guidance counselor was, but it bugged me all the same. Our school has an obsession about students getting into *good* colleges a.s.a.p. and knowing what they want to do with the rest of their lives (Terri and I call it the life-packaging syndrome). Anyway, this particular day I was coming out of gym on my way to study hall when Mr. Burnside, the guidance counselor, stopped me and started asking me all this stuff, like what my career goals were and had I decided what I wanted to major in in college.

What I said (only politer than it sounds here) was that how did I know what I wanted to major in when I didn't even know where I wanted to *go* to college. Mr. Burnside got a wild look in his eyes and started opening and closing his mouth so that all I could see was a shiny strand of spit running between his top and bottom teeth while he lectured me on how I was going about this whole college thing the wrong way. He said I should come into the guidance office someday and let him feed me into the

Mr. Burnside got a wild look in his eyes and started opening and closing his mouth so that all I could see was a shiny strand of spit running between his top and bottom teeth...

computer – well, not me exactly, but stuff like my grades, extra-curricular activities, and whether or not I needed financial aid.

"And what does your mother say?" he asked as he rooted in his pocket for a late pass to get me into study hall. "You'll certainly have it easier than anybody else in your class, or the school either for that matter – living with Dr. Emma Hart." He laughed that horselaugh of his and slapped me on the back. "She'll get right to the *Hart* of it." Another laugh. "Anybody else'd have to call her on the telephone." His laughter seemed to follow me all the way to study hall. I even heard it bouncing around in my head as I settled down to do my Spanish.

"Anybody else'd have to call her on the telephone," he had said.

"Anybody else'd have to call her on the telephone," he had said.

Why not? I thought as I was walking home from school.

Why not? I asked myself when Josh and I were eating popcorn and playing Scrabble on the living room floor that night.

And pretty soon *why not?* changed to *when?* The answer to that one was easy though, because spring vacation was only a week and a half away and that would give me the perfect opportunity.

The funny thing was that once I'd decided to do it, I never worried about getting through. Maybe that was because I'd heard Mom say plenty of times that they always liked it when kids called in to the show, and I guess I figured that unless everybody on spring vacation decided to call the Dr. Emma Hart Show, I wouldn't have any trouble. Besides, I practiced in the shower making my voice huskier than usual and just a little breathless, hoping that it would sound sincere and make an impression on Jordan, the guy who screens the calls and tries for just the right balance of men, women, and kids, with not too much emphasis on busted romances as opposed to anxiety attacks.

The next funny thing was that once I'd made up my mind to call Dr. Emma Hart, I began to feel like a wounded bird myself, and I was suddenly awfully glad that she cared about them the way she did. I had a little trouble deciding what I wanted to ask her on the show, and even before I could make up my mind I began to think of other things that bothered me too. Not problems, but stuff I'd like to talk over with Mom. Like Vietnam, for example. I'd watched *Apocalypse Now* on TV and there was a lot I didn't understand. And what about the sixties? – was Mom ever involved in sit-ins or walkouts or any of that? I somehow doubted it, but it would be important to know for sure. Finally it came to me: what I wanted to ask Dr. Hart about was not being able to talk to Mom because there she was all wrapped up with her wounded birds. Only the whole thing got confusing, one being the other and all.

I'd watched *Apocalypse Now* on TV and there was a lot I didn't understand. And what about the sixties? – was Mom ever involved in sit-ins or walkouts or any of that?

Anyway, I did it. I put the call in just before eleven on the Monday morning of spring vacation and almost chickened out when Jordan answered. I had met him a couple of times down at the studio, and I could almost see him now, looking like some kind of an intense juggler who is trying to keep everything going at once. I heard my voice, as if it were coming from somewhere far away, giving my name as Claire (it's my middle name) and outlining my problem. When I got finished, Jordan said that he was putting me on hold and not to go away, that Dr. Hart would be with me shortly.

And all of a sudden she was. I mean, there I was talking to my own mother and telling her how I couldn't talk to my mother, and how the things I wanted to talk to her about weren't actually big deals anyway, but still –

Dr. Hart let me go on for a while and then she broke in and said that it was important for me to know that my concerns were as real as anybody else's and it sounded as if my mother and I had a pretty good relationship that had just gotten a little off the track and what I had to do was be really up-front with her and let her know how I felt. Then she suggested that I make a date with my mother for lunch so that I could tell her (Mom) exactly what I'd told her (Dr. Emma Hart), and that I should be sure to call back and let her know how it worked out.

After that I said, "Okay," and "Thank you." Then I hung up.

The only trouble was that as soon as Mom got home that day I knew it wasn't going to work.

She was sort of coming unglued. It had been a bad day, she told me. One of her private patients was in the midst of a crisis; the producer of the show was having a fight with his wife and wanted to tell Mom all about it. She had a dinner speech to give Saturday night and didn't have a thought about what to say, and my uncle Alex had called from Scranton to ask Mom to try to talk some sense into his teenage son, who was driving them all crazy.

Then she looked at me and said, "Thank heavens you've got it all together."

Right away I knew I was going to break rule number one: I wasn't going to be able to be up-front.

Talk about guilt. Right away I knew I was going to break rule number one: I wasn't going to be able to be up-front.

The thing was, I knew I couldn't take what was already one rotten week for Mom and dump all my problems (which seemed to be getting bigger by the minute) on her. Even though I felt like I was going to explode.

By Friday I knew I needed another talk with Dr. Hart. After all, she'd said to call back, hadn't she?

Getting through Jordan was even easier the second time. All I had to say was that I'd spoken to Dr. Hart earlier in the week and that she'd said to let her know what happened.

"Oh, good, a success story," Jordan said right away, jumping to conclusions. I guess he knew what kind of a week it had been too. "Hold on; Dr. Hart will be with you soon," he said.

And there was Dr. Emma Hart again. And suddenly there *I* was, unloading about how what she had suggested wasn't going to work.

"Why not?" she wanted to know. "Did you try?"

"Yes – no," I said. Then I was going on again, all about Bad-breath Spellman, the guidance counselor, and how maybe my best friend had a thing for my boyfriend. She kept steering me back to the subject of my mother and why I hadn't arranged to have lunch with her.

I said that my mother had had a bad week. That she was swamped, preoccupied, distracted, and running behind. And then it happened. I mean, I heard the words sliding off my lips and couldn't stop them. I said, "The thing about my mother is that she has all these wounded birds who have really important problems and they take all the time she has."

When Mom finally spoke, her voice sounded choked, as if she had swallowed a gumball.

A silence ballooned up between us and was so loud I couldn't hear anything else – and if you know anything about radio, you know that the worst thing that can happen is silence. It lasted forever, and while it was going on I gave serious thought to running away from home, or at least hanging up.

When Mom finally spoke, her voice sounded choked, as if she had swallowed a gumball.

"We've been talking to Claire this morning, who is really Amanda," she said. "And one of the things we talk a lot about on this show is saying what you have to say – even if that's not always easy. Are you still there, Amanda?"

"Yes," I squeaked.

"If I know Amanda," my mother went on, "she would rather have run away, or hung up, but instead she did something harder. She hung on."

I gulped.

"Amanda is my daughter, and it seems we have some things to talk about, so what I'm going to do is to ask my assistant to make a reservation for lunch at the Terrace Garden." Then it sounded as though Mom had moved in closer to the microphone and was speaking just to me. "If you hurry, Amanda, I'll meet you at 1:30. So we can talk."

And we did: about Bad-breath Spellman, and Terri, and how it's okay not to know now what I want to do with the rest of my life.

We talked about saving the whales, and our two weeks at the shore this summer, and how some day we're going to Ireland. About books and movies and the time in fourth grade when I got the chicken pox and Mom caught them from me.

And we talked about how we had missed talking to each other and what we could do about it.

We ate lunch slowly, and took ages deciding on dessert, and ages more eating it.

We sat there all afternoon, until the light streaking in the windows changed from yellow to a deep, burning gold and the busboys started setting the tables for dinner. ▼

Only with the *AT&T Reach Out*® *World Plan.*

The sound of a loved one's voice. The laugh of a good friend. You can hear them again and again—and save with the *AT&T Reach Out World Plan.*

With this plan, it's easy for you to call family and friends in over 40 countries and areas, and save 20%* on your international calls.

Only the *Reach Out World Plan* gives you so much of the world in one plan with one low $3 monthly fee. And the savings begin with low per-minute costs—you can call Canada for 20¢, the United Kingdom for 59¢, Europe for 62¢, and the Pacific for 83¢.

With this plan you can call almost anytime—15 or more hours† a day during the week. And 24 hours a day on the weekends.

The longer you talk, the lower the per-minute rates go. Because the *Reach Out World Plan* lets you enjoy an additional 5% discount on that portion of your call after the tenth minute.

Even better, there's a 5% discount on state-to-state long distance calls made from your home.

And all your international calls will have the clear connections and superior customer service you've come to expect from AT&T.

Let AT&T help you go home, for less. Call today to sign up for the *AT&T Reach Out World Plan.*

Call 1 800 222-1776, Ext. 664.

*Average savings based on a 10-minute off-peak phone call when compared to AT&T International ... rates. Savings differ from country to country. Call us for a savings evaluation of the *Reach Out World Plan* and basic international long distance rates to Canada and Mexico. †Thirtee... urs to Ghana only.

Advertisements like this one promote the ability of the telephone line to bring distant family members together.

ACTIVITY 2
RESPONDING TO A STORY

1. Discuss the following questions with a partner.
   a) Why do you think Amanda feels she can't communicate with her mother? What is Amanda afraid of?
   b) Why is it important to Amanda to express herself?
2. At the end of "Amanda and the Wounded Birds," Amanda and her mother are able to communicate with each other. With your partner, improvise a scene of dialogue that might occur between them. Perform your scene for another pair of partners.
3. As a group of four, make a list of the elements you feel are necessary for effective communication. Compare your list with those of your classmates.

ACTIVITY 3
GETTING THE MESSAGE

1. With a partner, write a script for one of the following scenarios. To do this, consider what is difficult to convey in the situation, and how your characters could best overcome this difficulty.
   - two friends discuss running against each other in the student council elections
   - a parent or guardian and a son or daughter disagree about an environmental issue
   - a person tells a friend who has taken a part-time job that he or she is upset that they are spending less time together
2. Form a group with another pair. Perform your script, first as a telephone conversation and then as a conversation in person. Have your audience list your non-verbal behaviours during the second conversation. Refer to the infobox *Observing Non-Verbal Behaviour* on page 227. What effect did the non-verbal behaviours have on communication? Which conversation was more successful in solving the problem?
3. With your group, brainstorm a list of situations in which you might prefer to communicate in person. For what situations would you rather use a communications device such as a telephone, fax, or computer?

INFO BOX

Observing Non-Verbal Behaviour

To observe non-verbal behaviour effectively, you must watch out for various types of body language. This list provides some ideas about what to look for.

- What is the person doing with his or her hands? Are they in his or her pockets? Is the individual tapping a finger on a table? Are the arms crossed?
- What is the position of the body? Is the person leaning forward? leaning back? Is the body turned away from the other person?
- What is the position of the individual's legs? Are they crossed? Is the person tapping his or her foot?
- Where are the eyes looking? Are the two people keeping eye contact?
- Does the person smile? frown? yawn? cough?

THE MESSAGE OF THE MEDIA

The media – from television to radio to newspapers, books, and magazines – deliver information, ideas, entertainment, and popular culture. But how do the different forms of media affect how we communicate?

Consider television – a highly influential source of information and entertainment. Approximately ninety-eight percent of homes in North America have at least one television set. In fact, the average Canadian watches almost twenty-four hours of television a week. Read the article on page 228 and consider how television viewing habits affect how you interact with others.

"People watch television alone. It is mainly an isolating experience in American society."

TV TECHNOLOGY IS WOOING VIEWERS INTO ELECTRONIC COCOONS

Roy Shields

It is possible to spend years as a critic and observer of television and yet miss the most obvious and significant thing of all about the medium.

That's what happened to me. Either I had not thought about it, I told myself, or having done so, dismissed it as too self-evident to note. But now it rattles around in my brain and won't go away.

It is the memory of a program called *The Television Explosion* in the fine PBS series *Nova*.

Here we had the usual parade of industry experts, ranging from Les Brown, editor of the television magazine *Channels*, to Mark Fowler, chairman of the U.S. Federal Communications Commission. Most of the talk was about the new video technologies – 100-channel cable, videocassettes and discs, home satellite dishes, the works. They told us little that we didn't already know.

Then, in the midst of them, came a pert little lady whose words reverberated like the sudden clash of cymbals. She was Rose Goldsen, a professor of sociology at Cornell University.

"When the medium was first launched," she said, "we were told that it would bring families together, that the television set would be sort of like the central heart around which the family would gather.

"But, you know, today in the United States, more than forty per cent of us have more than two sets in the home and many, many families have three, four, and five sets in the home – one in the kitchen, one in the family room, the children have a set of their own, and so on.

"People watch television alone. It is mainly an isolating experience in American society.

"Moreover, the interacting goes from you to the screen. Even if you're sitting there watching in unison with other people, the dominating presence in the room is the television screen."

That fundamental fact must now be considered in the light of further isolation. Soon young people will have their own cable channels, old people theirs, and all the ethnic groups, the businessmen, the sports fans, women over thirty but under thirty-five, and so on.

Add to this the cassette libraries and personal computers linked to the TV screen and you have a situation in which people can almost avoid each other entirely except to mutter "Good morning" over the breakfast table.

"Of its role in the future only one thing is certain: It will be larger than ever before."

What's more, this isolation in your private world, protected from human contact by electronic distance, has great attractions. There doesn't have to be any inane small talk with friends, family, or associates, any emotional clashes, wounds, or waste of time. Why even leave the house to mingle with the masses and endure the traffic?

Nova concluded its program with this observation about television: "It has brought us together in times of national triumph and tragedy. And yet at the same time it has driven us apart, even in our own homes. Of its role in the future only one thing is certain: It will be larger than ever before."

The last words were left to Prof. Goldsen: "It means (it will affect) not just you and me, those of us who are on the face of the earth at this moment, it means (it will affect) the future generations...(who) come and inherit a world they never made.

"And we have to make the kind of a broadcasting system that will not contaminate what I call the 'thought environment' for future generations, but on the contrary, will bring out not the worst in people, but the best in us."

What is troubling about those words is the gnawing feeling that it is already too late, that we are beyond the point of no return. We will watch programs ranging from porno-pay to college courses alone in silence.

It will be a sad world indeed if future generations are born into electronic cocoons from which they rarely leave to eat, bathe, make love, or do violence, then retreat to the warmth of their isolation.

Are there no answers to this grim scenario?

ACTIVITY 4 CHANGING THE MEDIA

1. List the reasons Shields gives in "TV technology is wooing viewers into electronic cocoons" for his argument that television is an isolating influence. Write a paragraph in which you explain why you either agree or disagree.
2. Shields asks, "Are there no answers to this grim scenario?" What ways can you think of to use television to bring people together?
3. What strategies can you think of for using other media – for example, radio, newspaper, movies – to increase communication among people?

Some people feel that television – especially since the development of satellite technology – is creating a "global village" that will bring people from different places and cultures together.

Television coverage of the famine in Ethiopia brought awareness of the crisis to the Western world.

END THOUGHTS

Computers, cellular phones, and satellite dishes are among a few of the devices that have led to the rapidly expanding role of communications technology in society today. These new ways of communicating have many benefits. Communication is faster, easier, and more efficient. Workers, for example, may soon do their work from their homes, avoiding such problems as crowded buses and congested traffic. As with all new inventions, there are new problems. You have used your listening, speaking, writing, and non-verbal skills to help you think about the place of today's communication technology in your own life – to consider the impact of "instant communication."

ACTIVITY 5
EXTENSION IDEAS

1. Go to a computer store and ask a salesperson to demonstrate the latest in computer technology. Ask him or her what future developments can be expected. Also, ask how you might be directly affected.
2. Write a science-fiction story in which you imagine a world with new and sophisticated communications technology. What benefits would such a world have? What negative effects might there be as a result of this technology?
3. Interview a radio or television phone-in therapist, a talk-show host, or a program producer. How does he or she account for the rise in popularity of phone-in therapists? Present your findings to your class.
4. Conduct a survey of television viewing habits in your school. Prepare a report of your findings and present it to your class.
5. Home shopping channels, in which products are shown on television and people use their telephones to order the products, are an example of interactive television viewing. Write a script in which you imagine another possible interactive use of television. Videotape your script and show it to your class.

RADIO DRAMA
EXPLORING THE SCRIPT
FEEDBACK TO GROUPS
FIRST DRAFT
REHEARSAL
ON THE AIR!

UNIT 11

RADIO SCRIPTS

Radio is the medium of the imagination. Through a magical combination of words and sounds you can be transported instantly to any place or time. While television provides the pictures for you, radio places no limits on your imagination.

This unit invites you to enter the wonderful world of radio drama – a world in which anything can occur – even, as you will soon see, travel through time. The basis of the unit is a script first broadcasted on the CBC radio series called *Vanishing Point*. The activities based on this script will provide you with opportunities to explore and write yourself.

RADIO DRAMA

"Past Imperfect" is the title of a radio drama written by John Douglas. The first half of the play is included in this unit on page 236. Later in the unit you will take over the role of playwright and write the second half yourself. In writing the second half of the play, you will need to write in a style that is consistent with that of the first half. Therefore, as you read the script watch for the ways in which the writer makes the listener "see" what is happening in the story. Think not only about what is said, but the form in which it is presented.

The world of radio is part of our everyday lives – when we are at work or at play.

The mad scientist in the following radio play invents a time machine. In the movie *Back to the Future*, "Doc" creates a car that can travel through time.

ACTIVITY 1 GETTING READY

Before reading the script try the following activities. They will help you think about the theme of "Past Imperfect" and about writing radio scripts.

1. If you could travel back or forward in time, where would you go? In your notebook or journal make a list of the historical periods that you would like to visit. What would you expect to see and do? What are some things you would do in the past in order to change the present? Who would you want to meet?

2. Because radio is a medium for the ears, what do you think an author would have to keep in mind when writing for radio? In what ways would you expect radio scripts to be different from those written for television? In pairs or small groups brainstorm some suggestions that a writer could use to make a listener "see" what is going on in a play that will be broadcast on radio.

3. In small groups, brainstorm to produce a list of criteria for working effectively in groups. Try to generate as many items as possible. Review your list of criteria. Which criteria do you feel are the most important? Why?

PAST IMPERFECT

John Douglas

Cast:

Roger Pennithorne
Newscaster
Uncle Corliss Pennithorne
Man-eating plant
Andrea
Elihu, a Texas carter
Alistair McCourt
Herbert Nibbett
Sir Rupert McCourt
Captain Blunt
Mr. Markland
Messenger

(Man-eating plant through Messenger: appear in second half)

Scene 1: Short-Wave Radio
SOUND: FADE UP HEAVY STATIC, UNDER WHICH THERE COMES A PECULIAR SOFT RUSHING SOUND, MORE LIKE WHITE NOISE THAN ANYTHING ELSE

ROGER
(OVER SHORT-WAVE; POOR ACOUSTIC, VERY BAD STATIC) Is anyone there? ...one...there? (STATIC DIMINISHES STEADILY: ROGER'S VOICE BECOMES GRADUALLY ALMOST NORMAL) Can't...anyone hear me? For the millionth time...Anyone at all? No...of course not. If you could hear me, I'd never know it. Of course, some day someone else will find the way here, and who knows – (MAD GIGGLE) they may still find *me!* So listen, all you out there – Listen if you're born yet – and if you're not – (GIGGLE) listen anyway. Because one day, one day one of you is going to stumble on the same thing Uncle Corliss did, and learn what I did the day I visited his lab, (FADING, GLOATING) and *then* you'll be sorry...very sorry...oh, very, very, sorry.....

MUSIC: LIGHT, CYNICAL BRIDGE.
Scene 2: Uncle Corliss's Workroom. 1935.

SOUND: FADE UP BLEEPING AND BLOOPING, RHYTHMIC TONES OF A 1930'S LAB, IN BACKGROUND. SLOWLY FADE TO VERY LOW UNDER SCENE. SIMULTANEOUS WITH LAB, BACKGROUND, BRING UP NEWSCAST ON 1930'S RADIO SET.

NEWSCASTER
(FADING UP)... and here is the CRBC news for Wednesday, October 16, 1935. The newly-elected government of Liberal leader Mackenzie King is expected to take over office within the next few days from the Conservative party of defeated Prime Minister R.B. Bennett. Mr. King was not available for comment in Ottawa today, but a senior party official indicated that in his opinion, the transition of power was imminent...

CORLISS
(OVER END OF NEWSCAST) Roger, my boy! What a delightful surprise! Just turn off that mindless squawking will you?

SOUND: CLICK OFF RADIO SWITCH. CUT NEWSCAST.

CORLISS
That's better. (WORKING BUSILY AWAY ON HIS LAB TABLE) Just pass me those pliers, will you?

ROGER
(NATURAL SPACE) Of course, Uncle.

SOUND: CLINK OF PLIERS.

CORLISS
(BUSY) Thank you. You've never been the most devoted of nephews – to what am I to attribute this sudden excess of family affection?

ROGER
(GAMELY TRYING TO CONCEAL HIS DISTASTE) You know I'm always interested in whatever you're doing, Uncle Corliss. Science was always my favourite subject –

CORLISS
(CHEERFUL AFFECTION) In a pig's eye. I know that greedy look. Screwdriver!

ROGER
Here, sir.

SOUND: CLINK.

CORLISS
You're hoping for a loan if you butter me up enough, though I'm afraid in your case "snake-oil" is the more appropriate lubricant.

ROGER
(MEEK BUT SIMMERING) This isn't like the other times, Uncle. Really it isn't.

CORLISS
Nonsense. One more of your loose women howling for pearls and caviar again, of course.

ROGER
Uncle, this one is rich! If I marry Andrea I'll never have to ask for money again –

CORLISS
Forget it. Not a chance. The squalor of your character has been an unending delight to me ever since you could crawl, but there is a limit to how much I am prepared to pay for my entertainment. Wrench!

SOUND: CLATTER.

ROGER
If you think I came here just to be insulted –

CORLISS
I know you came here just to filch money. But now that you're here it occurs to me I *do* have a use for you. Wait a minute.

SOUND: CLATTER OF TOOLS SET DOWN ON WORKBENCH. SNAP OF MASTER SWITCH: MOST OF THE BLEEPING AND BLOOPING LAB SOUNDS DIE AWAY. PERHAPS A DISTANT RETORT STILL BUBBLES SOFTLY SOMEWHERE.

CORLISS
Now! I'm perfectly aware, dear Roger, that you haven't a bean to support the self-indulgence which you laughably consider your birthright. But if you're going to get any more money from me you'll earn it, shocking as the novelty may be for you. I pay cash on the barrelhead, but I'll have the barrel first, if you please.

ROGER
(AFTER A SULLEN PAUSE) What do you want me to do?

CORLISS
Be a guinea pig. In one of my experiments.

ROGER
Uncle Corliss, you're crackers.

CORLISS
Never saner in my life. If you follow instructions you should be perfectly safe. And a lot richer.

ROGER
(AFTER A PAUSE) Tell me about it.

CORLISS
With pleasure. Ever hear of a time-travel machine?

ROGER
(CONTEMPTUOUS SNORT) I don't read fantasy.

CORLISS
Fantasy, hell! Look on the table here in front of you. What's *that?*

ROGER
(PUZZLED) It looks like a pair of...earmuffs.

CORLISS
Idiot!

ROGER
Or...like those headphones they used to use on old crystal sets...

CORLISS
It's a radio transmitter and receiver. I found a way to make

everything tiny. Clips to your belt. (PROUDLY) I have invented the world's first portable radio device!

ROGER
That's what it is, a radio?

CORLISS
Not in the usual sense, dear nephew, you can't hear "Amos 'n' Andy" on it. I told you – it's a time-travel machine.

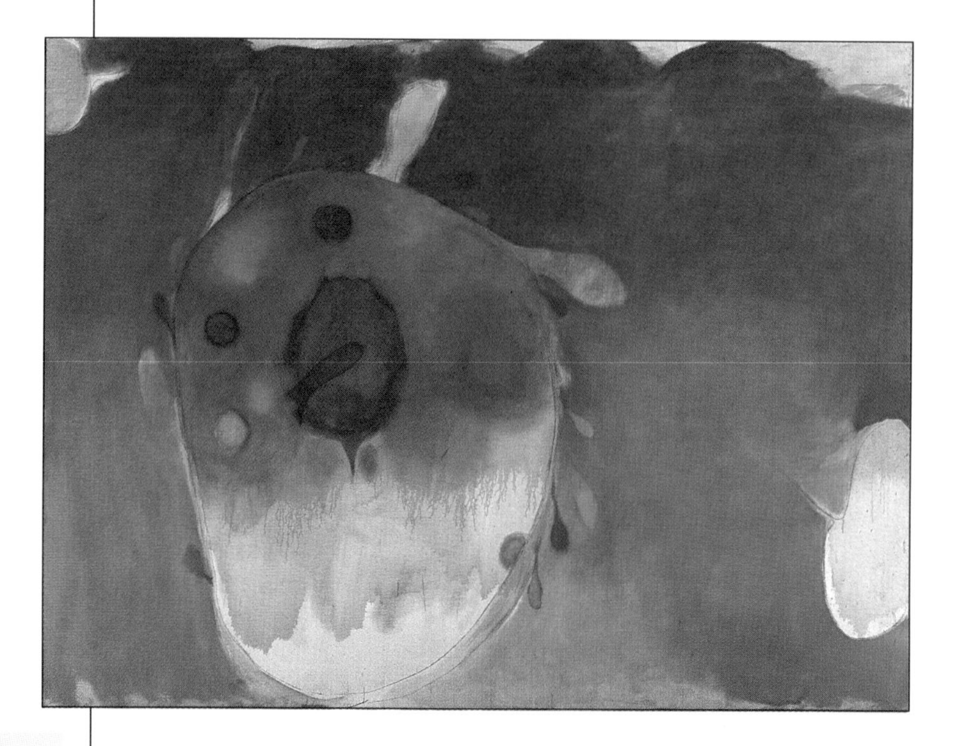

Joyce Wieland's painting *Time Machine Series,* 1961.

ROGER
That's impossible.

CORLISS
It's not. I've done it. Objects in time are affected by certain very high and very low frequencies that pass right through them. Certain rare sound waves, deliberately controlled, can *move people and things around in time.*

ROGER
And you've learned to do this?

CORLISS
Yes.

SOUND: LIGHT CLINK OF EARPHONES ON TABLE.

ROGER
The earphones...the sound waves come from them?

CORLISS
Just as they used to in the old gramophones – but at trillions of Kilocycles. Two intersecting beams – one from each ear-piece.

ROGER
And...if I put the headphones on...and turn on the machine...

CORLISS
Then you will travel back in time. The longer the sound waves are switched on, the farther back you go: two minutes, or two billion years, as you choose. Now put on the headphones.

ROGER
Why me? If you're so keen on time travel why don't you do it yourself?

CORLISS
Good heavens, my boy, I'm far too valuable to the world to risk myself that way. You're young, vigorous, and have a fine low animal cunning. Of course you're the one to go.

ROGER
Very kind of you. And just how would I come back to the present again?

CORLISS
Reverse the current – this button here –

ROGER
How do I know the damn thing won't do something terrible to me?

CORLISS
Would you use your head for something else besides showing off Brylcreem? I told you you'll be perfectly safe. Now alter the setting to broad-beam focus.

ROGER
Broad...?

CORLISS
Narrow focus, just what's between the headphones goes. *Broad* focus, the *whole machine* goes back with whatever – or whomever – it's transporting. Has to be that way, or a time traveller could never get back to his own time, d'you see?

ROGER
You mean...if he went back too far, without the machine, or anybody here to beam him back, he'd die of old age before, er, before he was born?

CORLISS
Exactly.

ROGER
Aghh.

CORLISS
Stop worrying. I'll show you it's harmless. Put on the headphones – and clip the power source to your belt.

ROGER
(UNEASY) Uncle, I'm not sure I, ah, want to –

CORLISS
Nonsense! You're only going back six or seven minutes – no more – to when you first came here just now. Come on then – be a good boy and do it. (PAUSE) Remember the pearls and caviar…for…Andrea.

ROGER
(SIGH) All right. I'll do it.

CORLISS
Wonderful what love can do for a boy's courage, isn't it?

ROGER
(FUSSING WITH CLIPS) Does it matter which side the power box goes on?

CORLISS
No. What matters is that you clip these lead soles on to your shoes.

ROGER
Wha – ?

SOUND: CLINK OF CLIPS AFFIXING LEAD SOLES.

CORLISS
The sound waves will take part of the floor with them if the lead doesn't block them. You don't want to go crashing into the past with a mass of kindling around your ankles, do you?

ROGER
No, actually.

CORLISS
Now get those headphones on your ears, and set the timer yourself.

ROGER
We'll try...seven minutes.

SOUND: BOOP BEEP BEEP BOOP.

CORLISS
Keep the powerband broad-focus, so the machine goes with you.

ROGER
Can hardly hear you – earphones too tight.

CORLISS
(LOUDLY) *Broad focus!*

ROGER
Oh. Okay.

CORLISS
(LOUDLY) Now come in here.

ROGER
(MOVING) Why?

CORLISS
(LOUDLY) Observation room. One-way glass. So you can see without being seen!

ROGER
Why?

SOUND: DOOR OPEN.

CORLISS
(LOUDLY) Why? Why? You sound like a three year old. Just get in.

ROGER
All right, but why?

SOUND: DOOR CLOSE.

Scene 2A: Enclosed Space.

CORLISS
(LOUDLY) So you don't scare yourself silly when you meet yourself seven minutes ago.

ROGER
What?

CORLISS
(LOUDLY) Never mind. It's 2:05 PM, you're going back to 1:58. Just push the activating button.

ROGER
Will you be coming too?

CORLISS
(LOUDLY) How can I, I'm already there!

ROGER
(BAFFLED AND HALF-DEAF) What?

CORLISS
(SHOUTING) Just push the bloody button!

ROGER
(SHOUTING) You don't have to shout!

CORLISS
(BELLOWING) *Push!*

ROGER
All right! All right!

SOUND: (1) BEEP! (2) DESCENDING NOTES (3) BRIEF RUSH OF WHITE NOISE, THEN SILENCE.

Scene 2B: Observation Room at Uncle Corliss's. 1:58 p.m.

ROGER
What – ? Uncle Corliss? Uncle Corliss? Where are you?

CORLISS
(TELEPHONE FILTER, CLOSE IN OUR EAR) Well, finally!

ROGER
Wha – how did you get in my earphones?

CORLISS
(FILTER) Loosen the damn headset. I can barely hear you.

ROGER
All right. (EFFORT)

SOUND: SNAP OF EARPHONES COMING OFF.

ROGER
I said how did you get in my earphones? Where are you?

CORLISS
(FILTER) (A LITTLE LESS CLOSE BECAUSE THE HEADSET IS NOW IN OPEN AIR) I'm right in the room beside you but I'm seven minutes in the future, dummy. The sound waves that

This scene from the movie *Time Machine* shows the main character in his invention.

brought you here carry *voices* across time.

ROGER
Oh. Yeah. (PAUSE) My God!

CORLISS
(FILTER) What is it now?

ROGER
We're both out there, on the other side of the glass! We're talking to each other!

CORLISS
(FILTER) Of course we are, you twit! It's seven minutes ago and you've just arrived!

ROGER
(DAZED) I have?

CORLISS
(FILTER) If you don't believe it, open the door, very softly, just a crack, and listen. But quietly. Remember your earlier self hasn't been told about time-travel yet. Don't scare him.

ROGER
(MUMBLING) No. God, no. Mustn't do that.

CORLISS
(FILTER) Wait! Stop! Which way are you facing? Will you see the door open?

ROGER
Which me? The Me-me, or the He-me?

CORLISS
(FILTER) What?

ROGER
The other one has his back to the door – he's talking to the past You.

CORLISS
(FILTER) He's talking past me?

ROGER
He-is-talking-to-the-1:58-you.

CORLISS
(FILTER) By-now-it-is-the-2-o'clock-me-but-never-mind. Just open the door very gently and listen.

ROGER
Well why didn't you say so?

SOUND: SOFT DOOR SOUND, SLIGHT OPENING.

FOREGROUND (2:07)
(BOTH SPEAK IN WHISPERS BUT MUST BE CLEAR OVER BACKGROUND)

BACKGROUND (2:00)
(EXACTLY AS IN SCENE TWO BUT OFF MIKE)

ROGER
Uncle, this one is rich! If I marry Andrea, I'll never have to ask for money again –

CORLISS
Forget it. Not a chance. The squalor of your character has been an unending delight to

ROGER
My God.

CORLISS
(FILTER) Believe it now, do you? Really believe you're back in time?

ROGER
I have to. (PAUSE) Two of me. Is there a third me back there with you?

CORLISS
(FILTER) Don't be absurd, Roger. When you went back in time there, you vanished from here.

ROGER
Thank God.

CORLISS
That's enough. Close the door now.

me ever since you could crawl, but there is a limit to how much I am prepared to pay for my entertainment. Wrench!

SOUND: CLATTER.

ROGER
If you think I came here just to be insulted – !

CORLISS
I know you came here just to filch money. But now that you're here it occurs to me I *do* have a use for you. Wait a minute.

SOUND: CLATTER OF TOOLS. SNAP OF SWITCH. LAB SOUNDS DIE.

CORLISS
Now! I'm perfectly aware, dear Roger, that you haven't a bean to support the self indulgence...

SOUND: DOOR CLOSES SOFTLY. VOICES STOP.

Scene 2C: Confined Room Ambience.

ROGER
(NORMAL VOLUME) How do I get back again? – quickly!

CORLISS
(FILTER) Cut the master switch first.

ROGER
Check.

SOUND: MASTER SWITCH OFF.

CORLISS
(FILTER) Now review your timer.

ROGER
Seven minutes.

CORLISS
Good. Now reverse the current to come back to the present.

ROGER
Check.

SOUND: SNAP OF SWITCH.

CORLISS
(FILTER) Main switch.

ROGER
(SHUDDERING) I never want to see myself in the past again.

CORLISS
(FILTER) Well, con-sidering all the idiot things you said, I'm hardly surprised. Master switch on!

SOUND: CLICK.

ROGER
It's not that.

CORLISS
(FILTER) Well?

ROGER
(WITH LOATHING) I – I look just like everybody else!

CORLISS
(FILTER) Shock, eh? Now flip the switch and come back here.

SOUND: (1) BEEP! (2) RISING SPROIINNG! (3) WHITE NOISE (4) POP!

Scene 2D: Back in the workroom. Present time, 1935.

CORLISS
(NORMAL ACOUSTIC) Now. See? Foolproof! But we must be very careful. Think what might happen if Hitler got hold of it.

ROGER
(BEGINNING TO THINK) Yes...foolproof. There are so many things...one could do...

CORLISS:
Roger Pennithorne, you can forget those little plans your conniving mind is developing, and listen to me.

ROGER
Yes, Uncle Corliss.

CORLISS
I'll have no get-rich-quick schemes or treasure-hunting in my bailiwick. And the past *is* my bailiwick – it's my invention opened it up, and my machine that keeps the key. Understand?

ROGER
Why of course, sir.

CORLISS
I'm going to use that machine purely to satisfy my curiosity about all sorts of things in the past: how the pyramids were built, and where Hungarians actually came from, and a thousand other things that actually matter.

ROGER
Isn't that clever! You've thought it all out, haven't you, uncle? So I'm only on...salary, eh?

CORLISS
Damned right you are.

ROGER:
(QUIET SMILE) In that case, Uncle, I guess there's nothing for me to do but give you...what you're asking for.

CORLISS
You'd better.

ROGER
Where...ah, in what part of history would you like to start?

CORLISS
(CACKLE) Why, at the very beginning, Roger, where else? Oh, say five million years ago? I'm sure something more or less human was walking around by then, a little chinless, probably, but then...your own chin, dear boy, is none too, ah...

ROGER
Why, of course, Uncle Corliss, if you'd just (EFFORT) show me how to put the machine on properly – the clip for the power source nearly came off, and I'm all tangled up in the headphone wires –

CORLISS
Good Lord, you're clumsy – here, watch –
SOUND: SNAP OF BELT CLIP.

ROGER
It looks better on you than it did on me.

CORLISS
Stop wasting time.

ROGER
(STRUGGLING) But I can't...loosen the bands on these...headphones when I can't see them...

CORLISS
Oh for heaven's sake – give them to me. Now pay attention while I adjust the clasps.

ROGER
Two million B.C., did you say?

CORLISS
I think we'll start you there, yes.

SOUND: VERY LONG SERIES OF QUICK BEEPS AND BOOPS.

CORLISS:
(PRE-OCCUPIED) You may find the climate a little damp back

Uncle Corliss is transported to a world like this one. In the next activity, you will have to decide what happens next.

then – I could loan you some galoshes, of course.

SNICK! OF SWITCH.

CORLISS
What? What are you doing? That's the *narrow-focus* switch, dimwit, (SUDDEN ALARM) Roger – what are you doing?

ROGER
Sending you to the hominids, Uncle Corliss – I do hope they weren't cannibals back then.

CORLISS
No! Don't touch the main switch – *Roger! Nooooo!*

SOUND: (1) BOOP! (2) RAPIDLY DESCENDING SPROINGGGG! (3) POP! AS UNCLE VANISHES. (4) RIPPING OF FLOORBOARDS.

ROGER
My God, he *did* take half the floor with him. At least the machine's still here...but *you*, dear Uncle, have gone, I fear, to join your fellow dinosaurs.

CORLISS
(FILTER FROM THE HEADPHONES, FURIOUS BUT FAR AWAY) Roger!

ROGER
(STARTLED) Wha – ? My God, you survived a five-million year jump?

SOUND: (FROM HEADPHONES) CRASHING AND SPLINTERING OF WOOD AS CORLISS TRIES TO GET PLANKS AWAY.

CORLISS
(FILTER) I'm not *going* to survive if I don't get this damn lumber off my feet! Get me out of here! Bring me back at once!

ROGER
(MOCK INNOCENCE) But I don't know how!

CORLISS
(FILTER) I *showed* you how, you – !

ROGER
But the machine is here with *me*. I seem to have got the wrong focus. What can I do? What's it like there, by the way?

CORLISS
(FILTER) It's horrible! Fog everywhere, and giant ferns. It's like a cross between a Turkish bath and a –

MAN-EATING PLANT
(SNAPPING ITS JAWS OVER FILTER) Krrrorwr- schluckkkk!

CORLISS
(CRY OF HORROR: RETREATS SLIGHTLY OFF MIKE)
Yeeeaaaaach!

ROGER
What is it?

CORLISS
(FILTER) (SLIGHTLY OFF) A plant the size of a Studebaker – it nearly ate me!

ROGER:
What a narrow escape for the plant.

CORLISS
(FILTER) (DESPAIRING WAIL) Rogerrrrr!

ROGER
And that, dearly beloved uncle, *that*...is where you were going to send *me?*

CORLISS
(FILTER) You? Why...ah, no, no, really dear boy, I didn't, I – (FREEZE) Roger!

ROGER
(OOZING SUGAR) Ye-e-e-s?

CORLISS
(FILTER) Roger, there are shapes coming near in the fog – they're walking on two legs, almost, – Roger – *help!*

ROGER
Good-bye, Uncle Corliss. I'm turning you off now.

CORLISS
(FILTER) No-o-o-o-o!
SOUND: SHARP SNICK CUTS HIS WAIL.

MUSIC: NASTY STING.

Scene 3: Narration.

SOUND: UP RUSHING HISS OF WHITE NOISE, HOLD UNDER.

ROGER
(NARR) (RADIO ACOUSTIC) Oh, I was so sure that the world was mine for the taking, or at least the past and future parts of it, once I had deposited Uncle Corliss back in the Great Evolutionary Playpen. Almost at once a wonderful idea came up and hit me over the head: everybody nowadays knows the richest areas of the world, but who can afford them *now?* But *I* could go back to a time before their value was known, and buy into them for a song, at a time when a thousand dollars was a fortune.

(cont'd...)

ACTIVITY 2
WHAT HAPPENS NEXT?

1. Imagine you are Roger. As you can see from the play so far, you are interested in making money and are not particularly concerned about how you get it. Now you have the means to make things happen – your uncle's time machine. How will you make this machine work for you? Make a list of all the places you could go to carry out the plan you announced at the end of the first half of the drama.
2. Form groups of four. Form these groups carefully because you will be helping each other with your scripts. Share your suggestions from number 1 with each other. Pick two or three ideas that the members of your group agree would make an interesting second half for the play.
3. The author has been careful to include a number of details that he can develop later in the play to provide an appropriate ending to Roger's plan. Make a list of these details. In your groups decide how you could use these suggestions and any others you can think of as the basis for an interesting ending to the play.

EXPLORING THE SCRIPT

Before you begin to write the second half of the drama, look at the script a little more closely. Focus on the following aspects of the play:

- the dialogue
- the sound and music cues
- the acting directions
- the structure of the script

Before television, radio was one of the main sources of entertainment.

ACTIVITY 3
THE ELEMENTS OF A RADIO SCRIPT

1. Have each member of your group of four pick one of the following assignments:
   a) **Dialogue**
   Because the radio audience can't see the characters, it is important that they be able to hear the differences in the characters. Look carefully at the words, expressions, and sentence structures used by Roger and his uncle. What makes them sound different? Use specific examples to illustrate your findings.
   b) **Acting Directions**
   The actors who perform the play will need specific suggestions about how the words should be spoken and the circumstances under which they are said. Make a list of the different kinds of directions that are provided by the writer. Include an example of each. Try reading the lines using the directions that have been provided.
   c) **Sound Cues**
   Because he is writing for radio the writer has included a large number of sound cues. Make a list of these cues and beside each one suggest how the sound could be created.
   d) **Script Structure and Format**
   As you can see, the play has been divided into a number of scenes and sub-scenes. Make a list of these scenes and briefly summarize what happens in each one. What is the basis on which the scenes are divided? How is the scene set up on the page? How are the characters, dialogue, cues, and directions indicated in the script?

2. Re-organize your groups so that all the students who chose the assignment on dialogue are sitting together, as are the students who picked acting directions, sound cues, and script structure. Complete the assignment with the other members of your new group.

3. When you have completed the assignment return to your original groups. Each group should now have someone who is an expert in each of the four aspects of radio scripts. Share your expertise with the members of your original group.

4. In your original group, use this expertise to prepare a guide to writers of radio scripts. In your guide include suggestions for writing dialogue, sound cues, acting directions, and the structure and set-up of the script.

FEEDBACK TO GROUPS

So far in this unit you have used groups to participate in an introductory activity, brainstorm ideas for the second half of the script, explore features of radio scripts, and prepare a guide for scriptwriters. Before going on to the next part of the unit, use the following activity to provide each other with some feedback on the group process.

Actors perform a radio play in this radio studio of the 1920s.

ACTIVITY 4
HOW DID WE DO?

1. Look back to the criteria for effective groups that you generated in Activity 1. Share your list with your group. Together determine the criteria on which your group will be rated.
2. Make a response form by listing these criteria down the left hand side of a sheet of paper. Leave several lines in between each one. Across the top of the page write the names of the members of the group. Using a scale of one to five (where five is the best mark), rate the group members on each of the criteria.
3. Below the ratings for the individual group members, comment on the performance of the group as a whole. Include some of the things that worked well and some suggestions for improvement.
4. Share your ratings and suggestions with each other. Was there general agreement about the individual and group performance? If you agreed that your group did well on the first half of the unit, pick a new set of criteria to use for the next set of activities. If the members of the group agree that more practice is needed on one or more of the first set of criteria, keep them in your list.

FIRST DRAFT

The activities that you have completed so far in this unit should make writing your first draft a fairly straightforward task. Remember the variables that a writer has to keep in mind and how these variables apply to a radio script.

- **Audience**
  Be sure to recognize the special needs of the radio audience. Always keep in mind that your dialogue has to enable your audience to "see" what is happening.
- **Purpose**
  Remember that the script was written to entertain a radio audience. The purpose of the second half of the script is to continue the first half by showing in an entertaining manner what happens to Roger.
- **Format**
  Set up your script using "Past Imperfect" as a model. Pay particular attention to how the speakers' dialogue, the directions, and the sound cues are set up.

ACTIVITY 5
FIRST DRAFT

Here are some suggestions for writing the first draft:

1. Improvise the rest of the play with a partner. As you are acting out what happens, keep a tape recorder running. Later you can use the best parts as the basis for your script.
2. Try taking Roger to several different locations and explore what might happen to him in each one. Pick the one you like best for your script.
3. It's probably easier to write the first draft individually, but if you work well with a partner you could try writing in pairs.

Modern deejays must be fast-paced and quick-witted to produce good radio programs.

REHEARSAL

In the real world of radio and theatre, scripts often get changed during the rehearsal period. As the director and actors start to work with a script they often discover that words that looked good on the page do not work well when they are spoken.

Furthermore, there may be aspects of the script that appeared clear to the author but which need further explanation for the actors and the audience. Revision and editing are a natural part of the production process.

ACTIVITY 6
REHEARSAL

In your groups of four, work through the following procedure.

1. Run off enough copies of your script for each member of the group and assign the roles to the members of the group. If there are several characters, some students may have to take more than one role.
2. Read through the play several times. As you read it aloud watch for things that are not clear, need further explanation, or can be improved.
3. Use the following questions as a guide to revision and editing:
   a) Is the dialogue appropriate to the characters? Do the main characters use words, explanations, and sentence structures that are consistent with the first half of the play?
   b) Are the directions to the actors clear and complete?
   c) Are the sound cues appropriate and do they help the listeners to visualize what is happening in the play?
   d) Are the scenes that you have added a logical and interesting extension of the first half of the play?
   e) Does the format of the play follow the model that has been provided? Are the dialogue, directions, and cues set up in the correct manner?
   f) Are the spelling, usage, capitalization, and punctuation correct?

ON THE AIR!

After several careful readings in your rehearsal groups, the scripts should be ready for broadcast. A radio production team usually includes:

- **Director** – the person who gives the directions to the actors
- **Producer** – the person who looks after the organization of the entire production and makes sure that everything that is needed is ready and available on time
- **Sound-Effects Person** – someone who prepares the sound effects and makes sure that they are cued at the right time
- **Script Editor** – the person responsible for making the script ready for broadcast
- **Technician** – the person who gets the equipment ready and ensures that it is operating properly

ACTIVITY 7
TURN ON THE TAPE RECORDER

1. Assign the various production roles to the members of your group. Each of you should have both an acting and production role. Assemble the equipment that you will need: a tape recorder, materials to create the sound effects, enough copies of the script for the actors and director, and music. When you are ready, begin taping.

2. Often members of the radio audience respond to their favourite programs by writing letters to the producer. After listening to the radio broadcasts on tape, assign various members of the class to write a letter to the producer of the play. In your letter comment on your reactions to some of the following:
   - the content of the play
   - the dialogue
   - the characters
   - the sound effects and music
   - the technical aspects of the production
   - the quality of the language
   - the actors and their voices

END THOUGHTS

Like all media texts, radio programs are careful constructions. Words, sound, and music are skillfully combined to make a single, coherent whole. As you become more aware of how media texts are constructed you will become an increasingly sophisticated consumer of media products.

ACTIVITY 8
EXTENSION IDEAS

1. Recordings of popular radio dramas from the Golden Age of Radio are often available at public libraries or record stores. Get a copy of a program such as "Amos 'n' Andy," "The Lone Ranger," or "The Shadow." Listen carefully to note the techniques that have been used to make the audience "see" what is happening.

2. Investigate the changes that have occurred in radio as a result of the coming of television. Be prepared to give a talk to your class about your findings.

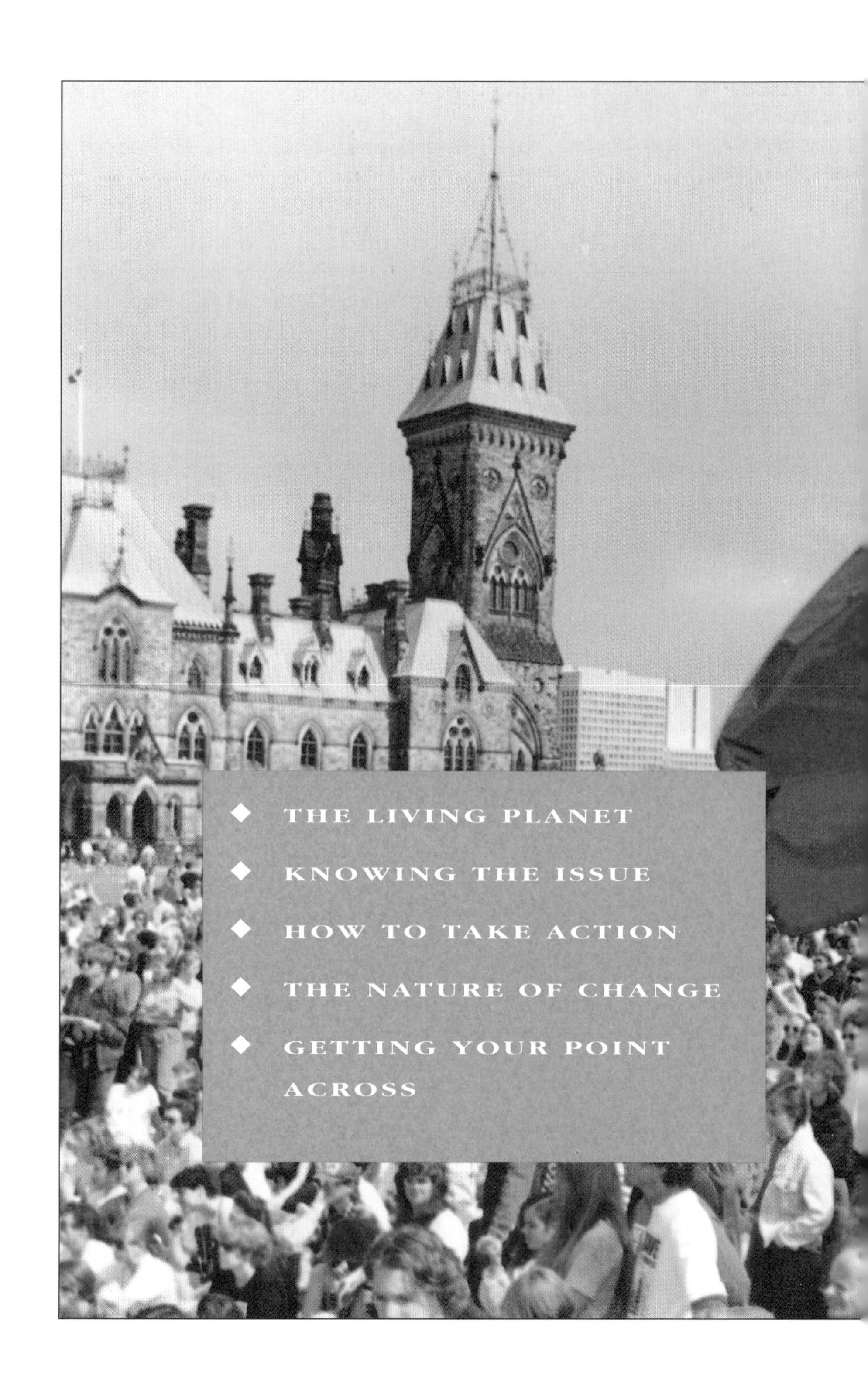
◆ THE LIVING PLANET
◆ KNOWING THE ISSUE
◆ HOW TO TAKE ACTION
◆ THE NATURE OF CHANGE
◆ GETTING YOUR POINT ACROSS

UNIT 12

EARTH FIRST

Acid rain, smog, global warming, polluted waters. Many scientists say that unless the process is reversed within the next ten years, the air you breathe, the food you eat, and the water you drink may not be sufficient to support life on this planet. To respond to this crisis you need to think "Earth First" by considering how your actions and those of others affect the environment. What can you do to preserve and protect the environment?

In this unit, you will use your group-interaction, negotiating, critical-thinking, and discussion skills to examine environmental issues.

THE LIVING PLANET

Our world is changing. In the late 1980s, in a small lake in Guatemala, the last of the giant grebes – a charcoal-coloured, flightless waterfowl – expired.... In the Philippines, dynamite razed a coral reef, turning an oasis of iridescent sponges and brilliantly coloured fish into a lifeless desert.... In 1989, an Alaskan beach once noisy with the sounds of gulls and otters was littered with oil-slicked, suffocating wildlife.

Not only is our world changing, but our view of the world is also changing. We work to save the Brazilian rain forest because we know its destruction threatens the survival of native cultures, wildlife, and the ozone layer that encircles our planet and keeps us alive. We call the rain forest the "lungs of the world" as if the planet were a single living body. This is because we are becoming aware that one part of the world affects the whole world.

Read the following selection written in 1854 by Chief Seattle. As you read, think about how the author views the relationship between humans and our planet.

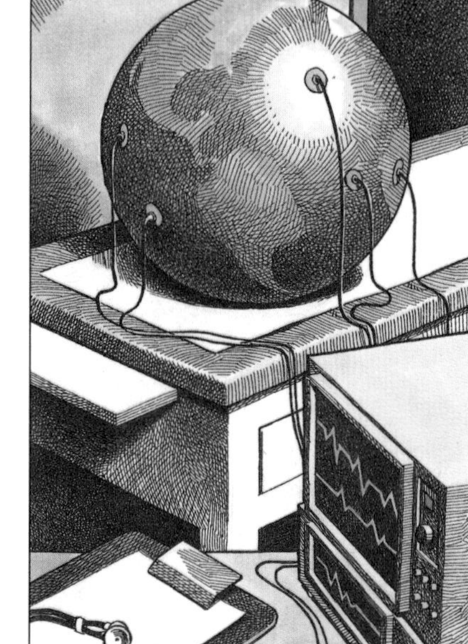

The Earth is a single habitat on which the health of each part affects the whole.

EVERY PART OF THIS EARTH IS SACRED

Chief Seattle

Every part of this earth is sacred...
Every shining pine needle, every sandy shore, every mist in the dark woods, every clearing and humming insect is holy...
All things are connected.
Teach your children that the earth is our mother.
Whatever befalls the earth, befalls the sons of the earth.
This we know: The earth does not belong to man; man belongs to the earth. This we know.
Man did not weave the web of life; he is merely a strand in it.
Whatever he does to the web, he does to himself.

We have contributed to the decrease in number of beluga whales. What will their destruction mean to us?

ACTIVITY 1
PARTS OF A WHOLE

1. Form small groups for the following activities.
   a) Chief Seattle describes the earth as our mother and humans as her sons. What other words does he use to describe the relationship between people and our planet?
   b) Can you think of some other descriptive words that do not appear in the poem that convey the same feeling?

2. In your groups, recall some environmental issues you have read about, seen on TV, or heard about on the radio.
   a) Do you think humans have been damaging the Earth? If so, how? If not, why not?
   b) Do you think we have hurt ourselves by our treatment of the Earth? If so, how? If not, why not?

3. Write your own poem about the Earth.
   a) Choose one of the issues that your group discussed in number 2 that most interested you. Use this issue as the topic of your poem.
   b) Before you begin to write, use a thought web to explore further your thoughts and feelings about the topic. Some of the descriptive words you brainstormed in number 1b) may be useful here.
   c) With reference to your topic, try completing some of the following thoughts:
      It reminds me of...
      It is like...
      It sounds like...
      It feels like...
      It smells like...
      It looks like...
      It makes me feel...
      What makes me angry is...
      What makes me laugh is...
      What makes me sad is...
   d) Pick the strongest words and images from the above sentences and use them in your poem.
   e) Share the first draft of your poem with a partner and consider possible improvements to the words and images. In what ways could they be changed to make the poem more vivid and original?

KNOWING THE ISSUE

In 1960, public outcry – fueled by a massive letter-writing campaign by school children across North America to the Prime Minister – saved the 250 wild horses of Nova Scotia's Sable Island from destruction.... In 1990, Kenyan women formed a tree-planting brigade to halt the spreading desert.... A community in Ontario pressured local politicians to help save the nearby Rouge Valley – a wildlife habitat – from developers' bulldozers.

In each case, concerned people – often anxious about problems in their own backyards – pooled their knowledge and resources to choose a plan of action and to carry out that plan. To make effective changes, protesters must find actions appropriate to the situation. They need a detailed understanding of all sides of an issue and the creative-thinking skills to consider alternatives. Once they clearly understand the issue, they can choose the most effective course of action. You can use the infobox *Understanding All Sides of an Issue* on page 268 as a guide to consider any action you might take for a cause.

This woman is taking action against the *Exxon Valdez* oil spill by shovelling oil at Pacific Rim National Park.

INFO BOX

Understanding All Sides of an Issue

These questions will help you think about environmental issues:

- What are the different elements involved? Consider, for example, the effects on the economy or on the local culture.
- How do the parts fit together? What is the impact of each element on the others?
- What are the alternatives? What are their impact on each of the elements identified?

Read the following article about Daniel Ashini. This selection illustrates how a social issue has an impact upon the environment. As you read, you will discover how the Innu of Northern Quebec have responded to military flights over their land.

"'This is a life-and-death matter,' says Ashini. As flights increase, chances for self-reliance on the land will decrease. If the Innu get no help to adjust – and none is forthcoming – they risk deteriorating rapidly as a society."

DANIEL ASHINI: NATIVE LEADER

John Goddard

While camped in southeastern Labrador in spring of 1989, Daniel Ashini and four other men decided to return to their village near Happy Valley-Goose Bay by canoe, instead of by small airplane with their families. "We took one of the elders who was familiar with the area," says Ashini. "We made our way down the river system and over some of the old portage routes for seven days and nights, sleeping in the open." Then, as they rounded the final bend near home, they could hardly believe their eyes. The entire community had camped on the beach to greet them. Most of the old people were dressed in traditional clothing, and a feast of caribou, duck and goose was waiting. "People were crying and dancing and beating drums," says Ashini. "It was the first time anybody had returned by canoe in twenty years."

"People were crying and dancing and beating drums," says Ashini. "It was the first time anybody had returned by canoe in twenty years."

Ashini is chief of the village of Sheshashit (the "i" pronounced "ee"), and he tells the story to illustrate how easily a spontaneous act of love for the land can lead to an emotional outpouring. Except for the southeastern campgrounds, almost all unceded Indian territory in Labrador and northeastern Quebec is under siege from low-flying bombers and fighter planes belonging to Holland, West Germany and Great Britain.

Nearly 7000 training flights a year now originate from the base at Happy Valley-Goose Bay, and the number is expected to more than treble by 1996. If the base becomes an official NATO Tactical Fighter Centre, as the Canadian defence department proposes, the number will reach 26 000 to 28 000 by 2001 – nearly seventy-seven flights a day.

"They're turning our homeland into a wasteland," says Ashini, a shy, even-tempered man who, despite a rounded, unprepossessing appearance, speaks directly, with integrity and determination. At the age of thirty, he has become a kind of hero to environmentalists, antimilitarists and aboriginal-rights supporters for his leadership of 10 000 of the area's Indians, who call themselves Innu.

Ashini's life story reads like that of many native leaders whose territories are being trespassed upon without prior land-rights agreements: he has struggled to learn new ways to perpetuate the old. Although born into a bush family, Ashini was encouraged in school, and he excelled, advancing to high school in Corner Brook, Newfoundland. After several years in band administration, he noticed a leadership vacuum and coped with his shyness enough to take the top job, becoming not only chief of Sheshashit but a key leader for fifteen other scattered Innu villages as well. His distaste for the limelight makes Ashini a better leader, not a worse one, people say.

The flights are massively destructive, says Ashini. Jets roar over Innu hunting camps at treetop level without warning, sending children screaming into the bush and dumping paddlers from their canoes.

The flights are massively destructive, says Ashini. Jets roar over Innu hunting camps at treetop level without warning, sending children screaming into the bush and dumping paddlers from their canoes. Aircraft exhaust can leave a film on the water's surface "like paint," and pilots occasionally release toxic fuel in emergencies. Proposed live bombing poses a forest-fire risk. Furthermore, the activities threaten, to varying degrees, the vast George River caribou herds, large populations of ducks and geese and scarce raptor species such as the gyrfalcon, osprey, bald eagle and peregrine falcon. "This is a life-and-death matter," says Ashini. As flights increase, chances for self-reliance on the land will decrease. If the Innu get no help to adjust – and none is forthcoming – they risk deteriorating rapidly as a society.

Ashini has gone to jail five times for demonstrating at the base and has helped to coordinate a public-awareness programme that has sent Innu families across the country and to Europe. He talked to the Pope recently and joined other Innu leaders in filing a lawsuit to stop the flights – a case expected to last several years.

Whenever he can, Ashini also joins other community members in the bush. "All the senses come alive out there," he says. "It's a very healthy, healing experience. It's important that the land not be damaged. People believe that in their hearts." ▼

ACTIVITY 2

UNDER-STANDING THE PROBLEM

For this activity, form a group of four people. Use the infobox *Understanding All Sides of an Issue* on page 268 to help you.

1. Have one person in your group use a chalkboard or a flip chart to record your responses to the following.
   a) List Ashini's reasons for opposing the military training flights over Happy Valley-Goose Bay.
   b) Brainstorm possible reasons for continuing the flights in that area.
2. Use the two lists you made in number 1 as the basis for role-playing negotiations between two Innu representatives and two military officials.
   a) To prepare, discuss and make notes of the arguments you and your partner will use. To help do this, refer to the following infobox, *Negotiating Skills.*
   b) Role-play your negotiations for your class.
3. Which argument does your class find most effective? Why?
4. With your class, discuss what happens when you negotiate. Did you feel you compromised too much? What different assumptions in values did each side make? What is required in order to find common ground?

William Kurelek's watercolour painting, *Subdue the Earth*, illustrates his vision of what our world is becoming.

INFO BOX

Negotiating Skills

The art of negotiation – of trying to reach an agreement – requires an understanding of both sides of the issue. Use the following tips to develop your negotiating skills.

- Know your arguments thoroughly. What points must you be able to make at the negotiating table?
- Know which of your points are critical and which are negotiable. Which of your points must not be compromised? Which, on the other hand, are you willing to bend on?
- Anticipate what the other side is likely to say or do. What points will they likely raise? And what can you say to reduce the impact of these points?
- Attempt to reach an agreement that will satisfy the most significant needs of both parties. To do this, you may need to give up something of lesser value.
- Keep your cool. Listen carefully when others speak and show that you have understood their concerns.

People around the world celebrated their love for the planet on Earth Day in April 1990.

HOW TO TAKE ACTION

As a concerned, aware citizen, you are ready to take action. As you plan your course of action, consider the following:

- How can you use your knowledge of the issue?
- Who can join forces with you to help?
- What resources are available to you, and how can you use them most effectively?

ACTIVITY 3
CONFRONTING THE PROBLEM

Form a small group of three to six people.

1. a) Choose one of the following problems and brainstorm the repercussions it has on humans and the earth itself. Think of all the ways in which the issue affects people and the planet, both positively and negatively. For example, consider how different people are affected economically by the issue.
   - endangered species
   - global warming
   - clear-cutting of timber
   - energy conservation
   - acid rain

   b) Using the lists you created in a), decide what stand your group will take on this issue. You may have to spend several minutes discussing the problem before you reach a consensus.

   c) Determine who can help you take action to solve the problem, that is, those who would agree with your group's view of how the issue should be resolved. These people may be concerned individuals or members of a special-interest group, for example. Also, decide who may obstruct your action to resolve the issue; these are the people who may gain from or see advantages to resolving the issue in a way contrary to your group's desire.

   d) Consider what specific actions you can take to put your campaign in motion. For example, you may start a letter-writing network or organize a group of volunteer fundraisers.

   e) Present your plan to your class. What suggestions can your class make to help you improve your plan?

THE NATURE OF CHANGE

How do your daily habits – and your values – affect the environment? Rethinking the various aspects of your day-to-day life is the start of a process that will protect and preserve the environment. To begin this process, ask yourself the following questions:

- What impact do my daily habits have on the environment? in the short term? in the long term?
- What changes can I make to help the environment? For example, what changes can I make as a consumer of food, and as a user of transportation and technology?
- How can I help others reconsider their lifestyle?
- How can I support laws that will enforce the protection of the environment?

Consider, for example, the by-product of your habits as a consumer: garbage. Every Canadian throws out over 15 kg of garbage each week. Much of this garbage is nonbiodegradable and so will occupy landfill sites for hundreds of years. In fact, since landfills are not designed to foster biodegradation, even paper products can last a long time. As well, disposal of hazardous household wastes contaminates soil, rivers, lakes – and drinking water. The following infobox suggests four methods of altering your garbage-producing habits.

The effective management of our natural resources? Dolphins, endangered sea turtles, and fish unsuitable for human consumption make up almost seventy percent of the catch in drift-net fishing. Most of the unwanted catch suffocate in the nets.

INFO BOX

Reducing Waste: The Four Rs

- Reduce your garbage by avoiding excessively packaged products. Avoid throw-away items. Buy bulk foods and economy-size products. Start a compost heap.
- Reuse glass jars, plastic containers, and storage bags. Give excess paint, motor oil, and other materials to your neighbours. Save gift wrap and ribbon to be used again.
- Recycle tin cans, newspapers, and glass jars. Hold a garage sale or donate your old clothes and furniture to charity. Take your old solvents and chemical products to special depots in your community instead of putting them in the garbage. Collect and save used white paper instead of throwing it out.
- Rethink your buying habits. Do you really need some of the products you buy? Buy products which are biodegradable or made from recycled materials.

Trees give life. Brazil has been condemned for destroying its rain forests but North Americans should be aware that our abundance of trees is also in danger.

The following article, "Recycling: The New Revenue" by Shannon L. Kodejs, discusses how Canada is becoming a recycling nation.

RECYCLING: THE NEW REVENUE

Shannon L. Kodejs

The facts are in: Canada is the worst recycler of any industrialized nation. At a two percent recycling rate, Canadians lag behind the Europeans, Americans and the Japanese, who, by the way, recycle an impressive fifty to sixty percent.

...Companies are becoming increasingly aware of public demand for less packaging and more environmentally friendly products.

Canadian businesses and industries are just beginning to take the recycling business seriously. Until now, it was more cost effective and less time-consuming to simply dispose of office waste, but times have changed. A combination of factors – consumer pressure, threatened government sanctions and profit potential in the buying and selling of recyclable goods – are influencing the business community to change.

As well, companies are becoming increasingly aware of public demand for less packaging and more environmentally friendly products. Proctor and Gamble recently introduced the "enviro-pak" – plastic pouches that can be placed in refillable bottles. In 1989, McDonald's restaurants began using styrofoam containers made without deadly CFCs (chlorofluorocarbons). In addition, the company is also testing trial recycling projects in Portland, Oregon and New York.

There's also a lot of money to be made by being environmentally friendly. Witness The Body Shop, an international, British-based cosmetics company which estimated its 1989 gross sales (including sales from seventy-five Canadian outlets) to reach $40 million by marketing environmentally sound products.

Diaper manufacturers are also scrambling to invent a better product. Sunfresh Limited has introduced an eighty-eight percent biodegradable disposable diaper, while two Canadian companies, Babykins and The Indisposables, are marketing a reusable cloth diaper, with easy-to-fasten velcro closures. Although initially more expensive than disposables, these Canadian-made diapers are more cost efficient over time and won't add to the 250 000 tonnes of soiled disposables that clog Canadian landfills each year. Another innovative Canadian company, Tryam Trading Inc., is working with the Anderson Diaper Service in Seattle to produce a recycling plan for disposable diapers. Soiled diapers are picked up bi-weekly at curbside, then washed at a processing plant where they are separated, sterilized and sold. The plastic is sent to the Far East while the remaining cellulose is used in fertilizer.

Without the necessary processing plants we must export out garbage, then buy it back after it has been processed, at greatly inflated rates.

Diapers are not the only item that can be recycled to produce different products. For example, Lafarge Canada Inc. utilizes shredded tires as a supplementary source of fuel, and Northwest Rubber Mats Ltd. also uses shredded rubber tires but to make floor mats for livestock stables. Computer paper is in very high demand and in the Ottawa area the federal government's office paper recycling program recovers 8 000 tonnes of paper per year which generates $800 000 of annual revenue. Other recyclables in demand are: batteries, glass, metals, various chemicals and hazardous wastes.

The big problem, however, is that Canada doesn't have enough processing plants for recyclable material. Without the necessary processing plants we must export out garbage, then buy it back after it has been processed, at greatly inflated rates. Newsprint is an excellent example of this as many Canadian newspapers would buy recycled newsprint, but the high import prices are too prohibitive.

Much of Canada's recyclables are sold to other industrial nations, namely Korea, Japan, Taiwan, Hong Kong, and even the United States who use it for a staggering amount of purposes – everything from memo paper to cars. Dick McCarthy, president of the B.C. Recycling Council, confirms that some of our garbage is even shipped to Europe, via the Panama Canal.

In order to rectify this situation the federal government will subsidize, up to fifty percent, any recycling costs that a non-profit company incurs under its Environmental Partners Fund.

That's a good start as the battle to change Canadian attitudes toward and habits concerning recycling slowly change for the better. ▼

ACTIVITY 4 CHANGING HABITS

1. Discuss the following questions in a small group.
   a) What steps are companies taking to reduce the impact of their packaging on the environment?
   b) What problems has Canada come up against in its bid to recycle?
   c) How is the Canadian government trying to encourage recycling?
2. Remain in your groups to answer these questions.
   a) How else should the federal government concern itself with environmental issues? Make a list of laws that you believe the federal government should establish to improve how Canadians treat the environment. Do you know if any of these laws exist already?
   b) How can each community help? In a small group, brainstorm a list of services that your community could offer that would make your area more environmentally friendly. Does your community already offer some of these services?
3. On your own, explore how you can contribute as an individual.
   a) Make a chart in which you list your activities for a typical day. Beside each, write down how you could perform that activity in an environmentally sound way. To help do this, re-examine the infobox on page 275. Your chart might look like this:

shower	use an energy-efficient shower head
breakfast	eat organically grown fruit
go to school	ride a bike
buy lunch	avoid buying food with plastic or styrofoam wrapping
wash dishes	use phosphate-free dish detergent

   b) Present your chart to your class. What other alternative methods can your classmates suggest?

GETTING YOUR POINT ACROSS

You have explored the environmental issues that exist and have investigated how you can take action to remedy our world's problems. But to make any significant effect on the situation, it has to be more than you who is involved. How can you convince others to care? You must develop your ability to argue the issue, that is, to get your point across. The following activity will require you and your classmates to use the knowledge and skills that you have acquired throughout this unit to effectively discuss your point.

ACTIVITY 5
LET'S TALK

This is a whole-class activity in which you will simulate a panel discussion for a TV talk show.

1. As a class, decide on the following:
   a) What will be the topic of discussion for the talk show? You might use one of the issues discussed in Activity 3, 1a), or you may wish to choose another one.
   b) What type of people will be the talk-show guests? Refer to the lists you made in Activity 3, number 1c), of people who would be interested in solving the issue and of people who may obstruct action against it. Choose four people from these lists to be the guests and decide who in the class will take these roles.
   c) Who will act as the talk-show host? This person will have to ask leading questions to stimulate discussion; encourage the speakers when the discussion is progressing well and redirect them when it is lagging; and allow for audience comments and questions.
   d) How will the audience members participate? Each member of the audience should have one or two questions to ask the talk-show panel.
2. Perform the talk show. You may wish to create a set and use props similar to what you would see on a real TV talk show. For example, you could place four chairs in front of the audience where the guests would sit and find a microphone for the host. Set a time limit for the length of the show.
3. After the show is over, as a class, discuss the arguments that the four guests presented. What were the strongest arguments? Why? Which questions, raised by the audience and the host, initiated the most discussion? Why? Were there any questions that no one was able to answer? What sources would you explore to find answers to these questions?

END THOUGHTS

Thinking "Earth First" occurs when you consider the effects of your actions – and the actions of others – on the environment. It involves an awareness of our planet as a living creature, the health of which depends on each of its parts – from the starfish to the northern forest to the ozone layer. Thinking this way often requires us to re-examine our consumer-oriented way of life in which we buy and dispose of goods with little awareness of the effect on the environment.

Thinking "Earth First" also requires careful analysis of the different aspects of an issue to choose the most effective action. In this unit, you have used your critical-thinking, group-interaction, negotiating, and discussion skills to explore issues and to examine methods of using your own resources to preserve and protect the environment.

ACTIVITY 6
EXTENSION IDEAS

1. Research an environmental issue and organize action in your school. For example, start a recycling program or adopt an endangered animal and initiate a fundraising and letter-writing campaign to help protect it.
2. Volunteer for an organization doing environmental work in your community. Prepare a video report in which you interview some of the people involved. How do they view the work they are doing? What do they hope to achieve? What personal satisfaction does their work give them?
3. The "green" consumer movement is resulting in a growing demand for environmentally safe products. Research the meaning of the following terms. Are companies who use these terms to promote their products making accurate claims about their effect on the environment? Report your findings to your class.
   - enzyme-free
   - chlorine-free
   - organic
   - CFC-free or ozone-friendly
   - phosphate-free
   - recycled or recyclable
   - biodegradable
4. Choose an environmental issue and invite two representatives from opposing sides of the issue to present their views to your class. Prior to the visit, prepare questions to ask them.

5. Prepare a booklet on environmental awareness for distribution in your school. Choose several areas in which people can change their habits to help the environment. Consider including a resource list of organizations where people can find additional information (such as Pollution Probe, Friends of the Earth, Greenpeace, or the Environment Canada Inquiry Centre). Include a description of the aims and methods of each organization on your list.
6. Consider planting a tree as a contribution to reforesting the Earth. Plant one in your own backyard or ask the principal if you may add one to your school property. You may wish to contact local businesses or the Ministry of Parks and Recreation to ask about other areas where you may plant a tree. Write a letter to the editor of your local newspaper to tell what you did and why you did it.
7. Arrange to visit a recycling plant with your class to see how it is done. After the tour, prepare a report on the different stages in the process of recycling.
8. Alone, or with a partner, brainstorm a list of hazardous wastes which you believe are being improperly disposed of. Think of better ways to deal with these wastes. Use a chart like the one below to organize your thoughts.

FORM OF HAZARDOUS WASTE	PRESENT METHOD OF DISPOSAL	BETTER SOLUTION

You may wish to do some library research or call Environment Canada to get more information. Create a poster to be displayed in your school using the information you gathered. It should encourage students to help solve a problem.

◆ AWARDS CEREMONY
◆ GRAD DANCE
◆ CAPTURING THE EVENTS
◆ GRAD BOOK
◆ PERSONAL BELIEFS ABOUT EDUCATION

UNIT 13

GRADUATION

Graduation – a time to take stock of the future and of the past. You may be relieved to get to the end of the school year and begin your future outside of high school. Yet you probably feel uncertain, worried, and maybe even a little afraid of what lies ahead. As you prepare for your graduation, you may find yourself reflecting on your high-school career. The things that happened to you, the people you know, your successes, your failures – all have helped to make you who you are. The unique design of this unit reflects its difference from the others in the text. You will engage in activities that will challenge your creativity and will give your graduation the attention it deserves. Congratulations. And good luck.

AWARDS CEREMONY

Better build schoolrooms for the "boy" than cells and gibbets for the "man."
– Eliza Cook, 19th century

What do the Oscars, the Junos, and the Genies have in common besides celebrities, tuxedos, evening gowns, and long thank-you speeches? They all recognize an outstanding achievement in a particular area – in an exciting and entertaining way.

Graduation, too, is a time of celebration and recognition of achievement. Use your imagination to create award categories for your fellow students. These awards should recognize achievement within your Language Arts class such as an award for the best poem written during the term, the group who performed the best dramatization, or the best peer editor.

Graduation cards have become a tradition.

AND THE WINNER IS...

- ❐ In a small group, brainstorm a list of awards that might be given to students in your Language Arts class.
- ❐ Choose the awards that you will present in your class. List the criteria for selection.
- ❐ Design the awards. Someone in the group might be able to make them in the school shop, art studio, or on a computer.
- ❐ When the awards are named and designed, show them to the class. Ask for nominations. Then hold a secret ballot to determine the winners.
- ❐ Plan the Awards Ceremony. Choose an MC. You may want to have guest presenters such as the principal or vice-principal. As well, you might want to invite another class or family and friends to attend your awards ceremony.

The shrewd guess, the courageous leap to tentative conclusion – these are the most valuable coins of the thinker at work. But in most schools, guessing is heavily penalized and is associated somehow with laziness.
–J.S. Bruner, 20th century

GRAD DANCE

Perhaps you think you would like to go to the grad dance but at the same time feel uncertain about committing yourself. You might wonder if you will have a good time, or if it will be worth spending the money. On the other hand, you realize that you might not have the chance to see all your classmates together again for quite a while.

To sort out how you feel, think about the pros and cons of attending the grad dance. Regardless of the outcome, you will find satisfaction in making a decision that is right for you.

Everyone carries good and bad memories of high school into the future.

Looking at both sides of an issue can help you decide what to do.

After you graduate, the ability to make decisions will help you make choices for your future.

Go–No Go List

Go	No Go
• sounds like fun	• cost – I'm broke
• sit with Mica and Tim at dinner	• no car to drive
• say goodbye to Ahmed and Tina	• have to wear a tie
• tell Ms. P that hers was my favourite class	• Julie isn't sure she's going
• thank Fara for helping me with math	
• go to Lock's after with L & A & T	

SHOULD I OR SHOULDN'T I?

- ❐ Use a chart like the one on the previous page to organize your thoughts on the grad dance. You could title the reasons for attending GO and the reasons for not attending NO GO. Or you could choose your own column titles.
- ❐ List the reasons for attending in one column and the reasons for not attending in the other column.
- ❐ Review your chart. Does one column contain more points than the other? Can one factor outweigh a number of factors in the other column? Which reasons are more convincing to you?
- ❐ Choose a position to argue, that is, that you should attend or you should not attend. Find a partner who has taken the other position. Try to convince your partner of your position. When you have finished speaking, listen to his or her arguments. Did either of you change your attitudes?
- ❐ Write a journal entry in which you reflect on your decision whether or not to attend the grad dance. State your reasons as clearly as possible. Did you find it useful to organize your thoughts by pros and cons?
- ❐ You might want to reconsider your decision one week before the event. Are you satisfied with your decision? What, if anything, would make you change your mind?

Train up a child in the way he should go; And when he is old, he will not depart from it.
–The Book of Proverbs

CAPTURING THE EVENTS

Whether or not you usually enjoy being photographed or videotaped, you'll probably want to capture the events of your graduation on film, and so will your family and friends. In the following activity, you'll have a chance to create some live pictures or tableaux of the events.

STRIKING THE POSE

- ❐ Form groups of three to five. Brainstorm a list of memorable scenes from your graduation ceremony and the events that surround it. For example, your list might include such items as receiving your diploma, being congratulated by family and friends, or arriving at the dance. The scenes could be humorous, formal, or casual.
- ❐ Decide on a sequence of scenes that illustrates the events and conveys the mood of graduation.
- ❐ Create live pictures or tableaux of the scenes.
- ❐ Practise moving from one tableau to the next in slow motion. Freeze in position for each.
- ❐ Perform your tableaux for your class.

GRAD BOOK

Although you are likely looking forward to graduating, you have probably thought about all the people you will miss. Creating a class grad book will help keep memories of your classmates fresh. Looking through it in the future will remind you of the good times you had with the people in your class.

PRESERVE A MEMORY

- ❒ As a class, decide on the content and form of your class grad book. What information would you like to include about each class member? Brainstorm a list of possible items. For example, you could include nicknames, favourite sayings, and favourite songs. Should the graduate profiles be humorous, serious, or a combination? Will you include photographs, sketches, or some other visual representation of each class member? Each student could prepare a profile of another classmate.
- ❒ To prepare a profile, interview the individual and his or her friends to find out more about this person.
- ❒ When you have collected all of the necessary information, word process, type, or rewrite your profile so it is neat, clear, and correct. Add any visuals.
- ❒ Compile the profiles. To make the grad book more attractive, someone in the class might create a cover. Other material could be added to the grad book. For example, you might include cartoons or poems about people or humorous events or short descriptions of class activities such as field trips.
- ❒ Make a photocopy of the grad book for each member of the class.

Experience keeps a dear school, but fools will learn in no other.
–Benjamin Franklin, 18th century

PERSONAL BELIEFS ABOUT EDUCATION

As you passed through school, you probably developed certain ideas about education, learning, and life in general. Now that you are getting closer to graduation, it is interesting to compare your own ideas with those of others. In the following essay, Robert Fulghum talks about his belief system, or credo.

You may have felt much the same way about homework and school assignments.

It's misleading to suppose there's any basic difference between education and entertainment.
–Marshall McLuhan, 20th century

THE CREDO

Robert Fulghum

All I really need to know about how to live and what to do and how to be I learned in kindergarten. Wisdom was not at the top of the graduate-school mountain, but there in the sandpile in Sunday School. These are the things I learned:

Wisdom was not at the top of the graduate-school mountain, but there in the sandpile in Sunday School.

Share everything.
Play fair.
Don't hit people.
Put things back where you found them.
Clean up your own mess.
Don't take things that aren't yours.
Say you're sorry when you hurt somebody.
Wash your hands before you eat.
Flush.
Warm cookies and cold milk are good for you.

Live a balanced life – learn some and think some and draw and paint and sing and dance and play and work every day some.

Take a nap every afternoon.

When you go out into the world, watch out for traffic, hold hands, and stick together.

Be aware of wonder. Remember the little seed in the Styrofoam cup: The roots go down and the plant goes up and nobody really knows how or why, but we are all like that.

Goldfish and hamsters and white mice and even the little seed in the Styrofoam cup – they all die. So do we.

And then remember the Dick-and-Jane books and the first word you learned – the biggest word of all – LOOK.

Everything you need to know is in there somewhere. The Golden Rule and love and basic sanitation. Ecology and politics and equality and sane living.

Take any one of those items and extrapolate it into sophisticated adult terms and apply it to your family life or your work or your government or your world and it holds true and clear and firm. Think what a better world it would be if we all – the whole world – had cookies and milk about three o'clock every afternoon and then lay down with our blankets for a nap. Or if all governments had as a basic policy to always put things back where they found them and to clean up their own mess.

And it is still true, no matter how old you are – when you go out into the world, it is best to hold hands and stick together. ▼

Graduation photos provide touching and humorous memories.

vin and Hobbes **by Bill Watterson**

ADVICE TO THE YOUNG

- ❒ What is your reaction to Fulghum's statement that everything he really needs to know he learned in kindergarten? Do you agree or disagree? Explain your response.
- ❒ With a partner or in a small group, discuss your school career. Think back over your elementary, middle, and high school. What would you do differently if you had the chance? What would you not change?
- ❒ What advice would you give to someone entering your high school next year? Decide on the tone and the form for your message. You could take a humorous or a serious approach. Your message might take the form of a letter, an essay, a poem, or an interview.
- ❒ Present your piece to the class.

Medieval education was supposed to fit people to die. Any school-boy of today can still feel the effect of it.
–Stephen Leacock, 20th century

The teacher does not try to prevent the learner from making errors... errors are valuable; they are the essential learning instrument.
–James Moffett, 20th century

END THOUGHTS

In this unit, you have reflected on your school career and your upcoming graduation. Although you are probably excited about what comes next, you may feel hesitant about the changes. Write a journal entry describing your feelings as you embark on a new stage of your life. Go ahead, be nostalgic. It is all right to be worried, insecure, and a little frightened. Change is never without its doubts and regrets.

When you educate a man, you educate an individual; but when you educate a woman, you educate a family. And that's what I'm going to do.
–Agnes Kripps, 20th century

The present preoccupations with body building and character molding are useless and may even be dangerous so long as we neglect and starve the mind.
–Hilda Neatby, 20th century

My goal as a teacher is planned obsolescence: to help each student reach the day when he or she will no longer need me.
–Mimi Garry, 20th century

Bodily exercise, when compulsory, does no harm to the body; but knowledge which is acquired under compulsion obtains no hold on the mind.
–Plato, c. 428-348 B.C.

Education is asking questions, not accepting answers.
–Janet Freeman, 20th century

A man should be jailed for telling lies to the young.
–Lillian Hellman, 20th century

Human history becomes more and more a race between education and catastrophe.
–H.G. Wells, 1920

High school is closer to the core of the American experience than anything else I can think of.
–Kurt Vonnegut, Jr., 20th century

- FOLLOWING THE PATTERN
- YOUR TURN
- WHAT ABOUT IT?
- ALL'S WELL THAT BEGINS WELL
- THE MIDDLE OF THE ROAD
- LAST BUT NOT LEAST

UNIT 14

WRITING AN ESSAY

Think of the last time you had a difference of opinion with someone. Perhaps you were sure that acid rain affects the health of people, not just trees and plants, but your friend believed this wasn't true. If only you knew the facts and could present them effectively to your friend, you might prove your point.

The ability to argue successfully is a useful skill. Being able to do this on paper means you have essay-writing skills. An essay is an argument that provides facts to support a position.

This unit is about writing an essay. Once you have completed it, you will have an ability that will help you in school, and at any time in your life, when you need to make your point.

FOLLOWING THE PATTERN

If ten people were told to draw a realistic picture of the same tree, each artist would come up with a slightly different result. The general form of the tree would be the same, but the style of each drawing would be unique. Similarly, essays tend to follow the same general pattern, although each author will bring his or her own style to the writing.

As a writer, you begin the essay with an opening paragraph which hooks a reader's interest and states the argument or main idea for the essay. The rest of the essay, or the body, presents the reasons to support the main argument. You set off each reason in a separate paragraph, and expand on these reasons by providing details, examples, or comparisons and contrasts. Then, you create a concluding paragraph to wrap up the essay. In this last paragraph, you usually do three things: repeat the main argument, sum up the reasons to support this argument, and provide a final comment to close the essay. The following article provides an example of an essay.

The following article about police dogs, "Collars and Scents," is an example of an essay.

COLLARS AND SCENTS

Heather Pringle

For years now, man's best friend has been one of the criminal world's worst enemies. With a sense of smell up to one million times more sensitive than that of humans for detecting such odours as butyric acid – an ingredient in human perspiration – dogs have long aided police departments in tracking down and identifying suspects. But the canine knack for crime solving has always been severely hampered by the clock. Most human fragrance disintegrates rapidly, often in a matter of hours.

No two human beings smell quite the same, and with their discriminating snouts, police dogs can easily distinguish one person's odour from another.

But a police-dog expert in the Netherlands has developed an ingenious way around the problem – a technique for collecting and preserving human odour. Employing such simple equipment as cotton cloths and sterilized glass jars, Sergeant Jan de Bruin of the Rotterdam police force has succeeded in banking human smells for up to thirty-six months. Moreover, he believes the technique could work for much longer periods: "The cloths can keep scents for years without changing much."

When arriving at the scene of a crime, de Bruin first wraps all articles carrying traces of the criminal's aroma – such as a forgotten cigarette lighter or an abandoned weapon – in chemically sterilized cotton cloths. Each swathed article is then transferred to a case containing an electric fan. As air circulates inside, skin follicles and scent molecules are deposited on and absorbed by the cotton. Twenty minutes later, de Bruin seals the odoriferous cloth in an airtight jar and carries it back to his laboratory.

Upon arrest, a suspect provides specimens of his personal scent by handling and holding a sterile cloth. No two human beings smell quite the same, and with their discriminating snouts, police dogs can easily distinguish one person's odour from another. "The suspect's scent sample," says de Bruin, "will then be compared with the samples taken from an object at the place of the crime."

To date, nearly sixty criminal scent cloths have been collected in the glass jars in de Bruin's scent bank, just waiting for suspects to be apprehended. Even so, the new $850 000 facility – now a national repository for the Netherlands – has room for 500 more. "I think we will use the method only for the big criminals," concludes de Bruin, "for the robbers, the murderers and the rapists." ▼

ACTIVITY 1
WERE YOU CONVINCED?

1. In your journal, record your reaction to the argument or main idea in the article "Collars and Scents." What do you think the argument is? Do you think it was discussed convincingly?
2. Form small groups to discuss and compare your ideas and feelings about the argument in the article. Note the similarities and the differences in what each group member got out of the article.
3. As a group, form a collaborative response to the question: What is the argument in the article "Collars and Scents"?

The ability to write effectively has become more and more important over the last century. This painting by Joseph Highmore shows a young woman writing in the 1700s.

YOUR TURN

The infobox *Essay Planning* outlines the basic parts of an essay. The real test in essay writing comes when you sit down to create one of your own. In the following activity, you will choose a general topic for an essay. You can use one of the suggested topics or come up with your own topic.

Each of the following sections in this unit will help you with the task of writing an essay. You will explore each of these components of an essay structure: thesis statement, introductory paragraph, middle paragraphs, concluding paragraph. When you put together your responses to the following activities, you will produce the first draft of an essay.

Essay Planning

Introductory Paragraph

1. Introduce your topic or main idea in the first few sentences.
2. Briefly mention the important supporting ideas that you might discuss in the middle paragraphs.
3. Present your thesis statement in the final sentence.

Middle Paragraphs

1. Each of the middle paragraphs begins with a topic sentence. (The ideas in each topic sentence should have been introduced in the introductory paragraph.)
2. Develop each topic sentence by providing facts and reasons to develop or prove your main idea.

Concluding Paragraph

1. Restate your thesis statement.
2. Briefly mention the supporting details that appeared in your introductory paragraph – and which make up the topic sentences in the essay. You will have to find another way of saying the same thing.
3. Provide a closing sentence to wrap up your essay in an interesting way.

ACTIVITY 2
CHOOSING A TOPIC

1. As a class, brainstorm several general topics for essays. Record any ideas that come off the top of your head.
2. Look over the topics brainstormed by the class and the ones listed below. Pick one that interests you and write in your journal why this topic attracted you.
   - Canada is a great country for young musicians.
   - Canadian people have to learn to live together.
   - My province is an interesting place to live.
   - Fashion is a growing industry in Canada.
3. With a partner, take turns talking about the topic that interested you and why. After one partner has finished, discuss between you how this person could approach the topic in an essay. Do the same after the other partner has spoken. Give each other ideas about how each topic could be narrowed to be appropriate for a short essay.

Virginia Woolf (1882-1941) was a famous essayist and author.

WHAT ABOUT IT?

After you have chosen a topic for your essay, you must narrow it into a thesis. When you create a thesis statement, you find the main purpose for your essay. One way of checking if you have a usable one is by asking this question: *What about it?* If you want to write an essay about the topic of school, for example, you need to narrow the subject by asking the question: *What about school?* Your answer might be *School is an important part of my life.* It is important to be able to recognize and to write a good thesis statement. A weak thesis statement is too general. It just doesn't get down to the job of answering the question *What about it?*

A thesis statement that is too general includes so many things that you cannot deal with all of them properly in an essay. For example, the thesis statement *Canadian musicians are very good* never answers the question *What about it?* You would need a book, not an essay, to deal with such a thesis statement. An appropriate thesis statement has a sharp focus. The following infobox provides examples of clear and fuzzy thesis statements.

Writing Thesis Statements

Read these models to get an idea of what is a workable thesis statement.

Incomplete statement: Ottawa is a beautiful city.
Complete statement: Ottawa is an interesting city because of its history.
Incomplete statement: Canadian athletes are very successful.
Complete statement: Because Canadian athletes can be very successful, the Canadian government should provide grants to support them.

ACTIVITY 3
WRITING THESIS STATEMENTS

1. In your notebook, practise writing a thesis statement for four of the general topics in this list:
   - the Canadian music scene
   - the Pacific Ocean
   - Niagara Falls
   - Canadian people
   - the Canadian fur industry
   - Canadian women in sports
2. As a group or whole class, examine your thesis statements. Make certain that each statement presents a topic and focusses it to answer the question *What about it?*
3. Find an essay that you have written for Language Arts or some other subject. Examine this writing to see what kind of job you did in stating a clear thesis statement. With a partner, decide how you could improve upon the thesis statement.
4. Write a thesis statement for the topic you chose for Activity 2, question 2. Examine this topic with a small group to make certain that you have defined it clearly. Then talk about your topic so that your group can help you generate more ideas about how to approach it in an essay.

It is seldom easy to start a piece of writing.

ALL'S WELL THAT BEGINS WELL

Things that begin well usually end well. So far, you have the ingredients for a successful beginning of an essay: a thesis statement that is clearly defined. You need to acquire another trick of the writing trade: the ability to lead your reader gently into the thesis statement. To do this, you need to learn to write a complete introductory paragraph. The following infobox outlines the components of an introductory paragraph.

An Introductory Paragraph

A good introductory paragraph will introduce the reader to the thesis statement in an interesting way. It contains the following components:

- an opening sentence (or sentences) that not only attracts the reader's attention, but also introduces the thesis of the essay
- a brief overview of the supporting arguments in your essay
- your thesis statement

While you are learning to write a short essay, you should include each of these components in your introductory paragraph in the order that they are listed here. You can experiment with the form of your introductory paragraphs as you acquire more skill in writing.

ACTIVITY 4
WRITING AN INTRODUCTORY PARAGRAPH

1. Practise writing interesting first sentences for four of the topics listed in Activity 3, question 1. Your sentences should both alert your readers about the topic and catch their attention.
2. In a small group, talk about your answers to question 1. Use the criteria set out in the above infobox to guide your discussion. Discuss each person's answers to decide what is the best introductory sentence that each person produced. Explain why you feel this way.
3. Write two or three different introductory paragraphs for the thesis that you created for Activity 3, question 4. Examine them with a partner or small group and decide which one is the best one. Save it.

THE MIDDLE OF THE ROAD

After composing an introductory paragraph, essay writers must develop each of the supporting ideas for the thesis statement. Each of these supporting ideas is developed in a separate paragraph. These become the middle paragraphs of an essay. The following infobox outlines the structure that middle paragraphs usually have.

Halfway through the process of writing your essay, you may experience writer's block. Don't let it discourage you. Discussing your problem with friends or brainstorming some ideas will help.

Structure of the Middle Paragraphs

- Each paragraph usually begins with a topic sentence that presents the content of the paragraph.
- The remainder of the paragraph develops the topic sentence by giving facts and proof.
- The content or idea for each topic sentence for these middle paragraphs is mentioned in the introductory paragraph. That is, the first supporting idea mentioned in your introductory paragraph becomes the topic sentence for the first middle paragraph, the second supporting idea becomes the topic sentence for the second middle paragraph, and so on.

ACTIVITY 5
WRITING MIDDLE PARAGRAPHS

1. Brainstorm some supporting ideas for one of the topics listed in Activity 3, question 1. Research or think up factual evidence to prove one of the supporting ideas.
2. Use the factual information that you produced in question 1 to write a middle paragraph.
3. a) Examine the introductory paragraph that you wrote for Activity 4, question 3. Determine what the supporting ideas should be for the thesis presented in this introductory paragraph.
   b) Show your supporting ideas to a partner or small group. Discuss your ideas to accumulate factual information about them.
   c) Using three of your supporting ideas and factual information about them, write the first draft of the three middle paragraphs for your essay.
4. Study an essay that you have written for another class. Note ideas about how you could have improved the way you organized your middle paragraphs.

LAST BUT NOT LEAST

In many ways, the last paragraph of an essay can be a mirror image of the first paragraph. When you write a concluding paragraph, you often begin with a rewording of the thesis statement. Some writers also use the conclusion to briefly remind the reader of the supporting ideas in the essay. Usually, you end with a general concluding comment about the topic.

As you work on your essay, you are improving your ability to argue effectively.

ACTIVITY 6
WRITING A CONCLUDING PARAGRAPH

1. Write a concluding paragraph for one of the topics listed in Activity 3, question 1.
2. In a small group or with the whole class, examine this concluding paragraph. Discuss each other's paragraph to decide how each one could be improved.
3. Look at a piece of writing that you did for another class. Does the concluding paragraph in this piece of writing match the introductory paragraph? Improve upon the concluding paragraph, if necessary.
4. In Activity 4, question 3, you wrote an introductory paragraph for a thesis that you created. Write a concluding paragraph to match this beginning paragraph.

ACTIVITY 7
WRITING YOUR ESSAY

1. Collect all of the writing that you completed in this unit on the topic that you chose in Activity 2, question 2. This writing provides you with the first draft of your essay. Find a partner and read each other's first draft. Discuss how the introductory, middle, or concluding paragraph could be improved. To help you with your revision, refer to the infobox below.

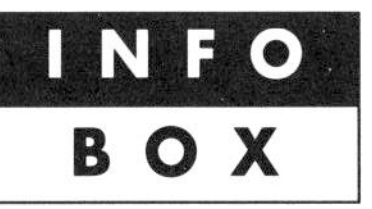

Techniques For Revising

Here are some techniques for revision that many writers use.

- Set the first draft aside for a period of time. When you return to it, you see it with fresh eyes. Of course, this requires, if you are writing to a deadline, that you write the first draft well ahead of the due date.
- Cut and paste. If you write your first draft on only one side of the paper, you will be able to cut and paste the draft. Add, take out, move, and change using scissors and paste or tape.
- When you are marking revisions on the page, use a different coloured pen or pencil to indicate additions, deletions, moves, and changes.
- Use a word processor, if possible. Revision will be easier because chunks of text can be added, deleted, moved, or changed by hitting a few keys. You can alter your first draft many times without making a mess of your pages and without having to recopy anything.

END THOUGHTS

This unit has introduced you to a powerful skill: the ability to make your point in a written essay. The next time you want to make a point when you are writing an essay, keep the following suggestions in mind:

Introduction

- Make your thesis clear.
- Try to hook your reader with an interesting opening statement.

Middle

- Support your thesis with convincing ideas.
- Develop your supporting ideas with plenty of evidence.
- Create paragraphs that flow naturally from one to the next.

Conclusion

- Don't leave the reader hanging – finish it off well by restating your argument, summing up your supporting ideas, and ending with a closing comment.

Now that you have mastered the skills of creating a first draft, you can move on to the next stages in the writing process: revising and editing your draft and, when you've shaped it to your satisfaction, publishing your essay.

- CREATING AN EFFECTIVE SHOT
- LIGHTING AND COLOUR
- EDITING
- SOUND
- STORYBOARD

UNIT 15

LIGHTS, CAMERA, ACTION

The scene opens in a noisy cafeteria. The camera zooms in on a table occupied by only one young man. The camera shifts to a close up of his neon-green high-tops tapping rhythmically on the floor. A medium shot reveals the young man bobbing his head to the music from his Walkman. The camera tracks back as the young man stands and strides towards the exit. A long shot emphasizes the distance between the young man and his schoolmates. The scene dissolves to black.

Not a word has been spoken and yet much has been told. Through the use of film techniques, the director has communicated a story. In this unit, you will read about and work with the techniques of filmmaking.

CREATING AN EFFECTIVE SHOT

When you describe a movie that you have seen, you probably talk about the plot, the characters, the action, and the dialogue. But other aspects of the film are also working to influence your response. Because film is a visual medium, filmmakers try to communicate ideas and feelings through visual clues rather than spoken words. To ensure that the visual messages reflect what they want to get across, filmmakers carefully compose each camera shot.

In this section, you will examine how the filmmaker uses the basic photographic techniques of *composition*, *camera distance*, *camera angle*, as well as the special qualities of *camera movement*, to create a shot that will affect you, the viewer, in a particular way.

Composition

The term *composition* is used to refer to the arrangement of objects, people, and places within a movie frame. By choosing to place some elements in the foreground and some in the background, the director of photography can influence the way you respond. Objects in the foreground will catch your attention and seem to have a greater importance.

The flowers in the foreground catch the viewer's attention more than the guitar in the background.

When the camera shifts its focus from the flowers to the guitar, the guitar gains importance in the picture.

Camera Distance

Camera distance is the distance from the camera to the subject. The choice of camera distance will contribute to the overall impression of the shot. Directors use *close-ups*, *long shots*, or *medium shots* to achieve different effects. Close-ups, for example, show the expression on a movie character's face, allowing the viewer to have a sense of sharing the feeling. A long shot shows the character in a particular setting, probably eliciting a more objective reaction from the viewer. A medium shot may be used to show this person in conversation with another character. Some of the background setting will probably be evident. As well there might be some information about the characters' relationship. For example, one character may be facing the camera while the other is turned away. This could indicate some tension between the characters.

Camera Angles

Camera angle refers to the angle at which the camera is pointed at the subject. The most common camera placements are *high angle*, *eye level*, and *low angle*. High-angle shots place the camera above the subject, making the subject seem small in the surroundings or emphasizing space and distance. For example, a lone character walking across the desert may be shot from a high angle to emphasize the great distance she must cover. In an eye-level shot, the camera is on the same plane as the subject so you see the character as you normally would. Television newscasters, for example, are usually shot at eye level to emphasize their sincerity. In a low-angle shot, the camera is below the subject so the viewer has a sense of looking up. A low-angle shot might be used to suggest that the character is threatening.

Camera Movement

The movement created by the camera as it films a scene also affects your perceptions. The rotation of the camera in an arc motion from side to side is called a *pan shot.* Panning may be used to follow action, to establish the setting, or to allow the viewer to see through the eyes of one of the characters.

The movement of the camera up or down is called a *tilt shot.* Tilting is often used when shooting from a high or low angle. Tilting up from a low angle often indicates that a character is powerful and somewhat threatening.

When the camera starts with a long shot and then focusses into a close-up shot, it is called *zooming*. This movement may be useful to show how a character feels about his or her surroundings or situation. The long shot establishes the setting and then the close up follows to reveal the expression on the character's face.

Sometimes the camera is mounted on some other vehicle so it can move at the same pace as the subject, or move towards or away from the subject. This is called *dollying* or *tracking*. This camera movement might be used to follow a long-distance runner. In this way, the viewer shares the runner's experience.

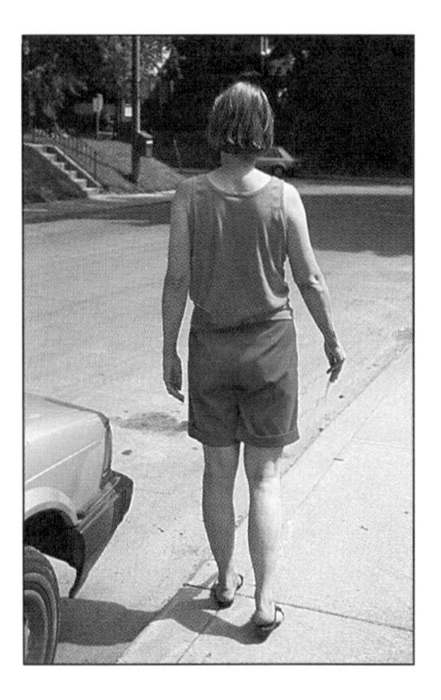
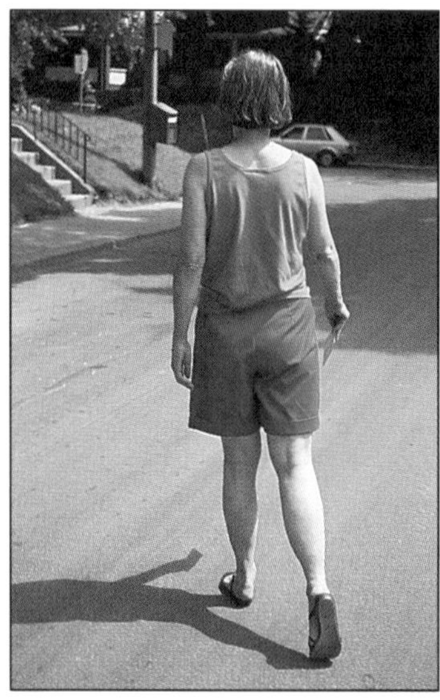

ACTIVITY 1
YOUR VIEWING EXPERIENCES

1. Form groups of four. Assign one of the elements of a camera shot mentioned above, that is, composition, camera angle, camera distance, or camera movement, to each group member.

2. Form a group with other individuals in your class who have been assigned the same subject. Consider the following questions for your subject:

   Composition
   Drawing on your own experiences as viewers, brainstorm a list of different ways that objects and people can be arranged in a photograph, ad, or movie still. Consider colour, shape, size, placement within frame, use of line or suggested progression, and sense of balance or imbalance as you prepare your list. Discuss the different effects created. If possible, collect pictures that illustrate these techniques or try to take your own shots.

   Camera Distance
   Try to remember some examples that you have seen of long, medium, and close-up shots used in ads, movies, television programs, music videos, and photographs. Discuss the different effects created. Try to find pictures that illustrate these techniques or take some with your own camera.

   Camera Angles
   Use your own experiences as viewers to brainstorm a list of different ways that high-angle, low-angle, and eye-level shots are used in ads, movies, television programs, music videos, and photographs. Discuss the different effects created. If possible, collect pictures that show these techniques or make some shots yourself.

   Camera Movements
   Drawing on your own exposure to this technique, brainstorm a list of different ways that the camera moves to follow action in movies, TV programs, music videos, and commercials. Remember the pan, tilt, zoom, and tracking shots. Discuss the different effects created. If possible, gather examples of these techniques.

3. Meet again with your original group. Share the contents of your brainstorm and any examples of the techniques you collected with the other group members. Report on your discussion about the different effects created.

4. As a group, discuss how these elements work together to create an effective shot. What combinations of techniques exist? How do elements work together to convey certain ideas and feelings?

LIGHTING AND COLOUR

Lighting, used effectively, can create a particular mood. A brightly lit scene, such as the sun-filled interior of a room, looks cheery and welcoming. The same room dimly lit with long-cast shadows seems menacing.

A subject may be shot with realistic light, that is, the actual available light. Or the lighting may be manipulated to create a particular effect. Refer to the infobox on page 315 for a detailed description of the *Effects of Different Lighting Sources.*

Colour is an important element in creating a particular mood. Colour can be used realistically, that is, depicted as it appears naturally. Most documentaries and situation comedies use colour realistically. Often movies and music videos utilize colour more expressively. Certain colours may be chosen to elicit a particular response from the viewer. For example, blues, greens, and violets are thought to suggest calm, quiet, and peace to the viewer. A scene of a garden party in which these cool colours are dominant has a very different effect from a scene dominated by warm colours such as reds and oranges.

Each scene creates a different effect because of the colours used.

INFO BOX

Effects of Different Lighting Sources

The lighting of a subject can be more important than the subject itself.

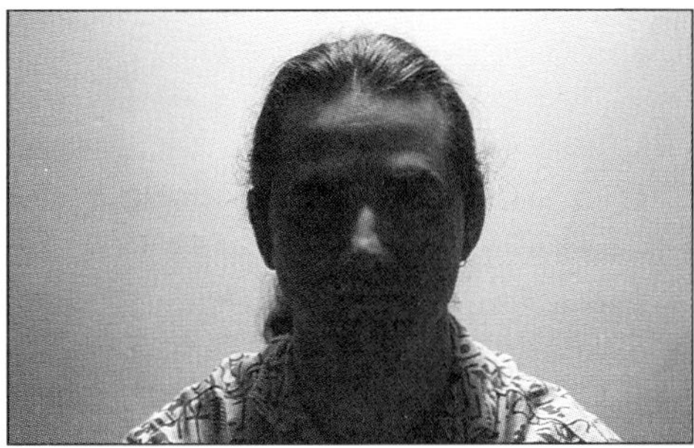

The use of available lighting on a subject suggests directness, honesty, and normalcy.

Lighting above the subject tends to create a halo effect which conveys spirituality.

A face that is only half lit may cast a feeling of ambivalence.

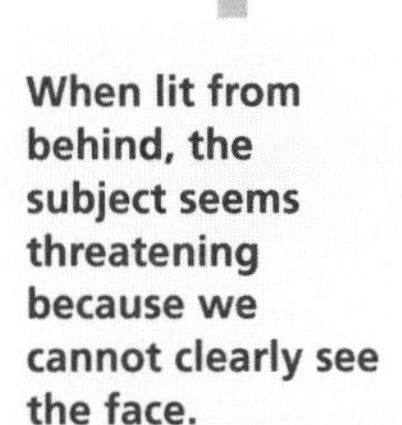

When lit from behind, the subject seems threatening because we cannot clearly see the face.

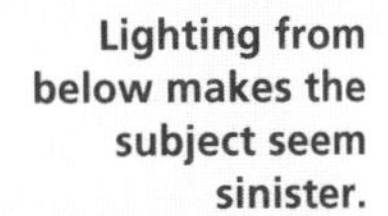

Lighting from below makes the subject seem sinister.

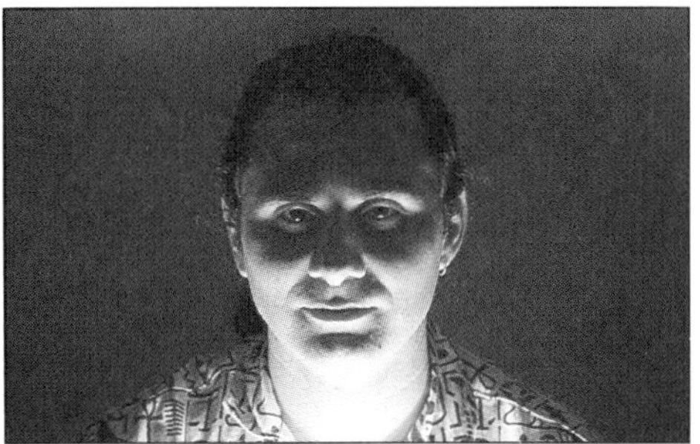

ACTIVITY 2
SETTING THE SCENE

1. Examine the following situations. Choose the lighting and colour for each. Remember that you are trying to create a particular effect.
   a) a child's birthday party
   b) the outside of a high-rise apartment building
   c) a couple sitting in a restaurant
   d) a modest living room
2. Share your choices with a partner. How does he or she respond to your choices of lighting and colour? Have you created the effect you wanted?
3. Some contemporary films are deliberately made in black and white, such as *Young Frankenstein*, *Zelig*, and *Down by Law*. Why do you think directors and producers sometimes choose to make their films in black and white rather than colour?

EDITING

Editing is an important element of filmmaking. Simply put, editing is the selection and arrangement of visual detail. The editor is responsible for viewing all the footage shot. Based on factors such as the final length of the film and the director's intentions, the editor will choose the shots and splice them together to create the final copy.

Editors also use techniques to create a particular effect. For example, an editor might interrupt a scene set in the present with shots of the past to show the viewer the connection between two events. Or the editor might cut from one character to another to show both of their reactions to a certain event.

The following shots might be used to make a commercial about drinking and driving. If you were the editor for this commercial, would you put the shots together as in Commercial A or Commercial B?

Commercial A

1. 

2. 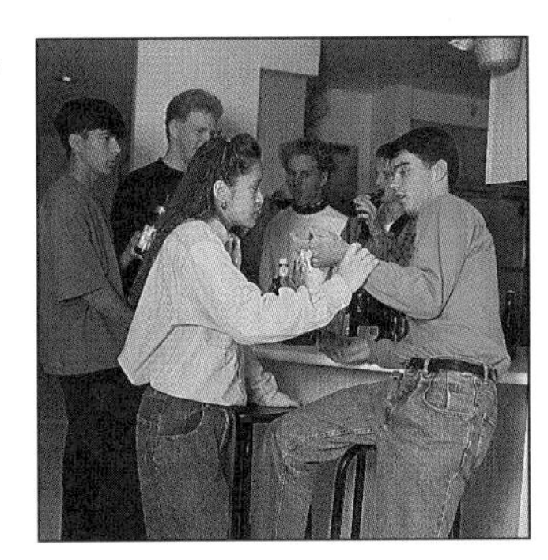

3. 

4. 

5. 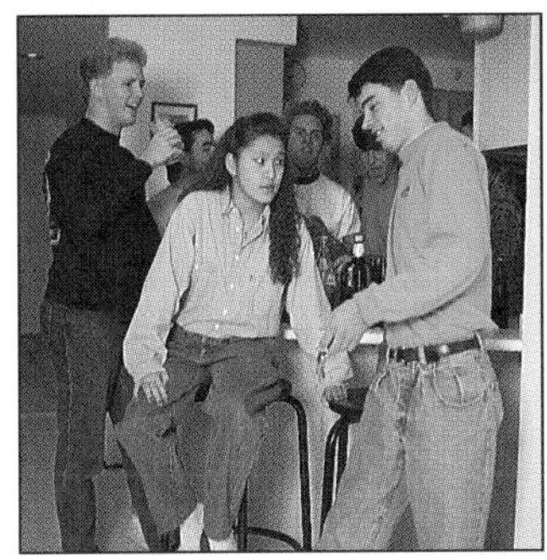

Commercial B

1. 

2. 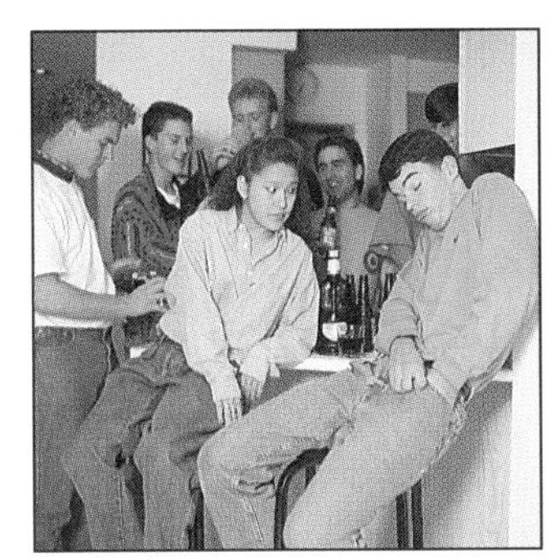

3. 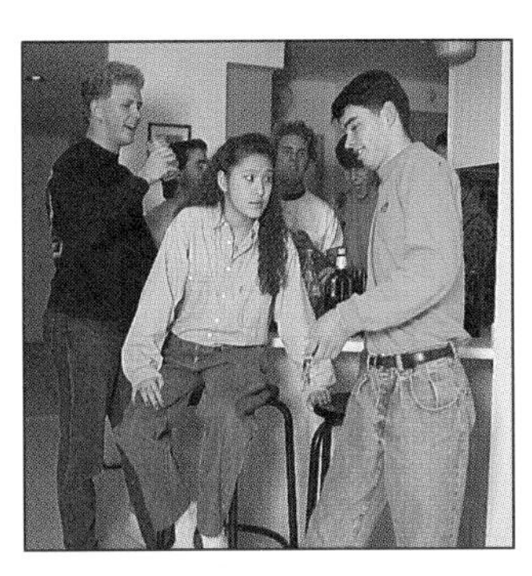

4. 

5. 

If you were to arrange the details as shown in A to create a visual message, your message would be unclear. Details are more clearly and logically sequenced in B and there is no mistaking the message in the commercial.

ACTIVITY 3
EDITING SKILLS

1. Create ten possible shots to communicate a visual message for one of the following (or if you prefer, create your own message):
   a) Smoking is bad for your health.
   b) Eating disorders are dangerous.
   c) Cycle safely.
   d) Protect endangered species.
2. Exchange your shots with a classmate.
3. Edit your partner's sequence. Select and arrange five of the shots your partner created to communicate the message.
4. Explain to your partner why you edited the shots in that particular way. Is your partner pleased with your edit? Why or why not? Do you agree or disagree with your partner?

A movie will sometimes become associated with a song in it. When you look at the still from the movie *Batman*, do you think of Prince's song *Bat Dance*?

SOUND

Sound is another important element of film. Sound effects, music, and dialogue are used to tell something about the action or the character. Suspense scenes often feature high-pitched sounds which make the listener feel tense. Scenes intended to glorify a character often feature uplifting music. Silence, too, can be used effectively to highlight strong emotions. Some films rely heavily on realistic background noise such as the chatter of people or the honking of horns.

ACTIVITY 4
SOUND EFFECTS

1. Create five fictitious titles for television programs or movies.
2. Exchange your list with a classmate.
3. Choose a popular song, past or present, to serve as theme music for each item on your new list. Explain your choices.
4. Share your musical choices with your partner. Explain your reasons for your choices.

STORYBOARD

The storyboard is one of the methods used to plan a film presentation. A storyboard is a series of sketches representing the images that will appear on the screen. A brief written description of the action, the dialogue, the camera work, the composition, and the lighting and colour accompanies each sketch. The storyboard helps filmmakers to visualize a film before they begin shooting.

ACTIVITY 5
CREATING A STORYBOARD

1. Think of the song for which you would like to create your own video or a scene from a short story or novel you would like to film. Choose one for which you have not previously seen a video.
2. Using the sample storyboard on page 320 as a model, create your own storyboard. Remember to consider the mood you want to create and use the film techniques you have learned about in this unit to create the desired mood.
3. If your school has video equipment, you may wish to shoot your music video or film adaptation.

An example of a storyboard. They are usually simple outlines of the scenes – colour is not necessary.

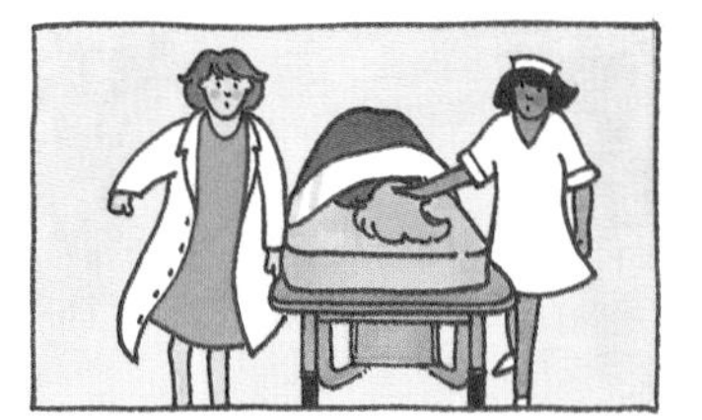

Patient is rushed down hallway.
Dolly, medium, eye-level shot.
Bright lighting.

Doctor: "It doesn't look too serious."
Medium, eye-level shot.
Bright overhead lighting.

Nurse takes blood pressure: "You're looking much better."
Zoom, medium, eye-level shot.
Available lighting from window.

Patient: "Can I go home, doctor?"
Medium, eye-level shot.
Direct lighting.

Doctor: "You can go as soon as I complete these forms."
Close-up, high-angle shot.
Direct lighting.

END THOUGHTS

In this unit, you have learned how film techniques are used to visually communicate ideas and feelings to you, the viewer. Now that you have some insight into these aspects of filmmaking, you may find yourself watching television, movies, and videos in a new way.

UNIT 16

READER RESPONSE

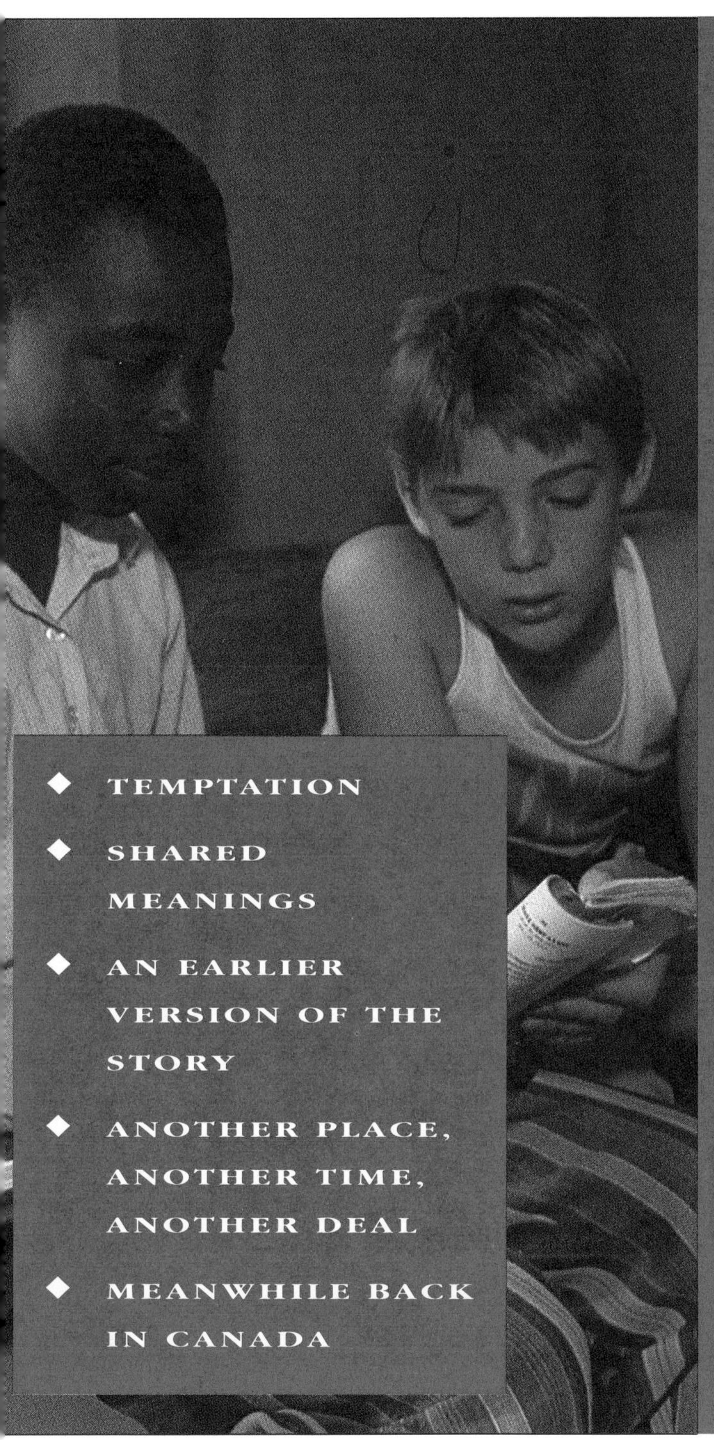

- TEMPTATION
- SHARED MEANINGS
- AN EARLIER VERSION OF THE STORY
- ANOTHER PLACE, ANOTHER TIME, ANOTHER DEAL
- MEANWHILE BACK IN CANADA

Once there was a teacher who wanted to show her students that people interpret things in different ways. One day, a man rushed into the class, ran to her desk, snatched her purse, and ran out again. At first the students were shocked. When the students calmed down, the teacher told them to write out a description of the thief. Then the teacher asked the students to compare what they had written down. There was little agreement. The teacher's next question was: "If we can't agree on something we all saw together, how can we expect to get the same meaning out of something we read? What factors influence the ways in which we interpret what we read?"

In this unit, you will explore these questions. It begins with your personal responses to a story and invites you to compare your reactions with those of other readers.

TEMPTATION

Have you ever been tempted? Have you ever wanted something very badly – money, trips, good looks, intelligence, fame, security? Have you ever said to yourself, "If only I could have..., I would...."? What words did you use to fill in the blanks?

There are age-old stories of people who have wished for their fondest dreams only to find that there is a price to pay for the privilege of having their dreams come true. The story in this unit takes this traditional formula and gives it a modern twist. Before you read it to find out how the young woman in the story meets and handles temptation, take a few minutes to think about your own dreams and wishes by completing the following activity.

ACTIVITY 1
WISH LIST

1. Complete each of the following sentences:
   a) If I could have anything in the world, I would wish for...
   b) If I could be anyone I wanted to be, I would be...
   c) If I could go anywhere I wanted to, I would go to...
   d) If I could do anything I wanted to, I would...
   e) If I could change anything I wanted to, I would change...
2. Use your answers to question 1 to make your personal wish list. Arrange the items in your list from most to least important.
3. What personal price would you be willing to pay to obtain the items on your list?
4. Get together in groups of four or five and compare your lists. Which items are similar? Which are different? How do you explain the similarities and the differences? What price were the various members of your group willing to pay in order to get these things?

SHEENA'S CONTRACT

Randy Howard

Sheena Macumrie was nearly sixteen before she was visited by serious temptation. She reported this immediately to her mother, who was modern in her parenting practices and deeply engaged at the time in an important career skirmish.

> He had long, wild, black hair, a young revolutionary beard, and was garbed in achingly beautiful son-of-motorcycle-jacket leathers.

"Sheena," she answered, when the temptation was brought up, "your character was well-formed by the time you were six. You're not asking now what's the difference between right and wrong, surely?"

"I guess not. But I thought you could, you know, talk it over with me a bit. Tell me how you felt about that sort of thing. What you'd do."

"Your life, baby. Don't be afraid to take charge of it, okay?"

"Okay," replied her daughter, with less than total enthusiasm, "if you say so."

With this counsel in mind she met the temptor the following day, after school. He had long, wild, black hair, a young revolutionary beard, and was garbed in achingly beautiful son-of-motorcycle-jacket leathers. His whole person was deliciously, perfectly unstudied. He could have been nineteen, even twenty.

"Hi, kid, you thought it over?"

"Hi, Bobby, sort of." He had Cokes before them as if by magic. "Thanks. Um, tell me the deal again, will you? I mean, it's kind of weird, isn't it?"

"Naw, it's been going on forever."

"Really?"

"Sure. The last generation did it all the time. They just don't talk about it to their children. It's like sex or getting high – too good for kids. They aren't mature enough to handle it, y'know?"

"I guess so. Anyway, tell me again what I have to do and what I'd be getting."

"You don't have to do a thing, kid, just enjoy your life. Except you'll have this incredible edge."

"The last generation did it all the time. They just don't talk about it to their children. It's like sex or getting high – too good for kids."

"I get a wish."

"Right."

"Anything I want."

"Anything. Except, you know, dumb things like living forever or more wishes. No cute stuff – it's gotta be a straight wish. But anything that's possible in the real world, you got it."

"Like being rich or famous or beautiful."

"You know it. No limit."

"And all I have to do is sign over my soul."

"Right, but only when you're all done with it. It's yours completely till after you're dead."

"Sure, but of old age? How do I know I won't have an accident twenty minutes after I sign?"

"Hey, we look after our own, kid. It's all in the contract. No funny business on either side. This is a very straight deal, with a very heavy organization. You think they'd risk word getting around that they cheated on a contract? No way. They'd be out of business in six months."

"I don't think I'm old enough to sign a contract, am I? Is it legal?"

"Hey, come on, that's prehistoric. As long as you know what you're doing, it's cool. It's your soul, nobody else's."

"That's what my mother says."

"Smart lady. Is she a client of ours, do you know?"

"I don't think so. She never mentioned it."

"Most people keep it pretty quiet."

"Bobby, my wish – I'd only get one, right?"

"Yeah, but it's a whopper."

"Well I'd be awfully afraid of using it by accident, I think. Like wishing my brother would shut up or something, without really meaning that to be *the wish*. Do you know what I mean?"

"Oh sure, that's all looked after. You got your own private personal code number. And when you want to use your wish, you have to write it down on a piece of paper and then burn the paper. And even then there's a safety. You'll get a registered letter with the wish typed out properly. You check it over and if it's exactly what you ordered, you sign it and burn it. That makes sure there's no slip-ups. Hey, they want you to get exactly what you asked for, kid. The whole thing. A fair deal's a good deal. That's how they stay in business."

"There's no time limit or anything?"

"Nope. As soon as you sign your number goes on file. It stays there until you decide to activate it. Any time for the rest of your life."

"You'll get a registered letter with the wish typed out properly. You check it over and if it's exactly what you ordered then you sign it and burn it."

"True?"

"Absolutely. So whad'ya say, we got a deal?"

"It sounds okay."

"Great." He had paper out from an inner pocket without seeming to unzip. "Here's the contract. You sign at the bottom there."

Sheena took the paper and turned it over. "That's not very big for a contract."

"Short form. The full one's got all the detail, but it's a sucker to wade through. You know, all legal language."

"Well, I'd like to read it before I sign it. My mom's a lawyer, so I know about fine print. I think I should read it first."

Bobby sighed and unzipped this time to reach into a deeper recess. "Whatever you say. This is the long form. All eighteen pages." He offered the bulky document to her, then put it on the table between them when she didn't take it. "What now?"

"Shouldn't you sign it first? I mean it's an offer to purchase, isn't it? So when I accept and sign, it's all done. Isn't that how it works?"

He flipped through the papers and signed in a couple of places. "There y'are. Happy now?"

She accepted the contract at this and turned pages for a couple of minutes. Bobby kept silent until she looked up.

"Well?"

"This blank space is where my number goes?"

"That's right."

"But it's blank."

"You haven't got a number yet."

"Isn't the deal that I give you my soul and you give me a

number for a wish?"

"That's it."

"So where's my number?"

He looked at her with a blank expression, opened his mouth to speak, closed it and scratched his ear. "Hang on and I'll check, okay? Have another Coke. I gotta make a phone call."

The Coke appeared, and he picked up the contract and walked with it over to the pay telephone by the entrance. She sipped and watched and tried to overhear the conversation. Bobby seemed quite agitated, waving his free hand and finally slamming the receiver into its cradle. He dug for another coin and dialed again. This time the conversation was very sedate. Bobby's body-English was almost...reverent. He wrote something, then hung up and returned.

He had paper out from an inner pocket without seeming to unzip. "Here's the contract. You sign at the bottom there."

"Whoo," he said as he sat, "any little thing outside of normal routine and they go nuts. Anyhow, I got your number, kid. So we're all set, right?"

"I still have to read it through."

"Oh yeah, right. Ah, when do you think you'll be done?"

"Are you in a hurry or something?"

In *The Witches of Eastwick*, three women succumb to the charms of the devil with dire consequences.

"No, no, it's cool. You take all the time you need. I'm here every day. Just drop it off when you've signed."

She smiled, folded the contract and tucked it into her tote bag, thanked him for the Cokes and left.

Two weeks later Bobby fell in beside her as she was walking to school.

"Oh, hi, Bobby. Where'd you come from?"

"Hi, Sheen. I was just in the neighborhood and saw you. How's it going with the contract? You done yet?"

"I got a call about your contract this morning. They're wondering what's happening, you know?"

"I got started, but you were right about the legal jargon. It's really hard to follow."

"Well, stick with it, kid. You know where I am. Soon as you've signed, just drop it off."

"I sure will."

"See you."

"Bye."

Almost a month after this encounter Sheena had a telephone call from the young man.

"Hi, it's Bobby. Ah, about the contract. You signed it yet?"

"You're awfully snappish today."

"Sorry, kid, things on my mind. I got a call about your contract this morning. They're wondering what's happening, you know?"

"You tell them I'll sign their contract when I'm ready to. Anyway, what's the panic over one little soul? I thought you said it was a great big organization."

"Oh sure, they're big. But they've got their way of doing things and they're on me about you, that's all."

"Well I'm the customer, so they can just wait until I'm satisfied."

"The thing is, Sheen, they've got staff tied up looking after you. You know, making sure you don't get run down sort of thing."

"Until I sign, then I'm on my own?"

"No, no, you get full protection for the rest of your natural life once you've signed. But in the meantime the rules are, you get double security so that you don't, you know, die before you sign."

"That's great."

"Well, they're not very happy about the delay. So, how about it?"

"They can be as unhappy as they like. I'm not signing anything that I'm not sure what it is."

"That's it?"

"You're darned right that's it. I'm just not going to be pushed and you can tell them that for me."

"Okay kid, I'll get back to you. *Ciao.*"

After school next day he was waiting for her. "You got a few minutes? We gotta talk."

"...You get full protection for the rest of your natural life once you've signed. But in the meantime the rules are, you get double security so that you don't, you know, die before you sign."

"I'm due home, but you can walk me."

"Okay. Bad news, kid. I gotta pick up the contract. They're cancelling."

She stopped cold and looked at him. "Just because I'm taking my time? That's not fair."

"I just work there, kid. Get me the contract and we'll call it quits, okay?"

They walked in silence the three blocks to Sheena's apartment building. In the foyer she stopped again. "No."

"What?"

"No, I won't give you back the contract."

"You gotta."

"No, I don't. I don't have to do anything of the sort. It's a signed offer to purchase and there's no date on it. You can't just change your mind and say, oh no, we take back the offer. No sir, I'm keeping it."

Her voice was quite loud by now, and a couple of men waiting at the elevator gave Bobby rather hard looks. He forced a smile at her and spoke soothingly. "This isn't the place to talk. Will you come to the coffee shop tomorrow afternoon? Please?" She agreed and he departed at speed.

Next day Bobby was at his usual table in the coffee shop, but not alone. His companion was an older man in a business suit. The first impression was fatherly but stern. Bobby introduced them as she sat. This was his boss, the Area Supervisor.

"I understand there's some problem with your contract, Miss Macumrie."

"No sir, no problem. I'm just not giving it back."

"Well, sign it then and let us get our books straight."

"When I've decided to."

"Young lady, do you know what kind of problems you're causing?"

"Bobby said you had to give me extra protection until I signed."

"Did he tell you that our big computer's all jammed up because a number's been issued that hasn't been recorded in the main files? *Your* number, miss."

"Not my fault if you can't look after running your own business. I'm just a customer."

The Area Supervisor got very red, but didn't change expression. He glared at her until his color came down somewhat, then spoke carefully.

The Area Supervisor got very red, but didn't change expression. He glared at her until his color came down somewhat, then spoke carefully.

"Let's be sensible, shall we? You've got no use for the contract if you're not going to sign it. So why don't we give you a little something for your time and call it even. How does that sound? Say, oh, $100?"

Sheena simply looked at him.

"Just to get this mess cleared up, I'm willing to be ridiculous and give you $1000 for that stupid contract."

She kept her silence.

"Well, what do you want then?"

"I sort of like being protected like this."

He sighed and nodded. "I guess we can do that."

"Double protection."

"All right."

"For the rest of my natural life."

His color was rising again. "Agreed."

"You know," she said, "I really wanted that wish. Could you throw that in too?"

He blinked, speechless, and she added in a thoughtful tone: "In writing, of course." ▼

Pol Turgeon created this illustration for the 1990 National Book Festival. Every person experiences a book in a unique way.

Eugene Delacroix's illustration depicts a man making a contract with the devil.

To illustrate the variety of ways in which students get meaning from a piece of literature, try the following activities in response to "Sheena's Contract."

ACTIVITY 2 PERSONAL REACTIONS

1. Complete each of the following sentences in your notebook:
   a) When I read the part of the story about ______________ I saw ______________ in my imagination.
   b) The story made me feel ______________. What made me feel this way was ______________.
   c) The story reminded me of ______________.
   d) A memory that occurred to me when I was reading the story was ______________.
   e) The part I liked best was ______________.
   f) The part I liked least was ______________.
   g) I thought the young woman in the story was ______________. I felt this because ______________.
2. Pretend that you are making a television program out of this story. Choose actors from current TV shows to play the people in the story. Who would you cast in the role of Sheena, the mother, Bobby, the Area Supervisor?
   a) What qualities do these actors have that you think suit them to the roles?
   b) Describe the set that you would use to shoot the program.
   c) What music would you use? At what points in the story would you use the music you have selected? Why?
3. Write your reactions to each of the following quotes from the story:
   a) "She reported this immediately to her mother, who was modern in her parenting practices and deeply engaged at the time in an important career skirmish."
   b) "Sure. The last generation did it all the time. They just don't talk about it to their children. It's like sex or getting high – too good for kids."
   c) "This is a very straight deal, with a very heavy organization. You think they'd risk word getting around that they cheated on a contract?"
   d) "Not my fault if you can't look after running your business. I'm just a customer."
   e) "I sort of like being protected like this."

SHARED MEANINGS

According to legend, there once were five blind people. Although they couldn't see, they were able to use their other senses to make meaning of the world around them. Often, they would travel together so that they could help each other along the way.

One day, as they were walking through a forest, an unknown object blocked their path. One at a time they tried to figure out what was blocking the way. The first one reached out and touched some wide floppy things and said, "It's a fan." The second one touched some thick wide things and announced that it must be pillars that were in front of them. The third touched the long stiff stick that ended in a tuft of fur and was convinced that it had to be a broom. The fourth one felt a hard, smooth object that tapered to a sharp point and declared that whatever it was, it carried a spear. The fifth one touched a long slithery thing and shouted, "It's a snake!"

Now they were really confused – a fan, pillars, a broom, a spear, and a snake. What could this thing be? Their problem, of course, was that each of them had glimpsed a part of the truth; each of them had one piece to the puzzle, but none of them had the complete picture.

Finally one of them had an idea.

"What fools we have been. Each of us has touched a different part of the thing. What we need to do is to put together all the pieces of information and then we will know what we are dealing with."

And this is exactly what they did. They asked themselves: what has ears like a fan, legs like pillars, a tail like a broom, tusks like a spear, and a trunk like a snake? And of course the answer was obvious – an elephant. Once they knew what they were dealing with, they were able to go up to the animal, grab its trunk, and lead it off to the side of the path so they could continue on their way.

When students read a story or poem, they are like these five blind people. If they read the story alone, they get one meaning – an interpretation that may be perfectly valid and appropriate, given who they are and the experiences that they have had. But how much more rich and varied their responses are when they share their perceptions with others.

Each person forms a unique interpretation of a story or poem.

ACTIVITY 3 OTHER EYES

To show how meanings can grow and develop as you share your responses with others, try the following activities in small groups:

1. a) Have each member of the group tell the others what he or she wrote down in Activity 2. As each member of the group reports, record the various responses on large chart paper. Place the title of the story in the middle of the sheet. From the centre of the paper, draw some lines that go out to headings such as feelings, memories, thoughts, likes, or dislikes. Under each heading, write down what each member of the group reports.
   b) Once you have all the personal reactions on the chart paper, have each member of the group state what caused his or her reaction. Try to be very specific about what incident, character, or sentence triggered the reactions.
   c) When each of the members of the group has had a chance to report, discuss the possible reasons for the differences. What in the background and experiences of the group members do you think caused these individual reactions? On another sheet of chart paper, make a list of some of these reasons.

2. a) Put the summary charts on the wall around the room. Have one member of the group summarize the group's responses for the rest of the class.
   b) When each of the groups has finished, compare the group summaries. Are there any patterns to the responses?

3. a) Individually, write down what you think the author is trying to say to the reader through the events, characters, and ideas presented in the story "Sheena's Contract."
   b) Form groups and take another sheet of chart paper. Make three headings: certain meanings, possible meanings, impossible meanings. As members of the group report, place their suggestions under each of the categories. Be sure to use evidence from the story to justify the category in which you place the various interpretations.

AN EARLIER VERSION OF THE STORY

There is a legend, over five hundred years old, about a brilliant but eccentric German scholar. The man was known as Dr. Johannes Faust or Faustus. Faust had devoted his entire life to acquiring knowledge about the world around him. He had studied the ancient arts of alchemy, astrology, and magic. Although he had learned a great deal, he was still dissatisfied. There was so much more to learn and experience and so little time in which to do it all.

One day a stranger made him a tempting offer. Faust could have anything he wanted – knowledge about the secrets of the universe, exotic pleasures, power over others – for a price. That price was his immortal soul. The stranger was, of course, the devil. According to legend, Faust was so hungry for ultimate knowledge that he willingly agreed. For a time, he had everything that he desired, but in the end the devil came to claim his due.

The British writer Christopher Marlowe, who lived about the same time as Shakespeare, used this German legend as the basis for his play *The Tragical History of Dr. Faustus.* On the next page is the speech Faust makes as the devil – or Lucifer – comes to claim his prize.

THE TRAGICAL HISTORY OF DR. FAUSTUS

Christopher Marlowe

(The clock strikes the half-hour.)
Ah, half the hour is past! 'twill all be past anon.
O God,
If thou wilt not have mercy on my soul,
Yet for Christ's sake, whose blood hath ransom'd me,
Impose some end to my incessant pain;
Let Faustus live in hell a thousand years,
A hundred thousand, and at last be sav'd!
O, no end is limited to damned souls!
Why wert thou not a creature wanting soul?
Or why is this immortal that thou hast?
Ah, Pythagoras' metempsychosis, were that true,
This soul should fly from me, and I be chang'd
Unto some brutish beast! all beasts are happy,
For, when they die,
Their souls are soon dissolv'd in elements;
But mine must live still to be plagu'd in hell.
Curs'd be the parents that engender'd me!
No, Faustus, curse thyself, curse Lucifer
That hath depriv'd thee of the joys of heaven.
(The clock strikes twelve.)
O, it strikes, it strikes! Now, body, turn to air,
Or Lucifer will bear thee quick to hell!
(Thunder and lightning.)
O soul, be chang'd into little water-drops,
And fall into the ocean, ne'er be found!
Enter Devils.
My God, my God, look not so fierce on me!
Adders and serpents, let me breathe a while!
Ugly hell, gape not! come not, Lucifer!
I'll burn my books! – Ah, Mephistophilis!
(Exeunt Devils with Faustus.)
Enter Chorus.

Chorus Cut is the branch that might have grown full straight,
And burned is Apollo's laurel-bough,
That sometime grew within this learned man.
Faustus is gone: regard his hellish fall,
Whose fiendful fortune may exhort the wise,
Only to wonder at unlawful things,
Whose deepness doth entice such forward wits
To practise more than heavenly power permits.
(Exit.)

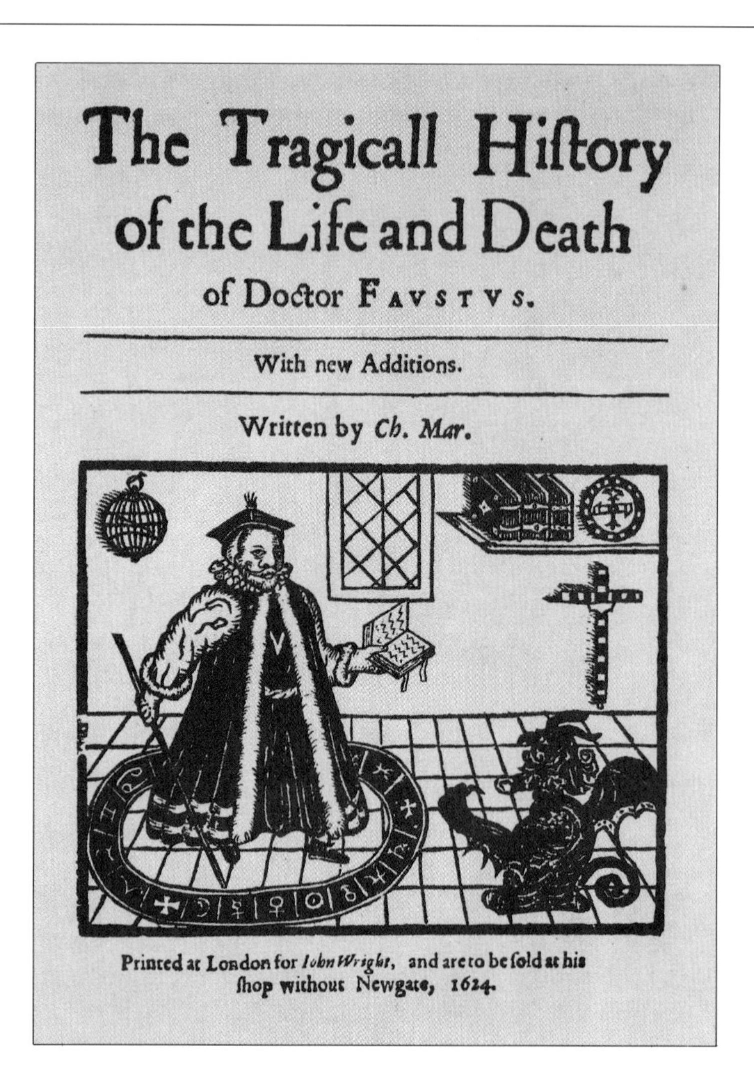
The Tragicall Hiſtory of the Life and Death of Doctor FAVSTVS.

With new Additions.

Written by *Ch. Mar.*

Printed at London for *Iohn Wright*, and are to be ſold at his ſhop without Newgate, 1624.

This illustration was created in 1624 as the title page for Marlowe's play *The Tragical History of Dr. Faustus.*

ACTIVITY 4
THE PRICE YOU PAY

1. What is Faustus' greatest fear as he faces the consequences of his deal with the devil? Why would he fear this?
2. What is the moral of the story, according to the chorus whose words provide the conclusion to the play?
3. Based on your reading of the excerpt from Marlowe's play, imagine what happened in Faustus' life before the devils took him away. How did the devil approach Faustus with his offer? Try to picture where Faustus was when the devil appeared and what the stranger looked like. Or, think about what Faustus did with the knowledge that was given to him by the devil. Was he wracked with guilt or did he revel in his new knowledge? Write a journal entry to record your thoughts or create a scene of a play using Marlowe's style.
4. Do Faustus' concerns and the moral presented by the chorus still have meaning for us today? In what ways would a modern audience see the problem in a different way? In what ways would the reactions be similar?

ANOTHER PLACE, ANOTHER TIME, ANOTHER DEAL

Over the centuries the legend of Dr. Faustus has been told and retold in many different forms. Although the main ingredients of the story remain the same, there are significant changes that occur as the story is told for a new audience in a new age.

A famous American version was written by Stephen Vincent Benet in a short story called "The Devil and Daniel Webster." The part of the story excerpted on page 339 tells how the deal is struck between the devil and Jabez Stone, a nineteenth-century farmer. As you read, think about how this version compares with the ones you have read so far.

The German scholar Goethe wrote a long poem called *Faust*, another famous version of the Faust legend, between 1770-1832. Reproduced here is an illustration from his work.

THE DEVIL AND DANIEL WEBSTER

Stephen Vincent Benet

There was a man named Jabez Stone, lived at Cross Corners, New Hampshire. He wasn't a bad man to start with, but he was an unlucky man. If he planted corn, he got borers; if he planted potatoes, he got blight. He had good-enough land, but it didn't prosper him; he had a decent wife and children, but the more children he had, the less there was to feed them. If stones cropped up in his neighbor's field, boulders boiled up in his; if he had a horse with the spavins, he'd trade it for one with the staggers and give something extra. There's some folks bound to be like that, apparently. But one day Jabez Stone got sick of the whole business.

"I vow," he said, and he looked around him kind of desperate, "I vow it's enough to make a man want to sell his soul to the devil! And I would, too, for two cents!"

He'd been plowing that morning and he'd just broke the plowshare on a rock that he could have sworn hadn't been there yesterday. And, as he stood looking at the plowshare, the off horse began to cough – that ropy kind of cough that means sickness and horse doctors. There were two children down with the measles, his wife was ailing, and he had a whitlow on his thumb. It was about the last straw for Jabez Stone. "I vow," he said, and he looked around him kind of desperate, "I vow it's enough to make a man want to sell his soul to the devil! And I would, too, for two cents!"

Then he felt a kind of queerness come over him at having said what he'd said; though, naturally, being a New Hampshireman, he wouldn't take it back. But, all the same, when it got to be evening and, as far as he could see, no notice had been taken, he felt relieved in his mind, for he was a religious man. But notice is always taken, sooner or later, just like the Good Book says. And, sure enough, next day, about suppertime, a soft-spoken, dark-dressed stranger drove up in a handsome buggy and asked for Jabez Stone.

Well, Jabez told his family it was a lawyer, come to see him about a legacy. But he knew who it was. He didn't like the looks of the stranger, nor the way he smiled with his teeth. They were white teeth, and plentiful – some say they were filed to a point, but I wouldn't vouch for that. And he didn't like it when the dog took one look at the stranger and ran away howling, with his tail between his legs. But having passed the word, more or less, he stuck to it, and they went out behind the barn and made their bargain. Jabez Stone had to prick his finger to sign, and the stranger lent him a silver pin. The wound healed clean, but it left a little white scar.

He didn't like the looks of the stranger, nor the way he smiled with his teeth. They were white teeth, and plentiful – some say they were filed to a point...

After that, all of a sudden, things began to pick up and prosper for Jabez Stone. His cows got fat and his horses sleek, his crops were the envy of the neighborhood, and lightning might strike all over the valley, but it wouldn't strike his barn. Pretty soon he was one of the prosperous people of the county; they asked him to stand for selectman, and he stood for it; there began to be talk of running him for state senate. All in all, you might say the Stone family was as happy and contented as cats in a dairy. And so they were, except for Jabez Stone.

He'd been contented enough for the first few years. It's a great thing when bad luck turns; it drives most other things out of your head. True, every now and then, especially in rainy weather, the little white scar on his finger would give him a twinge. And once a year, punctual as clockwork, the stranger with the handsome buggy would come driving by. But the sixth year the stranger lighted, and, after that, his peace was over for Jabez Stone. ▼

ACTIVITY 5
JABEZ AND THE DEVIL

1. What leads Jabez to make the deal with the devil? What does he get in return for his soul? Do you think the price is worth it? Why or why not?
2. a) In what ways are Jabez's reasons similar to or different from those of Dr. Faustus?
   b) How do you account for these differences and similarities?
3. The part you have read is just the beginning of the story. How do you think it ends? Write the ending of the story. You may use the ending of the Faust story you examined earlier or develop your own ending.
4. This famous story is often included in literature anthologies. For example, you can find it in *The Best Stories of the Modern Age*, edited by Douglas Angus (New York: Fawcett Work Library, 1969). Read the entire story. How did the ending you created in question 3 compare with the original?

All That Money Can Buy **is a movie based on the story "The Devil and Daniel Webster."**

MEANWHILE BACK IN CANADA

The story that you read at the beginning of this unit is a recent Canadian version of the Faust legend. Randy Howard, the author of "Sheena's Contract," was born in Victoria, British Columbia, and was educated in Toronto. Sheena, the main character in his version of this ancient legend, is a contemporary, street-wise young woman. The story takes place in a modern setting. What she wants out of the deal differs from the wishes of Faust and Jabez Stone. The biggest change is probably the way this modern character handles the devil. The following activity lets you compare "Sheena's Contract" to the traditional Faust legend.

ACTIVITY 6
SHEENA'S VERSION

1. Show that "Sheena's Contract" is a modern version of the Faust legend by considering the following:
   a) what the devil offers her
   b) what tempts Sheena
   c) Sheena's attitude to Bobby
   d) the attitude of Sheena's mother towards temptation
   e) what makes Bobby a modern devil
   f) how Sheena handles Bobby and the Area Supervisor
   g) the language used by the characters
   h) the end of the story

END THOUGHTS

A story that gets passed from one generation to the next often appeals to some universal qualities in human beings. Considering the versions of the Faust legend that you read in this unit, what do you think are the characteristics that make this story, in its various versions, survive for such a long time? What does it say about human beings – their hopes, their dreams, and their temptations?

UNIT 17

EXAMINATIONS

At the end of a course – or in order to gain entrance to a program of study – you might face an examination. Examinations allow you to summarize your knowledge of a particular subject, and to demonstrate that knowledge to others. In this unit, you will apply your organizing, thinking, and memory skills to the techniques that will help you prepare for an examination. These strategies include how to organize your notes, how to schedule your review time, how to review, and how to approach the examination itself.

- ORGANIZING YOUR NOTES
- SCHEDULING YOUR REVIEW
- EFFECTIVE REVIEWING
- APPROACHING THE EXAMINATION

ORGANIZING YOUR NOTES

Your notes are a crucial tool for preparing for an examination. They contain a great deal of information that you recorded because you felt it was important. Organizing that information so you can easily use it is an important stage in the review process. Try the following activity to learn how to organize your notes.

Exams give you the opportunity to demonstrate your knowledge to others.

Like a computer, your notes can act as your personal information system.

ACTIVITY 1
NOTEWORTHY

1. Make sure your notes are in order from the beginning of the course to the end. (If you have dated them, this will be easy.) To do this, try using your course outline or a partner's notes. What material are you missing? Use your partner's notes to fill in the gaps.
2. In the appropriate places, insert your essays, assignments, reports, and any other material related to the course (for example, teacher hand-outs). Tests can be a particularly useful guide; they indicate what information your teacher considers important. Place them with the material they belong with and check that all of the test questions have been answered correctly. Again, you might also use a partner's notes as a guide.
3. Once you have organized your notes, use dividers or paper clips to place the material into sections that can be studied in half-hour periods. Then count the sections and number each one. This will help you schedule your review.

SCHEDULING YOUR REVIEW

Scheduling your review time allows you to choose the best time to study. Planning also gives you an overview of *what* you need to accomplish and of *how* you will accomplish it. This overview will mean that you don't have to spend time in indecision and uncertainty about what to do next.

There are a number of methods for scheduling your time. It is important to choose one that is appropriate to your needs, and to stick with it. The following infobox provides you with some general hints for scheduling your review time.

Don't let the time pressure distract you from the task at hand. Creating a schedule will help prevent you from being haunted by time. Salvador Dali, *The Persistence of Memory*, 1931, oil on canvas (24.1 x 33 cm). Collection, The Museum of Modern Art, New York.

INFO BOX

Scheduling Your Review Time

- Consider when the best time for you to study is. Are you a morning person? If so, you might want to study in the morning before school. If you're a night person you might choose to study after dinner or work. Do you need peace and quiet? Then choose a study time when no one is around.
- Set a specific goal for each study session. For example, you might decide that you will review a unit of your course each session.
- Be realistic about what you can accomplish. For example, perhaps one particular course unit is lengthy or difficult. Review it in two study sessions instead of in one.
- Choose a specific time (for example, thirty to forty minutes) for concentrated review. When you finish your review time, reward yourself with a walk, a snack, or a few minutes on the telephone. Think of breaks as a necessary part of the studying process. In fact, some people need to drink, eat, or move regularly while studying.
- Try to vary what you study. For example, try to schedule different types of subjects after one another. Review your most difficult subjects during the time you work best. Try to spend more time on the difficult topics and less time on the easy material.
- Schedule time just to review the material you have studied in the past week.

ACTIVITY 2
YOUR REVIEW SCHEDULE

1. Start your schedule at least two weeks ahead of your first examination. Use a monthly calendar. On it, mark the date of your examination.
2. Create your review schedule for each day or night of the two weeks before your examination. You might choose to include some time on weekends, as well.
3. If you have divided your notes into sections, as suggested in Activity 1, schedule your study time for each section. Remember to schedule time to review a week's worth of study sessions.

4. As you schedule your review time, consider other important aspects of studying such as the place in which you study and the equipment you will need. Examine the following chart for suggestions. Then make a list of your equipment and place needs. Compare your list with a partner's.

Place	Equipment
• library	• desk
• kitchen	• textbooks
• bus	• notes
• bedroom	• dictionary
• somewhere with:	• extra pens, pencils, highlighters
– quiet	• study schedule
– proper lighting	

Cramming only places information in your short-term memory.

Roger crams for his microbiology midterm.

EFFECTIVE REVIEWING

There is no single best way to study. Everyone needs to have his or her own place, time, and system for studying. In fact, one of the most important conditions for effective studying is personal determination, which is a cross between wanting to do well and having the self-discipline to carry it out. Studying for examinations is only one aspect of this process.

When you review, examine the raw material or information in your notes and isolate the main points. Then organize supporting information around the major areas. Doing this will help you to grasp the relationship between different ideas or facts. This will, in turn, help you remember the information more easily when you need to express it during your examination.

There are several methods you can use to sort and remember key information. For example, try using a study sheet for which you select essential information and record it on a piece of note paper. Seeing your course "in miniature" will help you to focus on the essential points and to see how they are related. Making review cards is another useful method for summarizing information.

Techniques for remembering can include repeated reading of information; making lists of items to remember; creating an acronym to remember words in a series; and visualizing a situation that will remind you of the information. Repeated review of the same material will help you place the information in your long-term memory.

The following activity will help you use one of the techniques for sorting and remembering information – review cards.

ACTIVITY 3
REVIEW CARDS

1. Examine your notes for a course and identify the important information and concepts that you need to review. Use coloured markers to highlight this information, or make notes in the margins.
2. Make three or four index-size cards. On each card, write a question related to the information you have identified as being important. On the reverse side of the card, write the answer to the question. If there is more than one answer to the question, list some of the other answers, as well. Remember to include appropriate examples.
3. Make one review card for each section or unit of information and label it. Then place it with the appropriate cards. Hold each batch of cards together with an elastic band.
4. Use your review cards with a partner.

When you use review cards, you begin to transfer information from short-term to long-term memory.

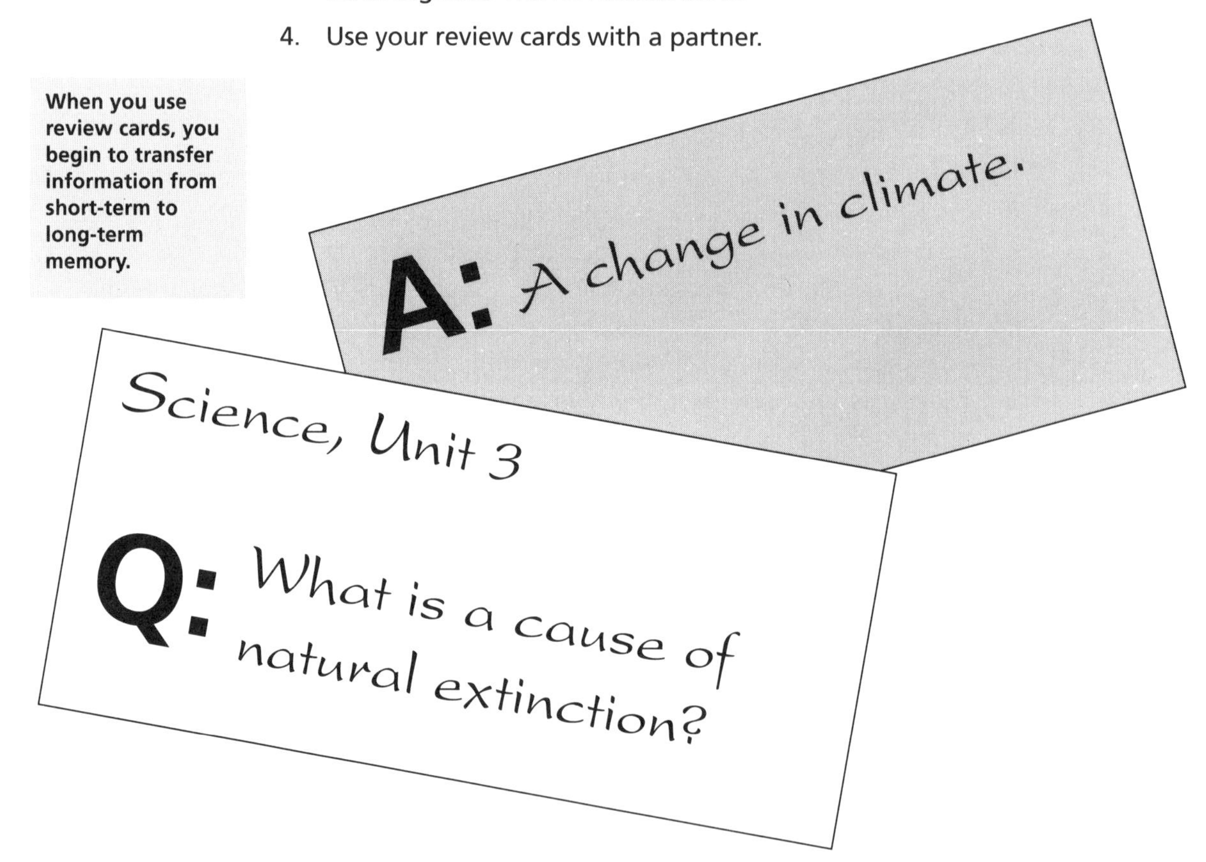

Another useful method for reviewing for an examination is to consider the structure of the examination. Keep in mind that each subject tends to have certain types of questions, and that some teachers favour certain types. The following activity will provide you with the opportunity to prepare for a variety of questions.

ACTIVITY 4
ABOUT EXAMS

1. With a partner, study old examinations prepared by the same teacher or for the same course. If these are unavailable, use your teacher's review sheet. This may be simply a list of topics.
2. With your partner, create a sample exam based on unit tests and classroom review. To do this, try to use different types of questions. Consider what each type asks you to do. Use the list of types of questions in the infobox on page 352 as a guide.

An organized method for reviewing prevents the necessity of last-minute cramming.

INFO BOX

Types of Questions

- **Short Answer Questions** require you to recall information and to fill in the blank with one or two words.
- **Sentence Answer Questions** require you to recall information and to respond by writing a sentence – usually a definition or a brief explanation.
- **Multiple Choice Questions** require you to recognize correct answers. Sometimes you must make computations before selecting the correct answer.
- **True/False Questions** require you to recognize whether a statement is true or false.
- **Matching Questions**, which provide two columns to match, require you to associate two items, often a word and its meaning.
- **Solving Questions** require you to apply formulas and problem-solving skills to find an answer. These are common, for example, in mathematics.
- **Labelling Questions** require you to recognize parts of a diagram and to recall the names of those parts.
- **Essay Questions** require you to recall information and to present it in an organized fashion. Often the method in which you will organize your answer is suggested by words in the test question such as *compare*, *contrast*, *explain*, and *give reasons for*. This type of question may also ask for an interpretation of facts or of a reading passage.

It is important to remember that there are many variations on these types of questions.

ACTIVITY 5
A SAMPLE EXAM

1. Make a list of the subjects for which you will write examinations. Beside each, list the *types* of questions that you have encountered on the tests for those subjects. Add any other types of questions that you anticipate will be on the examinations.
2. Choose one subject. Select at least one question for each major topic covered by your subject. Write your questions on a piece of paper in the form of an examination.
3. Try writing the examination. Then check your answers with the tests you have previously written.
4. Exchange sample examinations with a partner. Write your partner's examination. Again, check your answers.
5. Review the areas where you had difficulty.

If you are prepared for your exam, you will have the confidence to rely on your own knowledge to get through it.

APPROACHING THE EXAMINATION

Some people find examination time very stressful. You will find, however, that you will have increased self-confidence if you have reviewed for your examination systematically. And with self-confidence comes a more relaxed attitude. Examine the chart on page 356 for more tips on how to approach an examination with a positive frame of mind. The following infobox will help you as you write your exam.

Anxiety can hinder systematic learning and clear thinking. Thorough review will give you the self-confidence that will help you to relax.

Although your exam may not be humorous like this, try to stay in good humour. A positive attitude helps.

Final page of the Medical Boards

INFO BOX

Writing an Examination

1. Before you begin writing, read the whole examination. Underline, circle, or highlight the key words in each question. For example, mark words such as *list*, *evaluate*, *compare*, *contrast*, *state*, and *explain*, as well as other instructions such as *give three examples*.
2. Next, check the marking scheme. On the test paper beside each question, write the amount of time that you will devote to the question.
3. Think before you write. For long answers (for example, essay questions), use an organizer such as an idea web, a chart, or a list of details. Use this as a guideline when you write. This will allow you to remember important information and to present your ideas in an organized fashion.
4. If you reach a question you have difficulty in answering, try the next one. Because writing is a mental activity that stimulates your memory and other thinking skills, you might find you can return later to the difficult question and answer it more easily. In general, you may answer questions in any order; just remember to number your answers clearly.
5. Use all of the time allotted for the examination. Try to answer all the questions; since there is usually no penalty for wrong answers, an educated guess for multiple choice or short answer questions may earn you some marks.
6. If there is time, check your answers carefully and make sure you have followed instructions accurately. Try to improve what you have written. If you have written on every other line this will be easy to do.

The Night Before

- Study your review notes.
- Tape your review notes on a cassette and listen to them.
- Use your review cards or study sheets to refresh your memory.
- Try to get a good night's rest.

The Day of the Exam

- Avoid feeling rushed. Get to school on time.
- Make sure you have the necessary equipment.
- Try not to cram before the examination.
- Avoid anxious discussions with your friends.
- Be positive. Think of the examination as an opportunity to demonstrate how much you know.

ACTIVITY 6
PREPARING FOR EXAMS

1. Brainstorm a list of what you consider to be important examination preparation techniques under the headings "The Night Before," "The Day of the Exam," and "Writing the Exam."
2. Compare your list with those of others in your class. What can you add to your list?
3. Write a journal entry in which you express what you can do to improve your exam-writing techniques.

END THOUGHTS

Examinations are a useful way of demonstrating to yourself and to others what you have learned. You might encounter examinations at the end of a term or year for a course, or as a requirement for admission into a program of study in college or university. In this unit, you have used your thinking, organizing, and memorizing skills to learn how to retain information. These skills will help you deal with the stress of exams.

UNIT 18

THE RÉSUMÉ

When you apply for a job or for entrance to a program of study, people need information about you. They get this information in several ways: by examining your application form, by interviewing you, and by studying your résumé. Your résumé enables you to summarize what you think you can offer an employer or why you think you are suitable for a program of study. In this unit, you will use your reading, writing, and critical-thinking abilities to consider how to best present your skills and experience.

- TWO RÉSUMÉS
- IN YOUR OWN WORDS
- WRITING YOUR RÉSUMÉ

TWO RÉSUMÉS

Your résumé is a summary of your qualifications for a job or program. Think of it as a reflection of your skills and interests. To be effective, it should be well-organized and easy to read, error free, and short.

Examine the following two résumés. Both were written by student Steven Dombrowski. Which one do you think will help Steven be more successful in obtaining the job he wants?

There are job openings to be found; it just may take some initiative to see one that meets your interests.

Personal Data:

S. Dombrowski
1908 Spencer Street
Oshawa, Ontario

Position Desired:
any part-time job
Education: Grade 11, Central Collegiate
Oshawa, Ontario

Best subjects: none

Elementary School: Vincent Massey Elementary School, Oshawa, Ontario

Work Experience:delivering papers and working at

a summer camp and working in a store

Hobbies and Interests: sports and cars.Can cook.

References: none

Personal Data:	Steven Dombrowski 1908 Spencer Street Oshawa, Ontario K2Z 5B5
Telephone:	555-1234
Position Desired:	Short-order cook
Education:	Grade 11, Central Collegiate Oshawa, Ontario
Best subjects:	Food Preparation, Auto Mechanics, Social Studies
Work Experience:	September to June, 19 – : general helper, grocery store June to September, 19 – : volunteer cook at a summer camp for handicapped children
Hobbies and Interests:	Like all sports, especially hockey. Enjoy cooking and customizing cars.
References:	Available upon request.

ACTIVITY 1
COMPARING RÉSUMÉS

1. Read the two résumés on page 359. In a brief paragraph, state which one you think would be more effective, and explain why.
2. In your notebook list any errors in both résumés that you think Steven should correct.
3. List any other information that you think Steven forgot to include that might be helpful to an employer.

IN YOUR OWN WORDS

Both sample résumés on page 359 can be improved with positive action words, with phrases that give a concrete sense of your skills and experience, and with words that describe your personal characteristics. These action statements will leave your reader with a stronger sense of how your skills and experience are of value to the job or program for which you are applying.

Action Words

Examine the following list of action words. Used carefully, they will help you make a positive, favourable impression. Remember that it is important not to use a word in your résumé unless it truly applies to you.

competent	processed	resourceful
participated	qualified	sold
versatile	engineered	efficient
controlled	knowledgeable	guided
consistent	managed	experienced
directed	productive	supervised
effective	initiated	wide background
created	equipped	organized
positive	trained	investigated
coordinated	designed	analyzed
developed	repaired	maintained
expanded	built	specialized
established	communicated	

ACTIVITY 2
ACTION WORDS

1. Read the list on page 360 and be sure that you understand the meaning of each word. Use your dictionary, if necessary.
2. Select six words from the list that you feel apply to you. In a sentence for each word, explain why. For example:
   Managed: In grades ten and eleven, I managed the school canteen for twelve hours per week, supervising two other students.
   Versatile: I am versatile because I can perform several different tasks, instead of just one.
3. Exchange your list with a partner. Do you agree with his or her list? What other words can you suggest? Be sure to explain your views.

Personal Skills

Each person has a different background and, therefore, different training and abilities. Think about your own skills. Often, the skills you use in one type of activity can be applied in an entirely different situation. How would you describe your skills? And how could you suggest that your skills are applicable to a variety of situations?

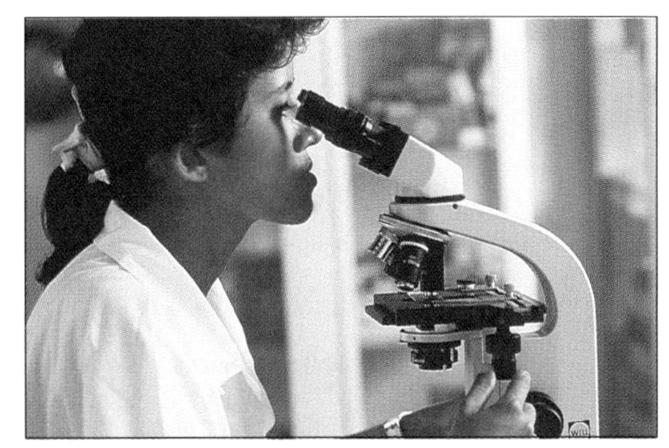

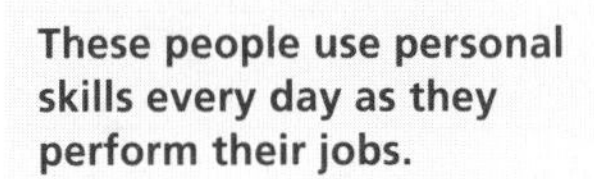

These people use personal skills every day as they perform their jobs.

The following is a checklist of skills. As you review the list, think about how these statements apply to you. On your résumé, only use those that accurately reflect your experience.

- analyzing data
- arranging social functions
- assembling apparatus
- budgeting expenses
- calculating numerical data
- checking for accuracy
- coaching
- collecting money
- compiling statistics
- constructing buildings
- coordinating people and tasks
- corresponding with others
- creating new ideas
- displaying artistic ideas
- distributing products
- dramatizing ideas
- entertaining people
- estimating space
- handling complaints
- interpreting languages
- teaching
- writing reports
- interviewing people
- mediating
- meeting the public
- monitoring progress of others
- listening to others
- motivating others
- operating equipment
- planning agendas
- problem-solving
- programming computers
- promoting events
- protecting property
- raising funds
- recording scientific data
- rehabilitating people
- repairing mechanical devices
- selling products
- sketching charts or diagrams
- speaking in public
- supervising others
- updating files

ACTIVITY 3
YOUR SKILLS

1. Reread the list on page 362. With your partner, discuss the meaning of any phrases you might not clearly understand.
2. Brainstorm a list of abilities you feel you have. Compare your list with that of a partner. Can you add any more skills to your list? to your partner's list? Be sure to explain your choices.
3. From your own list and from the list on page 362, choose six phrases that you feel apply to you, and in a sentence explain why. For example:
   Calculating numerical data: I was treasurer of the student council and learned to keep records and to prepare budget reports.
   Listening to others: I have been a peer counsellor at our school for two years and have learned to listen to the concerns of others.
4. Examine the photos of people at work on page 361. What personal skills do you think they need to perform their jobs?

Personal Characteristics

How would you describe your personality traits? Often, certain traits are useful for particular positions. Presenting those traits in your résumé will help explain how you are suited to a particular job or program. Do any of the words in the following checklist apply to you? Again, remember to use only words that accurately describe you.

hard-working	energetic	quick learner
enthusiastic	well-organized	patient
punctual	dedicated	thick-skinned
sensitive	creative	articulate
perfectionist	flexible	resourceful
analytical	people-oriented	innovative
work well alone	enjoy pressure	persevering
enjoy challenges	conscientious	thorough
open-minded	consistent	calm
discreet	firm	amiable

ACTIVITY 4
DESCRIBING YOURSELF

1. In your notebook, make a list of what you consider to be personal attributes or characteristics that accurately describe you. With a partner, examine each other's lists. If you disagree with your partner's self-description, explain why in a positive, constructive way.
2. Reread the checklist on page 363 and consider if you have or your partner has omitted any words that would be appropriate. Look up in your dictionary, and discuss with your partner, any words that you don't understand.
3. Select six words or phrases from your list and explain in a sentence for each how they apply to you. For example:
   Thick-skinned: I am able to accept constructive criticism without becoming upset.
   Punctual: In the three years I have been in high school, I have never been late for class.

WRITING YOUR RÉSUMÉ

Résumés may be as varied as the people who write them. Two common types are the chronological and the functional résumés. A chronological résumé lists items in order of the time when they happened, usually moving backward from the present to the past. A functional résumé is often organized around various skills.

Both kinds are effective. Which one you use is a matter of personal choice. Keep in mind, however, that a functional résumé can allow you to emphasize your personal skills even though you have little work experience.

Examine the following résumés. Note that the chronological one is that of a person who has completed a specific course that will qualify him for a particular job, while the functional résumé is that of a grade eleven student with no specific course.

Chronological Résumé

John Goldbergh
2064 Selkirk Avenue
Winnipeg, Manitoba M6V 8T3
(205) 555-1234

Position Desired:

Cook

Education:

September 19 – - June 19 – :
Grade 12, Riverhurst Vocational School,
Winnipeg, Manitoba R2W 2K8

- Took double preparation courses in Food Preparation in grades 11 and 12. Created original recipes; specialized in main courses.
- Best Subjects: Food Preparation, Mathematics
- Technical subjects: Can type or word process 35 wpm

Work Experience:

October 19 – to present:
Usher at Coronet Theatre, part time, evenings, and weekends.
Named "employee of the month" for punctuality and dedication.

May 19 – to June 19 – :
Delivered newspapers, babysitting

Personal Data:

Grade 12: Minor part in school musical
Grades 10-12: Involved in peer counselling

Hobbies: Cooking, music

References available upon request.

Functional Résumé

Emily Chan
3636 Hill Avenue, Regina, Saskatchewan S4S 5Z5 (306) 555-5678

Education: Grade 11, Vocational Course,
Central Collegiate, Rose Valley SOE 1M0

Demonstrated Abilities: I feel I have demonstrated the following abilities throughout my high-school years:

- Managing: In grade 11, I was appointed student manager of the canteen. This involved coordinating the work of two others, ordering canteen supplies, and balancing cash receipts at the end of each day. Also in grade 11, organized football team and planned schedules.
- Punctuality: I have never been late for class in three years at Central Collegiate.
- People-minded: I enjoy working with people, and in grade 12 was a peer counsellor.

Teachers have also told me that I have the following characteristics:

- I work well under pressure.
- I am easy to get along with.
- I follow instructions well.

In summary, I feel that whenever I have a task to do I always try to do it to the best of my ability. As well, I enjoy challenges and look forward to new experiences.

Other Experience: From grade eight to the present, I have been a volunteer for the Meals on Wheels program, bringing meals to the needy. I presently work part time as a cashier for Kelly's Grocery.

Skills: Typing, word processing: 50 wpm
Auto mechanics (Received highest mark for practical exam in Motor Shop, grade 12)

Personal Data: Elected school athletic rep. Enjoy swimming, reading, camping.

References available upon request.

ACTIVITY 5
LOOKING AT TYPES OF RÉSUMÉS

1. How are the chronological and functional résumés different? Which one do you prefer?
2. Which words from the lists on pages 360, 362, and 363 are used in each résumé? What other words from the checklists could you add to them?
3. Look once again at the résumés on page 359 by Steven Dombrowski. Write a new résumé for Steven using words and phrases from the lists on pages 360, 362, and 363.
4. To gain experience in writing a résumé, bring to class an ad for a job of interest to you. Write a résumé to apply for the job, using one or both of the sample résumés on pages 365 and 366 to guide you and the skills list you have developed in this unit to accurately and positively describe yourself.
5. Exchange your résumé with a partner and carefully proofread each other's. In order to make the best impression possible, redo yours until it is error free. Use the infobox on this page as a checklist for proofreading your own or your partner's résumé.

Checklist for Proofreading a Résumé

Is the overall presentation of the résumé effective and attractive?
Check for:

- erasures
- marks on the paper
- proper spacing
- orderliness

Is the résumé error free?
Check for:

- spelling
- punctuation
- capitalization
- complete sentences or phrases

Is the résumé well-organized?
Check for:

- present to past tense
- function

Is the résumé complete? Does it accurately portray the writer?

END THOUGHTS

Preparing your résumé is an opportunity to examine your abilities, experience, and personality and to consider how these might be of value to an employer or useful for a program of study. Keep in mind that as you develop new skills and gain more experience, you will need to change your résumé to reflect this.

Consider using a system that will allow you to easily update your résumé. For example, organize a page in your notebook with these headings: abilities, interests, personality traits, training, other experiences. As you become aware of new attributes during the year, record them under the appropriate heading. If you have access to a word processor, you can easily add or change information as necessary.

UNIT 19

THE INTERVIEW

Employers often use interviews to determine if you are a suitable candidate for a job. Or you may go on to some form of post-secondary education and face an admission interview. Knowing how to perform appropriately in an interview is a useful skill that requires thought and practice.

In this unit, you will use your speaking, listening, and non-verbal skills to gain confidence during an interview.

- PREPARING FOR AN INTERVIEW
- FIRST IMPRESSIONS
- LISTENING
- SPEAKING
- PRACTISING THE INTERVIEW

PREPARING FOR AN INTERVIEW

Being prepared will enable you to approach an interview with self-confidence and skill. To prepare for an interview, try to imagine the interviewer's point of view by considering the following questions:

- What do you think the interviewer is looking for?
- How can you meet the employer's needs or fulfill the requirements of a course of study?
- How can the employer or course meet your needs?

To consider these questions, read about the company or program in reference books in the library. If possible, consult people with knowledge of the company or program. Ask these people what they feel the company looks for in its employees or what the program looks for in its students. Also ask what services the employer offers its employees.

As you do your research, remember that an interviewer wants information about you. To do this, he or she will ask you questions – many questions – about yourself, ranging from the general to the very specific. Before your interview, try to anticipate the kinds of questions you will be asked and to consider the kinds of answers you will give. (Keep in mind that you are not required to answer any question that you feel is uncomfortably personal.) For example, an important question to anticipate is that of wages. As a general rule, wait until the interviewer raises this issue, but try to have a sense of what a fair wage would be.

When employers advertise a position, they usually desire certain qualities in an employee. When you look at career ads such as these, try thinking about them from the point of view of the employer.

GREENPEACE

An expanding development department in a growing organization of 300,000 members seeks an experienced fundraiser to make a contribution to a safer, cleaner environment.

Merchandise Co-ordinator: To develop a series of test merchandise programmes for Greenpeace Canada. Significant fundraising and mail-order merchandising experience required. Four to six month extendable position, may be based in Toronto, Vancouver or Montreal.

Bilingual (French-English) candidates preferred. Computer skills, activitist background are assets. Candidates must be compatible with the goals and approach of Greenpeace. This is a challenging and rewarding position for a highly motivated, self-starter. Some travel and overtime required.

Please submit a detailed resume with references to **Bob Penner, Development Director, Greenpeace Canada, 578 Bloor Street West, Toronto, Ontario M6G 1K1.**

Greenpeace encourages applications regardless of sex, race, religion or sexual orientation

Peripheral Operators

$528 - $584 per week

Excellent opportunities exist for three individuals with the ability to work as part of a team. You will: operate tape drives and printers; provide I/O scheduling, data control and tape-library services; ensure equipment is operating at optimal availability/performance levels, maintenance schedules are enforced and quality-control standards for output are met. You will work on a rotating-shift basis. **File GS-363/90.**

Qualifications: Experience and/or formal training in an MVS/JES2 operating environment, emphasizing tape, print and I/O procedures/techniques; good communication skills; ability to work as part of a team, handle large quantities of print stock and ensure adequate print-stock inventory to meet printing requirements.

Application/resume must be received no later than Oct. 15, 1990. Quoting relevant file number, send to: Human Resources Services Branch, Ministry of Government Services, 8th Floor, Ferguson Block, Queen's Park, Toronto, Ontario, M7A 1N3.

Dedicated to Employment Equity

Before you go for an interview, you must know what you want out of the job, and what the employer wants from you.

"I'LL TELL YOU WHY I WANT THIS JOB. I THRIVE ON CHALLENGES. I LIKE BEING STRETCHED TO MY FULL CAPACITY. I LIKE SOLVING PROBLEMS. ALSO, MY CAR IS ABOUT TO BE REPOSSESSED."

Often, when an interview is almost over, the interviewer will ask if you have any questions. Interviewers can learn a great deal about you from the kinds of questions you ask. Be ready by preparing two questions for your interview.

In the following activity you will have the opportunity to consider the kinds of questions you might be asked in an interview.

ACTIVITY 1 INTERVIEW QUESTIONS

1. Review the list of typical questions in the infobox on page 372. Into what categories can you organize these questions? For example, you might decide that some questions are personal, and that others seek to discover your work habits. List your categories and write the questions that you believe fit under each category. You may find that one question is appropriate to more than one category.
2. With a partner compare your lists and test each other's skill in analyzing interview questions. Choose a question from the infobox on page 372 and read it to your partner. Ask your partner to tell you what an interviewer would be trying to find out by asking this question. Talk about your partner's answer. Then switch roles.

INFO BOX

Typical Interview Questions

- What can you tell me about yourself?
- Have you ever done this kind of work before?
- Why do you want to work here?
- How do you think you will benefit from this program?
- Why did you leave your last job?
- What kind of salary do you expect?
- Why should we hire you instead of someone else?
- When can you start work?
- What are your greatest strengths and your greatest weaknesses?
- What five words describe you best?
- What do you do in your free time?
- What are your long-term goals?
- What kinds of equipment or machines can you operate?
- Can you work under pressure?
- Do you enjoy working in a group?
- What experiences have you had that would be helpful in performing the responsibilities we have talked about?

It is important not to memorize these questions. If you do, you may be lulled into a false sense of security. Instead, use this list to become familiar with the kinds of questions that interviewers ask.

FIRST IMPRESSIONS

According to an old expression, "You never get a second chance to make a first impression." In other words, an interviewer will often base his or her impression of you on what this person sees first. Look at a clock or watch. Note as ten seconds go by. It's not very much time, is it? Yet most job experts agree that the first ten seconds of a job interview determine a person's success as a candidate. What the interviewer is probably basing his or her assessment on is your non-verbal behaviour.

If you were an interviewer, what kind of impression would you get from this person?

At the top of the list of impression-makers is appearance. Job experts agree that it is important to be carefully groomed and appropriately dressed. Some experts suggest that you visualize yourself on the job, and then for your interview dress to look the part. Often this means choosing to wear "business" clothes in conservative colours, although other interviews might call for stylish, creative dressing. Keep in mind that chewing gum, smoking, and fidgeting also affect your personal appearance.

The infobox on page 374 provides some examples of non-verbal behaviour that will help you create a good impression during an interview.

Each applicant has dressed appropriately for the interview. Your dress should match the demands of the job.

Interview Etiquette

- a firm handshake and confident greeting
- steady eye contact to indicate self-confidence
- good posture while standing; leaning slightly forward while sitting
- displaying interest and enthusiasm
- good grooming and appropriate dress
- a friendly, positive attitude (whether it's toward your interviewer or toward his or her secretary)

Each person communicates an impression through non-verbal behaviour.

ACTIVITY 2
YOUR NON-VERBAL ABILITIES

1. For the next twenty-four hours observe the non-verbal behaviour of the people you are with. What – and how – do they communicate non-verbally? Discuss your observations with your class.
2. With a partner or in a small group, prepare a series of poses or tableaux to illustrate each of the tips in the infobox *Interview Etiquette* above. Have another group or your class describe the situations that you are presenting.
3. In a small group or with your class, add to the list of tips on how to act during an interview.

LISTENING

Regardless of the kind of job you want or program of study you are interested in, good listening skills are important. Photographers need to be able to understand what their clients or subjects want. Daycare workers or social workers need to listen carefully so that they can better understand people's concerns. Machinists need to clearly understand instructions for operating their machines.

Because listening skills are so important, interviewers often consider how well you listen. Think of your interview as a test of your listening skills and anticipate being asked some questions that may test your ability to listen. The following infobox provides some hints on how to improve your listening skills.

Listening in an Interview

To listen effectively in an interview:

- look at the person who is talking to you and concentrate on what he or she is saying
- ask questions
- let the interviewer finish speaking before you ask questions; don't change the subject
- keep your emotions in check
- respond appropriately (for example, by nodding)

ACTIVITY 3
YOUR LISTENING ABILITY

1. With a partner, improvise a scene that illustrates the *opposite* of each of the tips in the infobox on this page. Then redo the scene to show the right way to listen in an interview.
2. Present your work to a small group or your class. Ask your audience to use criteria such as the following to rate your scene: articulation, expressiveness, attentiveness, relaxation, friendliness, enthusiasm.

SPEAKING

For each of these people, the ability to speak well is important.

Most people love to listen to a good speaker. If the position for which you are applying involves working with other people – and most positions do – your interviewer will pay particular attention to the way you speak. The infobox below provides you with some suggestions on how to speak pleasantly.

Winnie Mandela speaking against apartheid.

Shakespearean actors perform at the Stratford Theatre in Ontario.

This man expresses his opinion through a bullhorn at a demonstration.

INFO BOX

Characteristics of a Pleasant Voice

During an interview, try to make your voice:

- articulate (clear and distinct)
- expressive (show different shades of meaning)
- pleasing (pleasant tone)
- relaxed (free from tension and affectation)
- personalized (appropriate to your age and image)

ACTIVITY 4
YOUR SPEAKING ABILITY

1. Use the list of speaking skills from the infobox on page 376 to think about your own speaking voice. Spend a day listening to yourself in formal situations such as in a classroom and in informal situations such as with friends. Try audiotaping yourself and using the items in the infobox to analyze your voice. Practise speaking until you are pleased with the result.

PRACTISING THE INTERVIEW

In the first section of this unit, you thought about how to prepare for the questions you might encounter in an interview. Then you considered how to present yourself non-verbally, how to listen carefully in an interivew, and how to use your voice effectively. Now use the activities in this section to refine your interview skills.

ACTIVITY 5
NON-VERBAL ABILITY

1. With a partner, plan a mock interview for one of the following positions or programs (or one of your own choice):
   - a salesperson in a retail outlet
   - a graphic arts course
   - a helper at an animal shelter
   - a food administration course
2. Use the infobox on page 372 to choose questions you might use during your mock interview.
3. Perform your mock interview. Have your class assess your non-verbal behaviour as the interviewee for each of the following categories:

a) handshake	poor	fair	good	very good
b) eye contact	poor	fair	good	very good
c) posture	poor	fair	good	very good
d) grooming	poor	fair	good	very good
e) appropriate dress	poor	fair	good	very good

ACTIVITY 6
LISTENING ABILITY

1. With another partner, choose a different situation from the one you used in Activity 5. Take turns being the interviewer and the interviewee.
2. As the interviewer, prepare a one-to-four-minute description of the duties and responsibilities that the job involves. (You might try working with a small group of interviewers who plan a similar situation.)
3. With your partner, practise the interview. As the interviewer, explain the duties and responsibilities of the job. As the interviewee, use effective listening skills. For information about listening skills, review the infobox on page 375.
4. As the interviewer, ask four or five questions about the duties and responsibilities of the job to test how effectively the interviewee listened. Was he or she a good listener according to the five points listed in the infobox on page 375?

ACTIVITY 7
SPEAKING ABILITY

1. With a partner, use the interview situation prepared in Activity 6 to conduct a third interview, this time focussing on the quality of the interviewee's voice.
2. When you have finished the interview, discuss how well the interviewee spoke. You may wish to use the form below to record your evaluation.

a) articulate	poor	average	great
b) expressive	poor	average	great
c) pleasing	poor	average	great
d) relaxed	poor	average	great
e) personalized	poor	average	great

END THOUGHTS

Kila walked confidently into the interviewer's office, remembering that lasting impressions are often made in the first ten seconds of an interview. She shook hands firmly with the interviewer, who noted approvingly her appearance, and sat alertly in her chair, her eyes focussed on the interviewer's. Kila listened carefully, periodically asking appropriate questions to clarify details. The interviewer's warm voice indicated an appreciation of her behaviour. At the end of half an hour, the interviewer shook Kila's hand and said, "Can you start Monday?"

Without doubt your non-verbal and verbal abilities are important in an interview. Take every opportunity to practise these skills. Remember that even if you are not facing an interview, becoming a better communicator develops abilities that can pay off handsomely throughout your life.

INDEX OF INFOBOXES

CREDITS

Every reasonable effort has been made to find copyright holders of the following material. The publishers would be pleased to have any errors or omissions brought to their attention.

UNIT 1

"Wendell Berry explains why he is not going to buy a computer" by Wendell Berry. Excerpted from *What Are People For?* Copyright © 1990 by Wendell Berry. Published by North Point Press and reprinted by permission.
"A Day in the Year 2060" by Rae Corelli. *Maclean's*, September 11, 1989, issue.
"Letter to a Future Generation" by Gwendolyn MacEwen. Reprinted with permission of the estate.
"Advice to the Young" by Miriam Waddington. From *Miriam Waddington's Collected Poems*, copyright © Miriam Waddington 1986.

UNIT 2

Career planning list adapted from *Chance or Choice*, ASCOT Work Group, Guidance Counselling Services, Toronto Board of Education, April 1984.
"When Are You at Your Best?" by Susan Perry and Jim Dawson. Reprinted with permission of Rawson Associates, an imprint of Macmillan Publishing Company from THE SECRETS OUR BODY CLOCKS REVEAL by Susan Perry and Jim Dawson. Copyright © 1988 Susan Perry and Jim Dawson.
"Unemployment Rates by Age, 1989/1990," "Income by Age, 1988," and "Income by Educational Level, 1988" from Statistics Canada.

UNIT 3

"Contact Lenses" by Audre Lorde from THE BLACK UNICORN, poems by Audre Lorde, by permission of W.W. Norton & Company, Inc. Copyright © 1978 by Audre Lorde.
"Nei um lung, ma? (Aren't you cold?)" by May Lee. First published in *Fireweed*, Issue 30 (1990). Reprinted with permission of the author.
"Golden Girl" by Janette Turner Hospital from *Dislocations* by Janette Turner Hospital. Used by permission of the Canadian Publishers McClelland and Stewart, Toronto.

UNIT 4

Quote from *Teaching the Media* by Len Masterman. London: Canadian Publishing, 1985. p. 229.
"Family Fun" by Catherine Dunphy. Reprinted with permission - The Toronto Star Syndicate.
Quote from THE PLUG-IN DRUG by Marie Winn. Copyright © 1977, 1985 by Marie Winn Miller. Reprinted by permission of the publisher, Viking Penguin, a division of Penguin Books USA Inc.
"Hooked" by John Cheever. From BULLET PARK, by John Cheever. Copyright © 1967, 1968, 1969 by John Cheever. Reprinted by permission of Alfred A. Knopf, Inc.

UNIT 5

"Run" by Barry Milliken. Reprinted with permission of author.
"Ulysses" by Alfred, Lord Tennyson.

UNIT 6

"Here Comes the Future" from *The Royal Bank Reporter*. Reprinted with permission of the publisher - *The Royal Bank Reporter*.
"Robots for Sale" by Jane V. Miller. Reprinted by permission from *SPACE AND SCIENCE FICTION PLAYS FOR YOUNG PEOPLE*, edited by Sylvia E. Kamerman. Copyright © 1981, 1985 by Plays Inc.
"The Chimney Sweeper" by William Blake. From *POETRY AND PROSE OF WILLIAM BLAKE*, ed. Geoffrey Keynes, London: The Bodley Head, 1939.
Quote by Alexander Ross from *Financial Post*, August 23, 1969, p. 7.

UNIT 8

"How Do I Love Thee?" by Elizabeth Barrett Browning.
"First Person Demonstrative" by Phyllis Gotlieb. Reprinted with permission of the author.
"The Demon Lover," Anonymous. From *THE POEM: AN ANTHOLOGY*, edited by Stanley B. Greenfield, A. Kingsley Weatherhead, Appleton-Century-Crofts, 1968.
"O Mistress Mine" by William Shakespeare from *Twelfth Night*, Act I, scene iii.
"A Red, Red Rose" by Robert Burns.
"A Birthday" by Christina Rossetti. From EVERYMAN'S BOOK OF ENGLISH LOVE POEMS, by John Hadfield, J.M. Dent & Sons Ltd., 1980.

"I Get Along Without You Very Well" by Hoagy Carmichael. Copyright © 1938, 1939 by FAMOUS MUSIC CORPORATION. Copyright renewed 1965, 1966 International Copyright Secured. Used by permission of Warner Chappell Music Canada, Ltd.
"I'll Never Smile Again" by Ruth Lowe. Words and Music by RUTH LOWE, © Copyright by MCA MUSIC PUBLISHING, A Division of MCA INC., New York, NY 10019. Copyright renewed. USED BY PERMISSION, ALL RIGHTS RESERVED.
"The Taxi" from THE COMPLETE POETICAL WORKS OF AMY LOWELL by Amy Lowell. Copyright © 1955 by Houghton Mifflin Co. Copyright © 1953 renewed by Houghton Mifflin Co., Brinton P. Roberts, and G. D'Andelolt Belin, Esquire. Reprinted by permission of Houghton Mifflin Co.

UNIT 9

"Why Canada Has to Beat Its Literacy Problem" by June Callwood from MORE THAN WORDS CAN SAY, published by McClelland and Stewart, 1990. Reprinted with permission of the author, June Callwood.
Quote from *Michele Landsberg's Guide to Children's Books* by Michele Landsberg. Markham, Ontario: Penguin Books, Canada, Ltd., 1985. Copyright © Michele Landsberg, 1985. Reprinted by permission of Penguin Books Canada Limited.
THE AMAZING BONE by William Steig. Copyright © 1976 by William Steig. Reprinted by permission of Farrar, Straus and Giroux, Inc.
"A Chat About Literacy" by Robertson Davies. Reprinted by permission of Robertson Davies.
Quotes from "Rock 'n' Roll and Reading," *The New Music* courtesy of MuchMusic/Chum City.

UNIT 10

"The Electronic Beehive" by Langdon Winner. Reprinted with permission of Langdon Winner, Professor of Political Science, Department of Science and Technology Studies, Rensselaer Polytechnic Institute, Troy, New York 12180-3590.
"Amanda and the Wounded Birds" by Colby Rodowsky, copyright © 1987 by Colby Rodowsky, from VISIONS by Donald R. Gallo ed., used by permission of Dell Books, a division of Bantam Doubleday Dell Publishing Group, Inc.
"TV technology is wooing viewers into electronic cocoons" by Roy Shields. Reprinted with permission - The Toronto Star Syndicate.

UNIT 11

Excerpt from "PAST IMPERFECT" - AN ORIGINAL PLAY FOR RADIO BY JOHN DOUGLAS.

UNIT 12

"Every part of this earth is sacred" by Chief Seattle from ALL MY RELATIONS, SHARING NATIVE VALUES THROUGH THE ARTS, reprinted with permission of the Canadian Alliance in Solidarity with Native Peoples.
"Daniel Ashini: Native Leader," article by John Goddard from January/February 1990 issue of *Equinox*, page 79.
"Recycling: The New Revenue" by Shannon L. Kodejs. Reprinted with permission of the author, Shannon L. Kodejs, and *Canadian Magazine*.

UNIT 13

"The Credo" by Robert Fulghum. Reprinted from ALL I REALLY NEED TO KNOW I LEARNED IN KINDERGARTEN by Robert Fulghum by permission of Villard Books, a division of Random House, Inc.

UNIT 14

"Collars and Scents" by Heather Pringle. Copyright 1990 Heather Pringle. Reprinted Courtesy of *Equinox* Magazine.

UNIT 16

"Sheena's Contract" by Randy Howard. Reprinted by permission of author.
"The Tragical History of Dr. Faustus" by Christopher Marlowe. From MARLOWE'S PLAYS AND POEMS, ed. M.R. Ridley, J.M. Dent & Sons (Every Man's Library), 1965, London.
Excerpt from "The Devil and Daniel Webster" by Stephen Vincent Benet from THE BEST STORIES OF THE MODERN AGE, by Douglas Angus, Fawcett World Library, 1969.

UNIT 18

"Action Words," "Personal Skills," and "Personal Characteristics" from Employment and Immigration Canada – Employment Services Branch. Counsellor's Manual for the Job Finding Club, 1983. pp. 120-122.

PICTURE CREDITS

Every reasonable effort has been made to find copyright holders of the following visuals. The publishers would be pleased to have any errors or omissions brought to their attention.

p. 6:	"Midnight Sun" solar car. Courtesy of University of Waterloo. Photo by Chris Hughes.
p. 7:	© Broadway Video International Limited. Photographer: Brian Hiltz.
p.8:	© Orion Pictures, 1987.
p. 9:	© ACDI/CIDA. Photo by David Barbour.
pp. 10, 11:	Photos by Susan Sopcek.
p. 12:	Ontario Science Centre.
p. 13:	© ACDI/CIDA. Photo by Pierre St-Jacques.
pp. 18, 19:	Miller Comstock/George Hunter
p. 20:	"Return of the Jedi" TM & © Lucasfilm Ltd., 1983.
p. 24:	© Monroe Leung/Rothco.
p. 25:	"Midnight Sun" solar car. Courtesy of University of Waterloo. Photo by Chris Hughes. Miller Comstock/George Hunter. Courtesy of Farm & Country.
p. 26:	Jensei Choh/The Image Bank Canada.
p. 33:	Courtesy of Soy City Foods. Photo by Richard Fenton. Canapress Photo Service.
pp. 38, 39:	Westend Machining.
p. 41:	Miller Comstock. Canapress/R.W. Lillans. Canadian Broadcasting Corporation. Westend Machining.
p.42:	Boardroom door at Ontario Craft Council by Gordon Peteran (Toronto). Photo by Jeremy Jones (Toronto).
p. 44:	Ontario Ministry of Skills and Development.
p. 49:	KJM Marketing/Associated Features Syndicate.
p. 52:	Douglas Fraser.
pp. 54, 55:	Canapress/Barbara K. Deans.
p. 56:	Norval Morrisseau, *Self-Portrait*, 1975. McMichael Canadian Art Collection. Joyce Wieland, *Self-Portrait*, 1978. Photography – Deborah Samuel.
p. 58:	Canapress/Barbara K. Deans. Cosmoda Inc./Swatch.
pp. 60, 61:	Canapress Photo Service.
p. 81:	Pablo Picasso, *Girl Before a Mirror*, March 1932, oil on canvas (162.3 x 130.2 cm). Collection, The Museum of Modern Art, New York.
pp. 84, 85:	Allarcom Limited, Edmonton, Alberta/SCTV.
p. 87:	Alan Grant, *Life Magazine*. © Time Warner Inc. Photofest.
p. 89:	Photofest. © 1989 Hanna-Barbera Productions, Inc./Hamilton Projects, Inc., New York.
p. 91:	Photofest. *The Toronto Star*/F. Lennon.
p. 93:	Allarcom Limited, Edmonton, Alberta/SCTV. © Broadway Video International Limited. Photographer: Brian Hiltz. Courtesy of MuchMusic/CHUM City. Photo by Fred Phipps/Playing With Time Inc. Photofest.
p. 94:	KKJ Graphix.
p. 97:	Courtesy of Rabo Video Productions. Photo by Aleksandar Sopcek.
p. 98:	Canapress Photo Service.
p. 100:	© 1989 Universal Press Syndicate. Reprinted with permission. All rights reserved.
p. 106:	The Far Side cartoon by Gary Larson is being reprinted by permission of Chronicle Features, San Francisco, California. © 1990 Universal Press Syndicate. Reprinted with permission. All rights reserved.
p. 111:	© Miller Services Ltd. Photo by Ed Carlin.
pp.114, 115:	Hollywood Book & Poster.
p. 116:	The Museum of Modern Art/Film Stills Archive, New York. Hollywood Book & Poster.
p. 117:	© 1939 Loew's Inc. Ren. 1966 Metro-Goldwyn-Mayer Inc. Evdon Films.
p. 118:	National Museums of Canada, Canadian Museum of Civilization.
p. 128:	The Bettman Archive.
pp. 132, 133:	Photo by Jack Weber. Courtesy of Cooper Lishman Production.
p. 134:	Photo by Jack Weber. Courtesy of Cooper Lishman Production. Sandia National Labs/*Discover Magazine*, 11/89.
p. 137:	Northern Telecom.
p. 138:	© Orion Pictures, 1987. "Star Wars" TM & © Lucasfilm Ltd., 1977. © 1956 Loew's Inc. Ren. 1984 MGM/UA Entertainment Co.
p. 144:	The Bettman Archive.
p. 146:	By permission of Johnny Hart and Creators Syndicate.
p. 147:	Drawing by Stevenson; © 1988 The New Yorker Magazine, Inc.
p. 148:	Canapress/Barbara K. Deans.
pp. 154, 155:	AT THE CREASE by Ken Danby, 1972, Private Collection.
p. 156:	Courtesy of the Royal Ontario Museum, Toronto, Canada.
p. 157:	*Web of Spiderman:* TM & © 1990 Marvel Entertainment Group, Inc. All rights reserved. AT THE CREASE by Ken Danby, 1972, Private Collection.
p. 158:	Canapress Photo Service/Gus Coral. The Bettman Archive.
p. 159:	Alfred Pellan (1906-1988), *Evasion*, 1949, Hamilton Art Gallery.
p. 161:	Bear Mask of Haida Indians, Carnegie Museum, (Fred Harvey Collection) catalogue number .3178/28.
pp. 164, 165:	The Stratford Festival.
p. 168:	Pablo Picasso, *Saltimbanque*, 1901. Photo by Edward V. Gorn.
p. 169:	The Bettman Archive. Troy Smith/LGI © 1988.
p. 173:	The Stratford Festival.
p. 174:	The Bettman Archive.
p. 175:	National Gallery of Art, Washington; Gift of Dr. and Mrs. Walter Timme.
p. 176:	Giovanni Boccaccio, *Le livre des cleres et nobles femmes*. French, 15th cent., Bibliothèque Nationale, Paris.
p. 178:	UPI/Bettman Newsphotos.
p. 180:	Canapress Photo Service.
pp. 182, 183:	Courtesy of Marci Lipman and *Canadian Living*. Illustration by Robert Kitchen. Photo by Cathy Bellesisles.

p. 184:	*Canadian Living*. Photo by Dimitri Mavrikis.
p. 190:	Sophie Pemberton, *Un Livre Ouvert*. Art Gallery of Greater Victoria, B.C.
p. 192:	Frontier College/READ Canada.
p. 193:	© 1986 Universal Press Syndicate. Reprinted with permission. All rights reserved.
p. 194:	THE AMAZING BONE by William Steig. Copyright © 1976 by William Steig. Reprinted by permission of Farrar, Straus and Giroux, Inc.
p. 201:	*Canadian Living*. Photo by Dimitri Mavrikis.
pp. 206, 207:	Courtesy of MuchMusic/CHUM City.
p. 210, 211:	Canapress/Uniphoto.
p. 212:	Canapress/Uniphoto. © Harvey Zane Helfand.
p. 215:	First Light/Jessie Parker. Miller Comstock/Barb and Ron Croll. Canon/Promanad Communications Inc.
p. 216:	Canapress Photo Service.
p. 225:	AT&T.
p. 230:	Canapress/Uniphoto Worldwide, 1989. © ACDI/CIDA. Photo by David Barbour.
pp. 232, 233:	Canapress Photo Service.
p. 234:	Miller Comstock/R. Lloyd, H. Armstrong Roberts, Inc.
p. 235:	© by Universal Pictures, a Division of Universal City Studios, Inc. Courtesy of MCA Publishing Rights, a Division of MCA Inc.
p. 240	© Joyce Wieland 1990/VIS*ART Copyright Inc.
p. 246:	© 1960 Loew's Inc. and Galaxy Films, Inc. Ren. 1984 MGM/UA Entertainment Co. and Galaxy Films, Inc.
p. 252:	Brian Franszak/*Discover Magazine*, 2/90.
p. 255:	Nina Leen, *Life Magazine*. © Time Warner Inc.
p. 257:	National Archives of Canada.
p. 259:	Canapress Photo Service.
pp. 262, 263:	Canapress Photo Service.
p. 264:	Doug Griswold.
p. 265:	Miller Comstock/Russ Kinne.
p. 267:	© Mark Hobson.
p. 268:	Greg Locke/Picture Works.
p. 271:	From the permanent collection of Laurentian University Museum and Art Centre, Sudbury, Ontario, Canada; courtesy of The Isaacs Gallery.
p. 272:	Canapress Photo Service.
p. 274:	© Braldt Bralds.
p. 275:	Canapress/Victor Englebert.
pp. 282, 283:	Canapress Photo Service.
p. 284:	Courtesy of Hallmark Cards. Photo by Susan Sopcek.
p. 285:	Reprinted with special permission of King Features Syndicate.
p. 286:	Canapress Photo Service.
pp. 289, 291:	© 1987 Universal Press Syndicate. Reprinted with permission. All rights reserved.
p. 293:	Art Resource.
p. 294:	Canapress Photo Service.
p. 296:	Art Resource.
p. 298:	National Portrait Gallery, London.
p. 300:	Reprinted by permission of UFS, Inc.
p. 302:	Porterfield by Joe Martin/Neatly Chisled Features, 2/16/90.
p. 304:	Miller Services Ltd./Eric Hayes.
p. 307:	Photo by Susan Sopcek.
pp. 308-312, 314, 315:	Photos by Susan Sopcek.
p. 317:	Photos by Cathy Bellesisles.
p. 318:	The Museum of Modern Art/Film Stills Archive, New York. © 1989 DC Comics Inc.
p. 320:	June Bradford.
p. 321:	© ACDI/CIDA. Photo by David Barbour.
p. 326:	The Museum of Modern Art/Film Stills Archive.
p. 330:	Pol Turgeon. Eugène Delacroix, French 1780-1863, *Méphistophélès à appraissant à Faust*, 1828, lithograph on chine collé, 40.8 x 30.3 cm (paper), 25.7 x 21.3 cm (comp). Art Gallery of Ontario. Gift from The Richard and Jean Ivey Fund, 1979.
p. 333:	© ACDI/CIDA. Photo by David Barbour.
p. 336:	Metro Toronto Library Board.
p. 338:	Illustration by Henry Clarke. Metropolitan Toronto Library Board.
p. 341:	The Museum of Modern Art/Film Stills Archive.
p. 343:	First Light/Louis Fernandez.
p. 344:	First Light/Louis Fernandez.
p. 345:	First Light/Jessie Parker.
p. 346:	Salvador Dali, *The Persistence of Memory*, 1931, oil on canvas (24.1 x 33 cm). Collection, The Museum of Modern Art, New York.
p. 348:	© 1987 Universal Press Syndicate. Reprinted with permission. All rights reserved.
p. 351:	© 1990 Universal Press Syndicate. Reprinted with permission. All rights reserved.
p. 353:	© 1988 Universal Press Syndicate. Reprinted with permission. All rights reserved.
p. 354:	Ontario Science Centre. © 1987 Universal Press Syndicate. Reprinted with permission. All rights reserved.
p. 357:	Canapress/Joseph Robichaud.
p. 358:	Photos by Susan Sopcek.
p. 361:	Canapress/Joseph Robichaud. © ACDI/CIDA. Photo by Pierre St-Jacques. © National Optical Astronomy Observatories.
pp. 365, 366:	Photos by Cathy Bellesisles.
p. 369:	Photo by Cathy Bellesisles.
p. 370:	Greenpeace. Ontario Public Services.
p. 371:	Reproduced by Special Permission of PLAYBOY Magazine. Copyright © 1979 by PLAYBOY.
pp. 373, 374:	Photos by Cathy Bellesisles.
p. 376:	Canapress Photo Service. The Stratford Festival/Robert O. Ragsdale. Canapress/G. Clarkson.